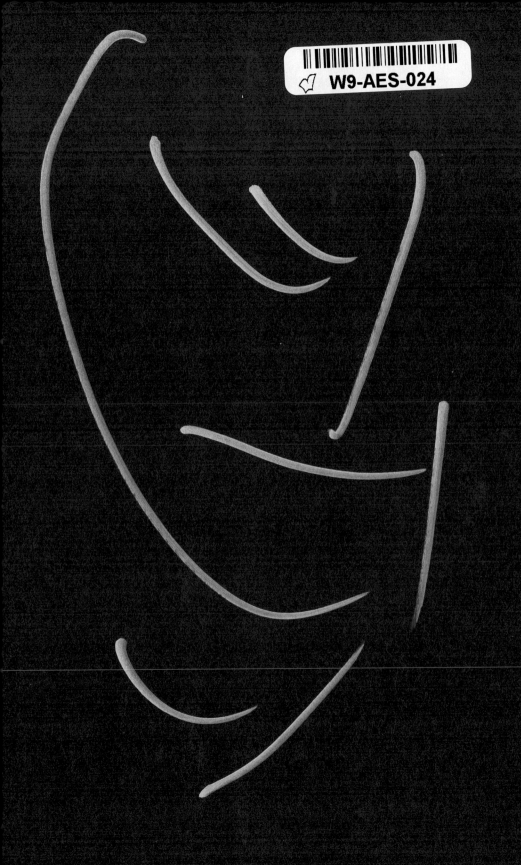

Fancy's Images

Contexts, Settings, and Perspectives in Shakespeare and His Contemporaries

Charles R. Forker

Southern Illinois University Press
Carbondale and Edwardsville

Copyright © 1990 by the Board of Trustees, Southern Illinois University

Edited by Teresa White
Designed by Shannon M. McIntyre
Production supervised by Natalia Nadraga

Library of Congress Cataloging-in-Publication Data

Forker, Charles R.
 Fancy's images : contexts, settings, and perspectives in
Shakespeare and his contemporaries / Charles R. Forker.
  p. cm.
 Includes bibliographical references.
 1. Shakespeare, William, 1564–1616—Criticism and interpretation.
 2. English drama—17th century—History and criticism. I. Title.
PR2976.F58   1990
822.3′3—dc20   89-21668
 ISBN 0-8093-1573-4   CIP

Frontispiece: Michelangelo Merisi da Caravaggio, *Narcissus* (c. 1596). Reproduced by
permission of the Galleria Nazionale d'Arte Antica, Rome, in cooperation with Alinari/Art
Resource, New York City.

The paper used in this publication meets the minimum requirements of
American National Standard for Information Sciences
—Permanence of Paper for Printed Library Materials, ANSI Z39.48-1984. ∞

For *Joseph Candido*

Contents

Illustrations

Preface

My title, borrowed from a comedy that makes much of problems of identity as well as of the interplay between actuality and our perception of it (*A Midsummer Night's Dream*, V.i.25), is intended to raise a capacious umbrella over this miscellaneous collection of papers—papers written over a considerable span of time and conceived originally as discrete pieces for professional conferences and journals. All of them, except the discussion of Perdita's flower speech in *The Winter's Tale*, have been published in earlier versions. The opening chapter on theatrical symbolism in *Hamlet* goes back to my student days and, although subsequently printed in 1963 and then anthologized in 1970, was first made available in manuscript and desposited as a prize essay in the Widener Library at Harvard in 1955. The final chapter on the theme of incest in Tudor and Stuart plays (including *Hamlet* of course) was published as recently as 1989. The intervening chapters, although not arranged strictly in the order of their composition, fall, temporally speaking, somewhere between these termini. As a group, therefore, the essays may be taken as fairly representative of my interpretive study of Shakespeare over a teaching career that began some thirty-five years ago.

It would be misleading—not to say naïve—to claim for any such collection the kind of cohesiveness or unity one expects in a book planned and executed as a single entity. My view of *Hamlet* today, to take but a single example, is rather less neat than it was when the earliest of these pieces was conceived. Nevertheless, anyone who thinks and writes about Shakespeare over something like half a lifetime is bound to discover in his own mind—not infrequently to his own embarrassment—certain thematic patterns and centers of interest (an unsympathetic reader might call them *idées fixes*) that reveal themselves progressively and come into focus most clearly when re-examined from a distance. Accordingly, I have divided this book into three sections, grouping essays together that seem to me to reinforce, extend, or in some way comment upon each other if only by implication. Those that make up the first part, to which the visual clue is the often reproduced vignette from William Alabaster's *Roxana Tragaedia* (see fig. 1), are all linked in one way or another by their common concern with theatrical self-consciousness and the problem of dramatizing human identity on stages that promoted great intimacy, physical as well as psychological, between actors and their audiences. These essays explore some of the dramaturgical implications of Shakespeare's attempt to imitate human nature powerfully, convincingly, even naturalistically, in a medium that, by definition, required the extensive use of symbolic artifice and the inherited conventions of illusion and poetic declamation.

The opening piece argues that the theatre metaphor itself becomes an organizing principle for Shakespeare's most popular tragedy as well as a locus for the tensions and interior divisions that characterize its mysterious and bafflingly complex hero. The second essay extends the study of *Hamlet* by comparing it to Shakespeare's earlier revenge play, *Titus Andronicus*. Here the emphasis falls on the rhetorical and gestic techniques employed to represent human suffering at its most intolerable and therefore least expressible, the apprentice and mature tragedies being both examined in the context of notable Elizabethan revenge plays by Kyd, Marston, Chettle, and the anonymous author of *Alphonsus, Emperor of Germany*. Whether these plays directly influenced Shakespeare's art or not, at least they set the tone and defined the rhetorical tradition in which the greater dramatist chose to work.

Chapter 3 turns to the consideration of stage-consciousness and mimesis in two contrasted Shakespearean comedies—the early, brilliantly farcical *Taming of the Shrew* and the final unassisted romance, *The Tempest*, arguably the playwright's profoundest handling of the illusion-reality puzzle. A comparison of these very different plays addresses the ways in which Shakespeare engages and detaches audiences emotionally— *on* as well as offstage; and it concludes, albeit tentatively, with the suggestion that the dramatist, as he approached the end of his career as an illusionist, moved from a greater to a somewhat more diminished faith in the power of the stage to represent the deeper truths of human experience. This shift, however (if we assume that it represents more than a surprising anomaly), far from signaling a loss of creative energy, seems rather to express a subtle alteration of priorities in the dramatist's way of looking at life. The final essay in the first sequence (chapter 4) takes up the part-Shakespearean play *Sir Thomas More*, trying to show how the theatrical motif not only helps to order a drama that has often been treated as a mere patchwork of collaborative carpentry but that also informs the central character's developing sense of his own integrity. More's self-dramatizing instinct, his awareness of the creative play necessary to control and sustain a public persona, becomes a way of coming to terms with the conflicting imperatives of serving king and country on the one hand and of remaining true to conscience and the higher demands of religious faith on the other. Here the idea of theatre touches upon concerns of a kind to which Stephen Greenblatt's influential work on Renaissance self-fashioning has recently drawn our attention. Nor will it escape the awareness of most readers that Greenblatt in his book on the subject chose the martyred Lord Chancellor for his first— and therefore definitional—example.

The second group of essays (beginning with a linking piece on *As You Like It*, a play that exploits the construction of identity through deliberately assumed personae) moves to consider the function of the green world in Shakespeare's comedies, histories, trage-dies, and romances. Central to these chapters are varied modulations of pastoral or simply natural settings, image patterns, and themes as significant factors in the dramatization of a romantic, political, or metaphysically hostile universe on the Elizabethan stage. The illustration chosen to accompany this cluster is an emblem of the walled garden taken from the *Parthenia Sacra* (1633) of Henry Hawkins, a Jesuit writer whose devotional and meditative iconography relates the world of plants through an elaborately developed matrix of symbols to the human world, to the physical universe, and ultimately to the divine and unseen source of all as mediated through Our Lady (the Mother of God or "Sacred Parthenes") whom the garden in all its aspects honors (see fig. 2). Although it is unlikely that Shakespeare shared the specifics of Hawkins's Marian religiosity or recusant sensibility (obviously he could not have read Hawkins's book), the garden emblem with its implication that divine order manifests itself in physical nature reflects a common Renaissance habit of mind and was equally popular with Protestant and Catholic poets, Spenser, Sidney, Herbert, Vaughan, Marvell, and Milton being obvious cases in point on the nonpapist side.

The discussion of *As You Like It* organizes itself around four sets of contrasting, complementary, and overlapping perspectives embedded in the play. These, it is argued, reveal the thematic fullness and complexity of Shakespeare's pastoralism and point to a comprehensiveness of vision characteristic of his mature comic art. Although the tensions of Nature versus Grace, Life versus Art, Time versus Timelessness, and Subjectivity versus Objectivity remain unresolved, the dramatist's pervasive, self-conscious reference to his own medium, the theatre, serves as a means of unifying the play. In addition to their use of stage imagery, a number of the characters are engaged in role-playing, and Rosalind-Ganymede, the master role-player, draws the various perspectives of the comedy together in a rich synthesis that allows us to enjoy the paradoxical effects of multiplicity and singleness at the same time.

The second of the green-world essays (chapter 6) surveys the ten chronicle history plays of Shakespeare, suggesting that their twin constructional principles of parallelism and contrast correspond in certain respects to the generic distinction between epic and pastoral. By invoking the natural world in a variety of ways—through literal and figurative speech, image patterns, settings, characterization, meditative pauses, and related strategies, the dramatist heightens ironic dichotomies between public and private life, between order and chaos, between war and peace, between escapism and realism, between behavior in tune with natural law and that which violates this standard. An important by-product of such thematic patterning is the juxtaposition of antithetical conceptions of the monarch—of the king as shepherd to his people (on analogy with the King of Heaven as *bonus pastor*) and of the king as warrior-hero or power-hungry aggressor. Also built into the structural irony is the double association (as in *Macbeth*) of the sacredness of royal blood and of bloody violence with the motif of vegetation.

A third essay (chapter 7) extends these ideas of the green world to the early tragedies and narrative poems of Shakespeare, with the accompanying suggestion that the philosophic view of nature that undergirds green-world comedies such as *A Midsummer Night's Dream* and *As You Like It* is essentially the same as that which informs works as different from each other and from the comedies as *Titus Andronicus, Romeo and Juliet, The Rape of Lucrece,* and *Venus and Adonis.* I argue here that it is chiefly with the later transitional examples—*Julius Caesar* and *Hamlet*—that a darker, more skeptical metaphysic begins to show up in the natural settings and imagery of Shakespearean tragedy: the green world, no longer serving mainly to mirror fallen human nature on the one side or to set it off by way of a foil on the other, begins to adumbrate a universe that is already bleak, hostile, irremediably contaminated, or unregenerative—and therefore increasingly less green. Gardens go to seed and are choked with weeds; landscapes breed poisonous herbs, grow barren, and become the proper settings for murder, suicide, treachery, madness, violent storms, and diabolical intrusion.

Applied to *The Winter's Tale* (which in many ways I take to be typical of the romances as a group), discussion of the green world and its symbolic resonances becomes the occasion for a close reading of Perdita's long flower speech in act IV (chapter 8). Embedded in the most pastoral scene of the play—a scene that stands in unmistakable contrast tonally to all that has gone before and will follow—this lyrical aria gives the superficial impression of being aesthetically independent, not to say dramatically inessential to the larger action; indeed it has sometimes been read as a symptom of Shakespeare's escapist fantasizing or poetical dreaming in the last plays, of his loss of interest in the stresses and strains of actual life. Suspending the forward movement of the plot as it does and setting up the basis for the debate with Polixenes on the legitimacy of grafting, the famous floral speech is typical of Shakespeare's dramatic lyricism in its frank appeal to the delights of the senses (musical and textural as well as visual) and in its implicit concern with the question of nature versus art. The analysis here attempts to show, however, that Perdita's much excerpted, often anthologized speech functions more integratively in the total drama than has usually been granted—that, appearances to the contrary, it subtly absorbs and synthesizes the major ideas of the play, invoking or portending through its green-world iconography and symbolism, as in a microcosm, past, present, and future actions. Perdita's speech also suggests a delicate fusion of conventional generic modes—pastoral, comic, tragic, and tragicomic—together with the different attitudes, perspectives, and expectations appropriate to each. In this way the speech utilizes a technique of impure or mixed genre not dissimilar from the combination of pastoral and epic already discussed in connection with the histories (chapter 6).

The final piece in the second sequence (chapter 9), although not concerned with pastoral or green-world settings per se, bears a relationship to the earlier essays in the group by virtue of its concern with ideas of time and temporality—a dimension as relevant to the meditative and visionary realm as the spatial. The earlier discussion of Shakespeare's chronicle plays as historical-pastoral notes that Henry VI, sitting on his molehill in the midst of internecine battle, not only longs to be a shepherd instead of a king, but also loses himself in the daydream of multiplying minutes, hours, days, weeks, and years under the aspect of eternity out of a desire for regularity and order—wishing to be delivered from the insistent pressures of time and hence from the threatening dynastic strife that makes his life, and the life of England, a present misery. Awareness of the timeless in a world of time is a motif that dramas as different from each other as *3 Henry VI* and *As You Like It* share. Accordingly, this essay takes up various intersecting concepts of time as these impinge upon the form and developing action of the second historical tetralogy (*Richard II, 1* and *2 Henry IV*, and *Henry V*). Two inherited models of the shape of time—the classical notion of historical sequence as cyclical and the medieval concept of it as teleological—produce fruitful ambiguities, especially when applied to the politics of the fourteenth and fifteenth centuries that Shakespeare found in Holinshed. And these points of view partly account, not only for conflicting interpretations of human character and motive, but also for the divided emphasis—even the balance—between comedy and tragedy in the history plays. Additionally in these dramas, Shakespeare effectively plays off an external and objective sense of time against more internal and subjective measurements of it, allowing his audience to be caught up in the frequently contrary implications of both a short- and long-term perspective.

The third and final section of the book (chapter 10) returns to *Hamlet* for its title phrase. But here the context is enlarged to encompass an extensive, historically based cross-section of Shakespearean and non-Shakespearean plays (including *Richard III,*

Measure for Measure, All's Well That Ends Well, Pericles, and *Henry VIII* as well as dramas by Webster, Beaumont and Fletcher, Middleton, Ford, Shirley, and Brome) to discuss ideas of dramatic engagement and disengagement, of intimacy, narcissism, and identity, as these crystallize around the stage treatment of incest, ties of affinity or consanguinity, and emotional relationships within the Renaissance family. Social historians of sixteenth- and seventeenth-century England have collected evidence, literary as well as nonliterary, to suggest that patriarchal authority, arranged marriages, inheritance customs, and other factors important to the economy and power structure of the family tended to promote emotional coolness between parents and children and between siblings of the same gender. As Caravaggio's famous but disturbing painting of Narcissus (c. 1596) may suggest (see the frontispiece), attraction to one's own image (or a close approximation of it in one's blood relation—sometimes even a twin brother or sister) implies the solipsistic incapacity to love freely or unselfishly and raises once again the centrality of self-consciousness in Renaissance art. This is an obsession, as we have seen already in the first group of essays, that is never far removed from Shakespeare's dramaturgy or indeed from Elizabethan, Jacobean, and Caroline drama as a whole.

The concluding chapter proposes, then, that incest, whether writers employed it literally or metaphorically, was a subject of the profoundest interest and concern to Renaissance society—an interest proved by the large number of dramatic plots and fictional situations in which it figures. Henry Peacham's amusing emblem, published in 1612, of the naked Ganymede riding a cock (an allegory of sodomy astride incest) illustrates the usual attempt in Shakespeare's culture to address forbidden desires by moralizing them (see fig. 3). But more sympathetic views of sexual involvement with family members and of the need for intimacy and emotional attachment that such desire can imply also found expression in the humanistic literature of the age (Marguerite of Navarre's *Heptameron* provides a suggestive example) as well as in the many historical marriages of the era that were ecclesiastically irregular as judged by the strictest standards of religion. Here the ancients (through classical myth and history) and the Bible were of paramount importance since both sources of cultural and moral authority sent contradictory signals about the permissibility of incest. Ovid, for instance, was famous for reminding Renaissance readers that neither the gods on Olympus nor the animal kingdom suffered under the same sexual contraints as modern Christian society, and the notorious controversies on the subject of incest to which Henry VIII's divorce from Katharine of Aragon gave rise made the problem a matter of learned theological and ecclesiastical dispute. Renaissance drama therefore reflects divided attitudes toward incest—unequivocally condemnatory in the tradition of Peacham's emblem but also somewhat more indulgent, like those expressed, in certain contexts at least, by the enlightened Queen of Navarre.

All the essays in this volume share a common interest in the relation of poetic or theatrical technique and of thematic patterning to dramatic structure. In this sense they fall generally under the rubrics and traditions of the New Criticism, now, of course, no longer "new." But insofar as they assume the importance of cultural contexts, they claim also to be historically oriented. Although I have made no attempt to revise any of the older pieces in major or substantive ways, I have in several instances made additions to the footnotes in the hope of alerting readers to scholarship and commentary more recent than my original composition. Also I have occasionally introduced cross-references at points where the discussion touches upon subjects that are treated elsewhere in the volume, usually (but not always) in a somewhat different context or with an altered emphasis.

Chapter 1 was first published in *Shakespeare Quarterly*, 14 (1963), 215–229, and later reprinted in *Essays in Shakespearean Criticism*, ed. James L. Calderwood and Harold E. Toliver (Englewood Cliffs, N.J.: Prentice-Hall, 1970), pp. 441–458. Chapter 2 appeared in *Hamlet Studies*, 2 (1980), 1–33. Chapter 3 is reprinted from *Shakespeare's Romances Reconsidered*, edited by Carol McGinnis Kay and Henry E. Jacobs, by permission of University of Nebraska Press. Copyright © 1978 by the University of Nebraska Press. Chapters 4, 6, and 7 were all published in *Shakespeare Studies*— respectively in vol. 13 (1980), pp. 85–104, vol. 1 (1965), pp. 85–104, and vol. 17 (1985), pp. 25–47. Chapter 5 appeared in the *Iowa State Journal of Research*, 54 (1980), 421–430, and Chapter 9 in *The Upstart Crow*, 5 (1984), 20–34. Chapter 10 was issued by *Medieval and Renaissance Drama in England*, 4 (1989), 13–52 and is reprinted here by permission of AMS Press, Inc. Chapter 8 appears in print for the first time here. To the editors of all the journals and presses in question I am indebted for permission to reprint. I must also thank the firm of Alinari/Art Resource of New York City for supplying me with a photograph of Caravaggio's *Narcissus* (housed in the Galleria Nazionale d'Arte Antica of Rome) and for permission to reproduce it as the frontispiece of this book. Last but by no means least, I owe a substantial debt of gratitude to my publisher, the Southern Illinois University Press—and especially to Kenney Withers, Director, and to Robert S. Phillips, Editorial Director, for their unfailing courtesy, encouragement, and support.

Unless otherwise noted the text of Shakespeare cited throughout is *The Complete Works of Shakespeare*, ed. David Bevington (Glenview, Ill.: Scott, Foresman, 1980). All other relevant editions are fully recorded in the documentary notes.

Part I

The Stage

1. Vignette of the stage, from the title page of William Alabaster's *Roxana Tragaedia* (London, 1632)

1

Shakespeare's Theatrical Symbolism and Its Function in Hamlet

I

A rapid glance at any concordance will reveal that Shakespeare, both for words and metaphors, drew abundantly from the language of the theatre. Terms like *argument, prologue, stage, pageant, scene, player, act, actor, show, audience, rant*—these and their cousins that evoke dramatic connotations occur again and again throughout his plays in instances that range from very literal or technical significations to highly figurative and symbolic ones. This constant recourse to dramatic vocabulary suggests an analogy in Shakespeare's mind between life and the theatre—an analogy that he himself makes explicit and that even the name of his own theatre, the Globe, reinforces. Examples are not far to seek. Everyone will recall the famous reference of Jaques ("All the world's a stage" [*As You Like It*, II.vii.138]) and Macbeth ("Life's but a walking shadow, a poor player / That struts and frets his hour upon the stage" [*Macbeth*, V.v.24–25]); and there are many others. Not infrequently the figure is associated with pain or death and the relation of man to the cosmos; hence, it becomes a natural focus for the idea of tragedy. The banished Duke in *As You Like It* speaks of the world as a "universal theatre" that "Presents more woeful pageants than the scene / Wherein we play" (II.vii.136–138); Lear with the penetration of madness bewails that "we are come / To this great stage of fools" (*King Lear*, IV.vi.182–183); and Richard of Bordeaux, the actor-king, glances back over his life to find it as unreal and as temporary as a play—"a little scene, / To monarchize, be fear'd, and kill with looks" (*Richard II*, III.ii.164–165).[1]

That Shakespeare should have conceived of man as an actor, the world as a stage, and the universe as its backdrop is not extraordinary, for, apart from the fact that he himself played the triple role of actor, playwright, and part owner of a theatre, the metaphor was of course a Renaissance commonplace. The motto of the Globe, "*Totus mundus agit histrionem,*" is only the most succinct expression of an idea extended to greater length in Montaigne, in Erasmus's *Praise of Folly*, in Romei's *Courtier's Academie*, and in the works of Shakespeare's fellow dramatists, as, for instance, the induction to Marston's *Antonio and Mellida*.[2]

The intention of this essay is to analyze some of the elaborate ramifications of the theatre symbol as it functions throughout *Hamlet*, to suggest that by reexamining the play with emphasis on the theme of acting, we may reach certain new perceptions about its dramatic architecture and see some of its central issues (Hamlet's delay, for instance, his disillusionment and madness, his intrigue with Claudius, his relation to his mother, his knowledge of himself) in fresh perspective. Before, however, we consider the one play of Shakespeare that embodies his most personal statements on the drama, let us make some further generalizations about the complexity of aesthetic response that theatrical imagery entails and the relation of this complexity to the idea and nature of tragedy.

S. L. Bethell points out that references to the theatre in a public performance elicit a double or "multi-conscious" reaction from the audience.[3] Devotees of the cinema may recall Howard Hawks's classic film *The Big Sleep* (1946) starring Humphrey Bogart and Lauren Bacall—a Warner Brothers dramatization of Raymond Chandler's crime novel, scripted (in part) by William Faulkner. At the climax of this wisecracking thriller, when Bogart (in the role of the detective Philip Marlowe) confronts the masterminding gangster Eddie Mars, he threatens him with a loaded revolver and the sarcastic quip, "What do you want me to do—count to three like they do in the movies?" At this point Bogart-Marlowe is actually echoing a grim joke with which Mars's "hit man" has similarly threatened a pettier crook earlier in the same film ("You want me to count to three or something—like a movie?"), thus making the allusion to a convention of Hollywood gangster films impossible to ignore. The chief effect of these pointed remarks is clearly to establish verisimilitude. We are invited to compare what is happening on the screen with cruder versions of the same thing that we have seen before, and the implication is that we know a hawk from a handsaw. But at the same time the reference to the medium distances the performance by reminding us that we are after all looking at a film and not at real life. The response is the same in Shakespeare, but its duality is more constant there, not only because the theatrical references are more frequent and the actors are people instead of pictures, but because the Elizabethans, lacking our naturalistic visual aids, had to rely much more than we are accustomed to do upon the symbolic suggestiveness of the spoken word. So, when Fabian comments in *Twelfth Night*, apropos of gulling Malvolio, "If this were play'd upon a stage now, I could condemn it as an improbable fiction" (III.iv.129–130), or when Cleopatra inveighs against her would-be captors with "I shall see / Some squeaking Cleopatra boy my greatness / I' th' posture of a whore" (*Antony and Cleopatra*, V.ii.219–221), the audience responds to the situation on a dual plane of reality. They are aware of play world and real world at once. The opposition between appearance and reality, between fiction and truth, is maintained; yet the appearance seems more real and the fiction more true.

In *Hamlet* this duality functions almost constantly, not only because there is so much reference to playing and to related aspects of the fictional world, both literally and figuratively, but because the center of the play itself is largely concerned with the arrival of the players at Elsinore and the "mouse-trap" that constitutes the climax or turning point of the plot.[4] Since Hamlet as a dramatic character is manifestly interested in the aesthetics of drama and its analogy to his own emotional predicament ("What's Hecuba to him, or he to Hecuba?" [II.ii.559]), the conflicts generated are teasingly complex. The theatrical references urge us to a sympathetic union with the characters, their actions and their feelings, and at the same time give them the objective reality of artifice through aesthetic distance. The world of the play becomes at once both more and less real than the actual world, and we are required to be aware of this relationship inside as well as outside the play.

The idea of theatre therefore embodies one of the mysterious paradoxes of tragedy, the impingement of appearance and reality upon each other. This is the very problem that obsesses Hamlet throughout the play and that eventually destroys both guilty and innocent alike. What is real seems false and what is false seems real. Spiritual growth, Shakespeare seems to say, is an extended lesson in separating out the components of the riddle and in learning to recognize and cope with one in the "role" or "disguise" of the other. Hence the theatre to Hamlet, to Shakespeare, and to the audience becomes a symbol for making unseen realities seen, for exposing the secret places of the human heart and objectifying them in a way without which they would be unbearable to look upon. We see into ourselves, as it were, through a looking glass. Thus the mirror image is connected in Hamlet's mind with acting and, by extension, with other forms of art that penetrate hypocrisy and pretense: "the purpose of playing . . . is, to hold, as 't were, the mirror up to nature, to show virtue her feature, scorn her own image, and the very age and body of the time his form and pressure" (III.ii.20–24). Later in the closet scene Hamlet verbally acts out his mother's crimes before her and teaches her by means of "counterfeit presentment" (III.iv.55) the difference between Hyperion and a satyr: "You go not till I set you up a glass / Where you may see the inmost part of you" (III.iv.20–21). In Ophelia's description of Hamlet as "The glass of fashion and the mold of form, / Th' observ'd of all observers" (III.i.156–157), the mirror and actor images coalesce as a symbol of truth reflected.

The very court of Denmark is like a stage upon which all the major characters except Horatio take parts, play roles, and practice to deceive. The irony is that Hamlet himself must adopt a pose in order to expose it in others. *All* the world's a stage. But for him pretense may entail revelation; Claudius "acts" only to conceal. Since, for Hamlet, the end of playing is to show virtue her feature and scorn her own image, he not only sees through false appearances ("Seems, madam! Nay, it is. I know not 'seems' " [I.ii.76]) but also feigns in order to objectify his inner feelings; he both uses and recognizes "honest" artifice. He welcomes the players enthusiastically and approves their art. One piece in their repertory, part of which he has memorized, he chiefly loves because there is "no matter in the phrase that might indict the author of affectation." It shows "an honest method, as wholesome as sweet" (II.ii.442–444). His antic disposition, although a smoke screen to protect him from his enemies, is also a dramatic device that allows Hamlet to express to himself and to the audience the nagging pain and disgust that the world of seeming has thrust upon him. It is by acting himself that he penetrates the "acts" of Polonius, of Rosencrantz and Guildenstern, of Gertrude, and even of the innocent Ophelia, upon whom her father has forced a role of duplicity.

The true appearances of things are revealed by phenomena from outside the world of Elsinore, by the Ghost who brings a vision of reality from the dead and by the players who bring another vision of truth from art. Thus the action of the play inhabits three kingdoms, and Claudius, a false king, is hedged on both sides by images of truth—on one side by old Hamlet, the "royal Dane" (I.iv.45), and on the other by a player-king.[5] It is one of the significant ironies of the play that the player's acting prompts Hamlet to action, that the action he chooses is a theatrical one, and that Claudius, himself perhaps the arch actor, is made to look upon his own deepest secret through the agency of drama. Thus, at one pole of the tragic magnet, the theatre is the symbol of inner truth. Just as the player's speech is true for Hamlet[6] and *The Murder of Gonzago* all too true for Claudius, so *Hamlet, Prince of Denmark* is truth for us. There is a sense in which the characters there are the abstract and brief chronicles of the time ("The players cannot keep counsel; they'll tell all" [III.ii.139–140]), and we are guilty creatures sitting at a play.

But if the stage stands for truth at its highest level, it also represents falsity at its lowest. Throughout Shakespeare's other plays but especially in *Hamlet*, "playing" is the stock metaphor for pretense and hypocrisy. The tragedy as a whole is a tissue of intrigue and counterintrigue, a scaffold for "unnatural acts" and "purposes mistook," all "put on by cunning and forc'd cause" (V.ii.383–386). The idea of falsity is therefore closely allied to the mention of actors, particularly bad ones, and indeed most references to them throughout Shakespeare are pejorative.[7] Actors all too often out-Herod Herod, strut and fret upon the stage, or tear a passion to tatters. They are false not because they imitate humanity, but because they imitate it so abominably. They pervert the dramatic function by concealing inner reality under a crude show of outward affectation.

When the analogy of acting (in this complex of associations) is applied to character, it of course implies moral weakness or corruption. It is this thrust of the metaphor that points to Claudius, Gertrude, Polonius, Laertes, and Osric as players on the world's stage, bad actors (with all the ambiguity the word contains) because they conceal the truth either from themselves or from their fellows or from both. Ophelia and Reynaldo are players with a difference, for they do not act as free agents like the others but have been cast in their roles by Fortune. Rosencrantz and Guildenstern occupy an ambiguous position between these extremes. Having no reason to suspect Claudius's secret crimes or, later on, his design upon Hamlet's life, they are obliged to carry out their sovereign's orders. Nevertheless, there is an unsavory side to their behavior that makes them more than simple dupes. They are natural meddlers, and as Hamlet says, "they did make love to this employment" (V.ii.57). Hamlet himself is symbolically the most complex type of the actor and therefore a special case, for Shakespeare has gathered up into his character all the self-contradictions and subtle paradoxes that the symbol can express. Hamlet is caught in a maze of antinomies. He both chooses his "role" and has it forced upon him by fate. He must live in the divided worlds of good and evil, of fact and fiction, of actuality and feigning, of spectator and performer. His part requires of him both action and passivity, and he is constantly stepping out from behind his mask to serve as chorus to his own tragedy.

The figure of the actor in *Hamlet* may therefore be viewed as a symbolic focus for the idea of tragic conflict—man divided against himself, forced in his brief hour upon the stage to play conflicting roles and torn between the compulsion to act (*to do*) and the need to pretend and hence *not* to do. Man as actor must reconcile reason with passion, the beast with the angel, the will with the imagination, and his dignity with his wretchedness. And as tragedy, for the audience, represents the ordering of its own inner divisions, so "acting" for Hamlet is his way of objectifying the various modes of his own self-awareness. The theatre audience can preserve a comforting detachment, for its involvement is purely imaginative. The spectators know that *Hamlet* is only a play. But Hamlet, the character, is not so sure, for the action in which he takes part is real from one point of view and unreal from another. Claudius's relation to theatrical performance is something else again, for he is tented to the quick by it. At one point, he cannot maintain any detachment at all. The extent to which acting is real or illusory depends largely upon the position of the observer, and we, like Hamlet himself, are permitted to shift position in our imaginations and look upon the fiction from both sides of that hypothetical curtain that divides the stage from the pit. Claudius does not have that privilege.

It will surely be apparent by this time that the various facets of the theatre-life equivalence (particularly when it is dramatized upon a stage) constantly threaten to blur into one another. The blurring results, in part, from the critic's method of abstracting meanings that Shakespeare embodies organically, and it should remind us that tragedy is a mystery to be shared rather than a problem to be solved.

To sum up, the symbol of the actor is important and implies (particularly in *Hamlet*) a good many meanings: metaphorically, he may stand for both true and false seeming and for doer and pretender; at times he may serve as audience to his own performance and to those of the other actors on the stage or as chorus to both. He may function both as the observer and the observed, playing in more than one sphere of reference at once. Lastly, he can symbolize tragedy itself—man as ephemeral, man as Fortune's fool, man as self-aware, and man divided against self. If we keep these generalizations in mind, it should be possible to trace the dramatic structure of Shakespeare's most popular play in terms of its theatrical symbolism and to see its progress (metaphorically as well literally) as a series of "scenes" and "acts" in which the characters "play" to each other, combining and alternating between the roles of spectator and performer.

II

The overriding symbol of Elsinore as a stage upon which the people do not always recognize each other in their shifting roles is immediately hinted in the nervous first lines (spoken upon a "platform") of the opening scene:

> *Bernardo.* Who's there?
> *Francisco.* Nay, answer me. Stand and *unfold* yourself.
> (I.i.1–2; emphasis added)

Marcellus and Horatio enter presently, and it soon becomes apparent that they are there to *watch* an appearance of some kind. This is, of course, the Ghost, which Horatio successively refers to throughout the course of the scene as "fantasy," "apparition," "image," and "illusion" (I.i.23, 28, 81, 127). Already at the very outset, we are shown a scene within a scene. The Ghost is a kind of show, and the other characters onstage are its audience. This relationship immediately raises the mysterious appearance-reality question in our minds, for we do not know as yet what to make of the apparition. Horatio, who serves throughout the play as a medial figure between stage world and real world, a kind of *raisonneur* whose reactions we watch as a guide to our own, fills in the political background for us, and the scene ends with the decision to acquaint Hamlet with the supernatural phenomenon just witnessed.

The next episode, played, we discover, in the king's *audience* chamber, gives us our first glimpse of the Danish court and its dominant figures. This, too, is a kind of performance, although it only emerges as such very gradually in the light of details that are added later. Claudius makes a formal speech from the throne, putting as fair a face as possible on his "o'erhasty marriage" (II.ii.57) and "our dear brother's death" (I.ii.1). In its extensive use of doublets the speech may communicate a hint of duplicity. After the ambassadors are received and Laertes has been granted his suit, our attention turns to Hamlet, the solitary and silent auditor who refuses to be drawn into Denmark's "act," remaining on the periphery to comment bitterly on the difference between "seems" and "is" (I.ii.76). When his mother remarks about the "nighted color" (I.ii.68) of his mourning costume, he replies in a metaphor from the stage:

> These indeed seem,
> For they are actions that a man might play.
> But I have that within which passes show;
> These but the trappings and the suits of woe.
>
> (I.ii.83–86)

Hamlet is not deceived by the "cheer and comfort" (I.ii.116) of the king's eye nor persuaded by the queen's plea that he "look like a friend on Denmark" (I.ii.69). In the soliloquy that follows he acts as chorus, emphasizing to the audience the discrepancy he feels between fictional reality, or absent truth, and actual, present hypocrisy. He compares himself to Hercules, Gertrude to Niobe, the dead king to Hyperion, and Claudius to a satyr. His speech ends with the realization that he too must play a role, and we understand that "acting" represents inner conflict: "But break, my heart, for I must hold my tongue" (I.ii.159). Now Horatio "delivers" the "marvel" (I.ii.193–195) of the apparition to Hamlet, which the prince receives excitedly in contrast to the words he has just heard from the king and queen. He will be a willing spectator to this appearance, and he enjoins Horatio to adopt his pose: "Give it an understanding, but no tongue" (I.ii.248). Thus Hamlet is already involved in a double role: he will be both "actor" and "audience" at once.

The theme of acting is now echoed in the underplot. Laertes, about to depart for France, adopts the role of worldly-wise big brother and warns Ophelia not to take the appearance of Hamlet's love for truth. Her best safety lies in fear (a euphemism for pretense), for "The chariest maid is prodigal enough / If she *unmask* her beauty to the moon" (I.iii.36–37; emphasis added). Ophelia sees through his performance, however, and counters with her own distinction between the "ungracious" role of pastor and the "puff'd and reckless libertine" beneath it (I.iii.47–49). Polonius now enters to give his son some fatherly advice in the same tone Laertes had used to his sister. The roles are reversed and actor-father now performs to auditor-son. His counsel is a lesson in cautious appearance: "Give thy thoughts no tongue, / Nor any unproportion'd thought his act" (I.iii.59–60). His concluding words, "This above all: to thine own self be true" (I.iii.78), ironically point up to the audience the contrast between "seems" and "is." After Laertes' departure, Polonius repeats his son's warning to Ophelia, and since Hamlet's vows are but "springes to catch woodcocks" (I.iii.116), he orders her to play a part unnatural to her and to refrain from conversation with the prince. Acting for Ophelia, as for Hamlet, symbolizes inner division. She too must hold her tongue.

In terms of the theatrical symbolism, the situation onstage at the Ghost's second appearance is the same as before, with the difference that Hamlet is now the principal spectator at a performance to which Horatio (in an earlier scene) had spoken the prologue. To the verbal part of the Ghost's revelation, he is sole auditor. Although Hamlet is not quite certain intellectually of the Ghost's "honesty," the emotional effect both for him and for us is that of truth disclosed: "Pity me not, but lend thy serious hearing / To what I shall *unfold*" (I.v.5–6; emphasis added). The Ghost also refers to Gertrude's hypocrisy, calling her "my most seeming-virtuous queen" (I.v.47). After the apocalyptic disclosure, Hamlet's answer to his father's words, "Remember me," is:

> Ay, thou poor ghost, whiles memory holds a seat
> In *this distracted globe*.
>
> (I.v.97–98; emphasis added)

Thus Shakespeare, in a triple pun (one meaning of which is unfortunately lost in modern performance) gathers up several aspects of reality into a single phrase and allows the audience to respond multi-consciously. The "distracted globe" (literally "mind" or "head") represents Hamlet's inner world, his divided self, his microcosm; and by extension, it connects the real world, the macrocosm, with the theatrical world through the mention of the very theatre in which the play was being performed. Hamlet's reaction to what the Ghost has told him underlines the crucial split between actor as true and false seeming. The Ghost himself plays the first role in this ambivalent situation and, by doing so, turns Hamlet's attention upon the false actor, the usurper who "may smile, and smile, and be a villain" (I.v.109). Hamlet is caught between the two illusions, that which reveals and that which conceals the truth. In order to reconcile the two symbolic worlds, for they are "out of joint" (I.v.189), he must act in the true world by "acting" in the false one. The "antic disposition" (I.v.173), then, is truly to be a double role. To Hamlet himself and to the real audience it will mean one thing; to the court audience at Denmark it will signify quite another.

The opening of act II takes us back to the underplot with Polonius sending Reynaldo to spy on Laertes in Paris. His directions to the servant are truly a lesson in "seeming," and the speech may be regarded as a humorously ironic counterpart to Hamlet's later lesson to the players on how a "bait of falsehood" may take a "carp of truth" (II.i.60). Ophelia enters to recount to her father (now in the role of audience) the scene of Hamlet's distracted appearance to her in the guise of a madman. This instance of Hamlet's behavior is a scene (like the queen's description of Ophelia's drowning) that the audience sees at one remove from actuality through the speech of an actor as narrator. But it is clear from Ophelia's words that Hamlet has already assumed his dual role, for the sincerity of true feeling shows through the guise of affected madness. The tone of the speech also indicates that Ophelia is moved, although she does not understand what lies behind the "antic disposition." The prying Polonius is fooled by his daughter's recital, and Hamlet's performance conceals from him what it reveals to us.

In the next scene we are introduced to Rosencrantz and Guildenstern attending upon the king and queen. The two carbon-copy courtiers are told of Hamlet's transformation, informed that neither "th' exterior nor the inward man / Resembles that it was" (II.ii.6–7), and assigned the job of spying on him, even as Reynaldo had been charged with a similar task in the preceding scene. Claudius, the actor who hides behind a mask of smiling, enlists two other actors who will attempt to "play upon" (III.ii.363) Hamlet; and we know that he too is wearing a mask. A chain of "playings" is thus set in motion in which the disguises on both sides will either succeed or fail depending on how much the opposing side knows.[8] The theatre audience, of course, may enter into these "playings" more and more omnisciently as the plot unfolds.

After Voltimand and Cornelius report the news of Norway's alliance to Denmark and Polonius with more "art" than "matter" (II.ii.95) has mistakenly diagnosed the cause of Hamlet's madness to the royal pair, the theatrical parallel is again apparent in the decision to "find / Where truth is hid" (II.ii.157–158) through what amounts to another little play-within-the-play. In this production Polonius and the king will play audience "behind an arras" (II.ii.163), and Ophelia will act the ingénue in order to trap Hamlet into a confession of his true feelings.

Now Hamlet enters playing his role of distractedness, and the king and queen withdraw to let Polonius "board him" (II.ii.170). "Actor" confronts "actor," and Shakespeare, for the first time, fully exploits the tragicomic possibilities of Hamlet's dual role—Hamlet playing to himself and the audience and Hamlet playing to Polonius. Throughout this episode and the next (which substitutes Rosencrantz and Guildenstern for Polonius in the symbolic pattern), the ironic disjunction between pretense and sincerity is stressed again and again as Hamlet penetrates the disguise of his opponent:

> *Polonius.* Honest, my lord?
> *Hamlet.* Ay, sir. To be honest, as this world goes, is
>   to be one man pick'd out of ten thousand.
>   (II.ii.177–179)[9]

And Hamlet to the stage twins: "there is a kind of confession in your looks which your modesties have not craft enough to color" (II.ii.280–281).

A little later the players are announced to the prince. If man delights not him, they do, and it is at this point that Shakespeare begins to play explicitly upon the paradoxes of the theatrical process itself. Since the players' art for Hamlet symbolizes a kind of artifice that is at least potentially "good," being at once more true and more unreal than the "acting" of the court, the company serves as both contrast and parallel to the people who surround him. The actors have come to Elsinore by reason "of the late innovation" (the current popularity of the "little eyases" [II.ii.333–339]), and Hamlet can identify himself with them because he too is suffering from a late innovation of a different sort.[10] Also the reference to the war of the theatres may remind the Globe audience that they are witnessing symbolically another kind of theatrical warfare on the stage of Denmark. At any rate, Hamlet likes honest actors because feigning is their job (as it is now his own) and has for its object, ideally at least, the revelation of truth, so that, from one point of view, a bond of sympathy exists between him and them. But the changing fashion of their profession also suggests to him the symbolic link between acting and the hypocrisy of the real world that so disgusts him, and he comments bitterly on this idea by drawing a parallel between the fickleness of the public's response to adult and child actors and the fickleness of Danish subjects to a good and bad king (II.ii.363–368). In both cases, fashionable appearance rather than true worth is the criterion of value. Polonius, of course, although he is indeed an actor in the world of hypocrisy and likes to account himself a critic of the drama ("That's good. 'Mobled queen' is good" [II.ii.504]), sees no such fine distinctions, as he proves a little later by his reaction to the player's speech. For him theatrical art is just make-believe.

The players enter and Hamlet asks for a taste of their quality, specifying a particular speech he loves from "Aeneas' tale to Dido" (II.ii.446). The significance of this speech and its content are, of course, integral to the theatrical symbolism of the play. Harry Levin has already given it such exhaustive analysis in the essay previously cited[11] that I should only be repeating him to discuss the matter at length. It is necessary to point out, nonetheless, that this episode constitutes another of our plays-within-the-play, with this difference—that the artifice here is quite literal as well as figurative in effect.[12]

Hamlet begins to recite the speech, and the players and Polonius serve as audience. After thirteen lines, Hamlet breaks off, directing the first player to continue, so that the audience-actor relationship is reversed on the stage. The fact that Hamlet himself gives part of the speech indicates how closely he identifies himself and his own situation with its content; for the lines dramatize for him, both through contrast and parallelism, the very feelings about which he is otherwise constrained to be silent—grief for his murdered father, his mother's lack of grief, his uncle's cruelty, and the pressing necessity for revenge. Not only does the speech make real to him "the very age and body of the time" (III.ii.23–24), revealing, as the Ghost had done, truth beneath the appearances of things; it also forces upon him the depressing realization that the player's speech was but "a dream of passion" (II.ii.552), a mere fiction, whereas his own motive for passion is horribly real. Art is seen, then, as having both more and less reality than life itself, and our relation to *Hamlet* is precisely analogous to Hamlet's relation to the player. Hence the speech provides Hamlet with a cue for action. Stepping once more out of his role as actor (by convention of the soliloquy), Hamlet clarifies the meaning of the player's speech to the audience and tells them that the play's the thing wherein a player-king will catch the conscience of a real king. But even as he moves toward action, he is encircled by more doubts:

> The spirit that I have seen
> May be the devil; and the devil hath power
> T' assume a pleasing shape.
> (II.ii.599–601)

The Ghost, too, may be a kind of "actor." We are caught up in paradox within paradox. As commentator, Hamlet stands upon a stage in London; as tragic protagonist, standing upon a stage in Denmark, he wrestles with three worlds of seeming and looks backward to the Ghost as he looks forward to the play.

In the third act, which contains the play's crisis and *recognition*, the theatrical stratagems, up to now so carefully rehearsed, are brought to the test of actual performance. Mask confronts mask under conditions of intensified psychological pressure; thus "acting" turns to action, and the faces behind the masks are made (partially, at least) to disclose themselves to each other. After Claudius, with ironic satisfaction, receives from Rosencrantz and Guildenstern the news of Hamlet's interest in the players, the first bout of the "mighty opposites" (V.ii.62) follows immediately as Polonius and the king withdraw behind the arras to observe Hamlet's behavior toward Ophelia. Polonius gives a last stage direction to his daughter:

> Read on this book,
> That *show* of such an exercise may *color*
> Your loneliness.
> (III.i.44–46; emphasis added)

Even as he does so, Polonius's recognition of duplicity provides Claudius with a flash of insight into his true self that prepares us for his breakdown later. Characteristically, the first proof of the king's guilt comes in the form of the aside, the usual device (along with the soliloquy) that Shakespeare employs to make it clear that the actor has temporarily dropped his persona: "O, 'tis too true! / How smart a lash that speech doth give my conscience!" (III.i.50–51).

Already the disclosures are beginning. Hamlet's soliloquy intervenes before Polonius's prearranged "act," and the prince (again as commentator) states in more fundamental terms than before the deeply rooted conflicts of being and not being, of appearance and reality. The "nunnery scene" itself reveals to Claudius that "Love" (III.i.165) is not the cause of Hamlet's madness; his suspicions about the nature of Hamlet's attitude toward him are strengthened, and he therefore determines to send his nephew to England, since "madness in great ones must not unwatch'd go" (III.i.191). To Ophelia, who takes the antic disposition for genuine lunacy, the scene is also a revelation, though a very partial one. It turns her eyes upon herself, showing her the hopelessness of her love. For the audience in the pit, it portends her eventual collapse. What is pretense for Hamlet will be all too real for her. After the "show" is over, Polonius comes out from behind the arras. But he would pry yet deeper into dangerous secrets, and now he plans what is to be his last theatrical venture—the closet scene.

Hamlet's advice to the players underscores the difference between good and bad acting and states the principle (which we are about to see operating in *The Murder of Gonzago*) of theatre as the reflection of inner truth. All the while, Hamlet, like the player he advises, is learning to "suit the action to the word" (III.ii.17). Before the play scene, however, Hamlet has his brief interview with Horatio, who exists outside the world of hypocrisy and symbolizes the kind of human relationship where truth resides divorced from "acting." Now the "mouse-trap" itself begins—the crux of theatrical symbolism in which the two great opponents face each other, each playing the dual role of actor and audience. The relationship is very complex. Claudius himself is actor to Hamlet and the others of the court audience, but he is also spectator to the actors of the "mouse-trap." Hamlet is also pretending; he wears his "antic" mask to Claudius and the others, but at the same time he is carefully observing the players' performance and that of Claudius, which the play-within-the-play will presumably affect. Audience watches audience. The observed are the observers, and the observers are the observed. Meanwhile the theatre audience is identifying itself with all these points of view at once. At a crucial moment, Claudius cracks under the strain, revealing his guilt. Ironically he calls for light, as he tries desperately to retreat into his world of moral darkness. This constitutes the major disclosure of the act, and Hamlet has triumphed in a way, for he now *knows* what he had only *suspected* before. But he has also exposed himself, for Claudius is beginning to see through Hamlet's mask too. The player-king has ironically stated the truth of the situation for both segments of the stage audience: "Our wills and fates do so contrary run / That our devices still are overthrown" (III.ii.209–210). Hamlet's strategy is defensive—to draw the enemy into his own territory—but after he has done so, pretense alone will no longer suffice. On both sides of the conflict, there is now the necessity *to do*.

The remainder of the third act is devoted to a few lesser skirmishes and Claudius's soliloquy, which manifests his own tragic inner division as a self-aware actor. Hamlet again (more explicitly this time) exposes the hypocrisy of Rosencrantz and Guildenstern by showing them that to play upon him "is as easy as lying" (III.ii.356), and Polonius, who follows their appearance on the stage, is made the unconscious victim of his own "seeming" through the comic dialogue on camels, weasels, and whales (III.ii.375–381). Thus the appearance-reality theme is stated throughout the tragedy in almost all of the character relationships and strands of plot, extending in an emotional spectrum that includes a great variety of "serious" and comic colors. Hamlet ends the scene as chorus, stating his willingness to obey the Ghost and analyzing his function as "actor" in the approaching encounter with the queen: "I will speak daggers to her, but use none. / My tongue and soul in this be hypocrites" (III.ii.395–396).

In Claudius's long and self-searching soliloquy (III.iii.36–72) we see that the enforced hypocrisy that is destroying Hamlet is also destroying the king. He too is caught between the irreconcilable claims of this world and the next. Pretense will only do for this life: "'tis not so above. / There is no shuffling; there the *action* lies / In his true nature" (III.iii.60–62; emphasis added). But he has chosen his role, and he must act it out to the world, however transparent it may be to heaven. Hamlet enters and faces the problem of whether or not to kill him now. As Claudius struggles vainly to reconcile earthly sin with his consciousness of heavenly judgment, Hamlet struggles to reconcile passion with reason. Deciding for the latter, he moves on to his mother's closet and another "staged" episode, which, like the play-within-the-play, will result in a disclosure of truth.

Polonius has again set up the "scene" and is ready (once more from behind the arras) to watch Gertrude play her assigned part. Hamlet's entrance, however, suddenly reverses the whole proceeding, because he plays an unexpectedly active performance to them. Polonius cries out in surprise. The wily actor dies ironically as audience to his own play—in an action for which his theatrical experience as a university student in the role of Julius Caesar ("I was killed i' th' Capitol" [III.ii.101–102]) seems to have prepared him most inadequately. But as auditor to the moral drama of Hamlet's confrontation with his mother, the meddling politician is curiously parallel to his master the king, both, in their different ways, being caught in a "mouse-trap." When the Ghost appears in this scene, Gertrude does not see it, continuing to think of Hamlet's madness as genuine. Thus the queen, too, is involved in the illusion-reality dilemma, and this may be Shakespeare's way of dramatizing the idea that she is so used to corrupt appearances that she still cannot recognize the truth when it is present.[13] Hamlet must teach her *dramatically* the difference between true and false illusion by means of the two portraits. The final irony is that Gertrude, when she is made to realize the truth about herself, must immediately reassume her mask. To be sure, she will now "act" for the sake of virtue— *if* we can believe that her change of heart is more than temporary. But the pretense must go on, and for Claudius she will have to wear the same costume. Gertrude, like both her husband and her son, must continue to live upon the world's stage.

Act IV combines playacting with real acting. The queen relates the events of the closet encounter to Claudius in her new role. Claudius tries to send Hamlet to England, arranging for a little tragedy there with an actual victim as protagonist, but Hamlet unexpectedly changes the ending and returns to Elsinore. Fortinbras's army moves against Poland, and the innocent go to their deaths "for a fantasy and trick of fame" (IV.iv.61). The feigned madness of Hamlet produces real madness in Ophelia, and her sad performance seems to the queen "prologue to some great amiss" (IV.v.18). Laertes returns, prepared in his rage to act openly, but is wooed to the king's side by a masterfully controlled bit of "seeming" and then involved in the plan for another dramatic production (the fencing match) in which the actor is to show himself his "father's son *in deed* / More than in words" (IV.vii.125–126; emphasis added). Claudius emphasizes the necessity to play the part well:

> If this should fail,
> And that our drift look through our bad *performance*,
> 'Twere better not assay'd.
>
> (IV.vii.150–152; emphasis added)

The act ends with Gertrude reciting to the stage audience an elegy on Ophelia's death in which artifice and sincerity are one.

In the last act of the play, all the paradoxes of appearance and reality merge and are mysteriously resolved in death. This final harmony is ironically foreshadowed in the graveyard, where Hamlet looks upon the skull of Yorick and the court buries Ophelia. In the end, all appearances come to dust; the actors on the world's stage must have exits as well as entrances, and let them paint an inch thick, to this favor they must come. The joking of the clowns gives a tragicomic emphasis to the contrast between the hypocrisies of life and the realities of death. By a fantastic paradox, Death, the leveler, makes a bid to social appearances and distinctions: "And the more pity that great folk should have count'nance in this world to drown or hang themselves, more than their even-Christen" (V.i.26–29). Hamlet's relation to the gravedigger (the one who remains) is at first that of audience and later, when he engages him in conversation, that of actor, for the clown does not identify him. There is a grim irony on the other side too, since Hamlet does not know that the grave before him is to be Ophelia's. The theatre audience, again, sees the relationship from both points of view at once. Then Hamlet (in his remarks to Horatio and the address to the skull) performs the choric function, generalizing on death in terms of the dead—Yorick, Caesar, and Alexander (V.i.183–216).

As the funeral procession enters, Hamlet and Horatio withdraw, playing unseen audience to the ceremony in which the others take parts. Laertes usurps the stage and vents his grief with the passionate diction and exaggerated gesture of the "deep tragedian," to borrow Buckingham's phrase for the melodramatic thespian (*Richard III*, III.v.5). Hamlet reacts to the performance as if a bad actor were tearing a passion to tatters, and the reaction in turn impels him to outdo the "player" in a dramatization of his own grief—to express theatrically the passion circumstance has heretofore compelled him to repress: "Nay, an thou'lt *mouth*, / I'll *rant* as well as thou" (V.i.283–284; emphasis added). The leaping into the grave is symbolic too, for the histrionics point forward to a final "scene" from which neither actor will emerge alive. The words of the king are more prophetic than he knows: "This grave shall have a living monument. / An hour of quiet shortly shall we see" (V.i.297–298).

The following episode discovers Hamlet narrating his sea adventure to Horatio by means of theatrical imagery:

> Being thus benetted round with villainies,
> Or I could make a prologue to my brains,
> They had begun the play.
>
> (V.ii.29–31)

The metaphor summarizes Hamlet's tragic predicament and indicates his progress through the drama—the symbolic advance from thought to action that we have noted. In the soliloquy that concludes act II, Hamlet had said, we remember:

> About, *my brains*!
> Hum, I have heard
> That guilty creatures sitting at a play
> Have by the very cunning of the scene
> Been struck so to the soul that presently
> They have proclaim'd their malefactions.
> (II.ii.588–593; emphasis added)

Preparing for the "mouse-trap," Hamlet had been concerned with "playing" in the aesthetic sense and its symbolic relation to his own spiritual conflict. Now he is caught in a play he did not begin. He finds himself upon a real stage where the symbols are turning to facts and the actors are making their exits one by one. Polonius and Ophelia have already made theirs, and now Rosencrantz and Guildenstern "go to 't" (V.ii.56).

Hamlet now expresses regret to Horatio for having forgotten himself to Laertes, for "by the image of my cause I see / The portraiture of his" (V.ii.77–78). Both are faced with the problem of avenging a murdered father. As the Pyrrhus speech and *The Murder of Gonzago* had shown the observers their inner selves, so now Hamlet learns to adjust himself to Fortune's role by an increase in imaginative sympathy for the roles of others. This growth is conveyed by his cheerful reception of Laertes' challenge, brought to him by Osric (who ironically says of Laertes that "his semblable is his mirror" [V.ii.118]), and by his recognition that "to know a man well were to know himself" (V.ii.139–140). This is the quietness of mind that allows him to observe that "the readiness is all" (V.ii.220).

The final episode of the play takes the form of another "show," a sports event in which the stage audience, as well as the performers, unite ironically in the same last "act," which is death.[14] It is noteworthy that the fencing match begins with an attempted reconciliation and that Hamlet, in his speech to Laertes, speaks both truth and falsehood at once. In his apology, Hamlet lies about the cause of his outburst and pleads his madness, for he must continue to "act" so long as the revenge remains unaccomplished. But he also speaks from his heart, for he bears Laertes no enmity. Sincere emotion radiates through the persona. Here, then, the actor is seen explicitly as symbol of the man divided against himself, the man who would play one role but is forced by fate to play another. Moreover, Hamlet's "disclaiming from a purpos'd evil" reminds us again of the theatrical terms in which the final spectacle is to be witnessed by his reference to "this *audience*" (V.ii.238–239; emphasis added). "Audience" here refers to the court group but, by extension, of course to the theatre audience as well.

As the performers *"prepare to play"* (V.ii.263), Claudius (now in the double role of actor and audience) announces a ceremonial accompaniment to the bout. He will drink to Hamlet, and the kettles, trumpets, and cannon will echo each other in a chain of cosmic reverberations. Ironically, these are to be a death knell rather than a proclamation of victory, and they therefore point ahead to the final words of the play, "Go, bid the soldiers shoot" (V.v.405). The fencing match proceeds but not according to plan, for "acting" is no protection from the mysterious operations of chance. What begins as "entertainment" ends in a spectacle of death. The illusion becomes reality suddenly and in violence. Gertrude drinks the poisoned cup before Claudius can properly warn her; that he does not snatch it from her hands shows us not only that he has steel nerves but also that he, like Hamlet, must play out his role to the end. Laertes wounds Hamlet with the unbated rapier (as prearranged by the royal stage manager), but the foils are mistakenly exchanged, and the actor-son, like his actor-father, is justly killed by his own treachery. The masks drop off, and for the first time in the tragedy the characters confront each other without disguise. Laertes lays bare the stratagem; Hamlet immediately carries out his revenge upon the king and exchanges forgiveness with his informant. Shakespeare tells us what our emotional reaction to this holocaust should be by the dramatic terminology in which Hamlet's dying speech is couched, for we are now at one with the stage audience:

> You that look pale and tremble at this chance,
> That are but mutes or audience to this act,
> Had I but time—as this fell sergeant, Death,
> Is strict in his arrest—O, I could tell you—
> But let it be.
>
> (V.ii.336–340)

Even in death, Hamlet is eager to speak—to "tell all" like a player, to uncover the truth for those who remain. And so he deputizes Horatio, whom he wears in his heart of hearts, as official epilogue for the drama:

> O God, Horatio, what a wounded name,
> Things standing thus unknown, shall I leave behind me!
> If thou didst ever hold me in thy heart,
> Absent thee from felicity awhile,
> And in this harsh world draw thy breath in pain
> To *tell my story*.
>
> (V.ii.346–351; emphasis added)

When Fortinbras and the ambassadors enter as audience to the tragic spectacle, Horatio fulfills Hamlet's urgent wish. As Cunningham has noticed,[15] it is almost as though Horatio were speaking the prologue to the play we have already witnessed:

> give order that these bodies
> High on a *stage* be placed to the view,
> And let me speak to th' yet unknowing world
> How these things came about. So shall you hear
> Of carnal, bloody, and unnatural *acts*,
> Of accidental judgments, casual slaughters,
> Of deaths put on by cunning and forc'd cause,
> And, in this upshot, purposes mistook
> Fall'n on th' inventors' heads. All this can I
> Truly deliver.
>
> (V.ii.379–388; emphasis added)

Fortinbras answers:

> Let us haste to hear it,
> And call the noblest to the *audience*.
> (V.ii.388–389; emphasis added)

The play ends as it had begun—in terms of the theatrical symbol: "Bear Hamlet, like a soldier, to the *stage*" (V.ii.398; emphasis added). An actor-audience beholds an actor-spectacle upon a scaffold. Through death, the conflicting worlds of "seeming" and "being" coincide; Hamlet and the Ghost are strangely united as we become one with the living actors on the stage. Distinctions are intentionally blurred in the tragic mystery of art. As we are drawn emotionally into this union, we gain a deepened awareness that we, too, are actors playing roles and that our world is a theatre. We know that

> the great globe itself,
> Yea, all which it inherit, shall dissolve
> And, like this insubstantial pageant faded,
> Leave not a rack behind. We are such stuff
> As dreams are made on, and our little life
> Is rounded with a sleep.
> (*The Tempest*, IV.i.153–158)

2

Titus Andronicus, Hamlet, and the Limits of Expressibility

> *Hippolytus.* Animusne cupiens aliquid effari nequit?
> *Phaedra.*   Curae leves locuntur, ingentes stupent.
> —Seneca, *Hippolytus*

> A heavier task could not have been impos'd
> Than I to speak my griefs unspeakable.
> —*The Comedy of Errors*

I

Interested (as inevitably they were) in exploiting passions upon the stage, Elizabethan dramatists could hardly avoid confronting the fundamental problem of what language can and cannot express. Sooner or later the playwrights were bound to encounter that linguistic barricade that Marlowe's Tamburlaine defines so poignantly for us:

> If all the pens that ever poets held
> Had fed the feeling of their masters' thoughts
> And every sweetness that inspired their hearts,
> Their minds and muses on admired themes;
> If all the heavenly quintessence they still
> From their immortal flowers of poesy,
> Wherein as in a mirror we perceive
> The highest reaches of a human wit—
> If these had made one poem's period
> And all combined in beauty's worthiness,
> Yet should there hover in their restless heads
> One thought, one grace, one wonder at the least,
> Which into words no virtue can digest.
> *(Tamburlaine, Part I*, V.i.161–173)[1]

Less theoretically than Marlowe, Shakespeare gives us numerous instances of the dramatic situation in which words are inadequate to their supposed function. Bottom's verbal helplessness upon awakening supplies a comic example:

> I have had a most rare vision. I have had a dream, past the wit of man to say what dream it was. Man is but an ass, if he go about to expound this dream. Methought I was—there is no man can tell what. Methought I was—and methought I had— but man is a patch'd fool, if he will offer to say what methought I had. The eye of man hath not heard, the ear of man hath not seen, man's hand is not able to taste, his tongue to conceive, nor his heart to report, what my dream was.
>
> > (*A Midsummer Night's Dream*, IV.i.203–212)

Lear, in the painful incoherency of his response to filial ingratitude, shows us the breakdown of language in its tragic mode:

> No, you unnatural hags,
> I will have such revenges on you both,
> That all the world shall—I will do such things—
> What they are, yet I know not, but they shall be
> The terrors of the earth. You think I'll weep;
> No, I'll not weep.   *Storm and tempest.*
> I have full cause of weeping; but this heart
> Shall break into a hundred thousand flaws
> Or ere I'll weep. O fool, I shall go mad!
>
> > (*King Lear*, II.iv.278–286)

The tragedies of revenge raise this issue with peculiar urgency, for specializing as they do in sensational crimes and outraged responses under the most dangerous and frustrating of conditions, they tend to present emotion at an unnaturally high pitch, to show its polar extremes. The revenge plays depict collisions between horror, atrocity, the most violent forces of psychic disruption, and those civilized, orderly values of which eloquent articulation has always been a major evidence. By the very nature of their subject such plays necessitated techniques of dramaturgy in which Tamburlaine's "immortal flowers of poesy" might somehow be accommodated to situations and states of feeling for which the primal scream or dumb-struck impotence would, in the nonfictional world, be the truly commensurate reactions. Imbalances or disproportions between factual stimuli and the verbal responses to them are scarcely to be wondered at in such dramas. Therefore, when T. S. Eliot judged *Hamlet* to be flawed by its failure to achieve a satisfactory "objective correlative" for its own emotive content and its hero to be "dominated by an emotion which is inexpressible," perhaps he was pointing less to an aesthetic deficiency in Shakespeare's tragedy than to a feature indigenous to the revenge play as a genre.[2]

If there is truth in this hypothesis, we may profitably reexamine Shakespeare's two dramas of revenge with the purpose of learning more about how the greatest poet-playwright of his age addressed the limits of expressibility. Comparing *Titus Andronicus* (1589–94) with *Hamlet* (c. 1601) in this context has the obvious historical advantage of juxtaposing a very early work with a tragedy of the dramatist's maturity. But, apart from the opportunity afforded to study yet another aspect of Shakespeare's artistic development, the two plays, by a curious irony, represent the very antipodes of popularity in the canon. By almost universal agreement *Titus* is the most rebarbative and shunned of Shakespeare's plays, while *Hamlet*, if the number of performances and bibliographical entries is any guide, remains the world's unchallenged favorite. Some suggestion as to why this is so may emerge as a by-product of our investigation.

II

Before isolating the two Shakespearean tragedies of revenge, it may be useful to consider briefly the few other plays that comprise the immediate context of the genre in which Shakespeare was working. Kyd's *Spanish Tragedy* (1582–92) appears to be the earliest of the extant revenge plays and is generally regarded (together with the lost *Ur-Hamlet*) as the progenitor of the type. The anonymous *Alphonsus, Emperor of Germany*, although not published until 1654 (when it was mistakenly attributed to Chapman), probably dates from 1594 to 1604. Marston's *Antonio's Revenge* can be narrowed down to 1599–1601, and Chettle's *Tragedy of Hoffman* seems to have been written about 1602.[3] Marston's play may be later than *Hamlet*, and Chettle's almost certainly is, but taken together, these four dramas are the only surviving tragedies of revenge—apart from plays marginal to the genre such as Marlowe's *Jew of Malta* (1589–92) or the anonymous *Lust's Dominion* (1600)—that could conceivably have antedated Shakespeare's Danish masterpiece. All of them dramatize atrocity, and all necessarily show suffering in its most extreme and violent forms. Although of course they vary greatly in dramatic skill and effectiveness, these plays, for the most part, tend to present intensity of feeling, especially outrage, in two related but opposite ways. On the one hand, we hear characters *in extremis* venting their griefs in the most voluble, most elaborately artificial and rhetorical of speeches; on the other, we observe them reduced to frenetic irrationality, disjunctive utterance, or even mute gesture.

The twofold pattern appears with greatest clarity in Kyd. Hieronimo's discovery of his hanged son in the arbor prompts a soliloquy of thirty-three lines replete with syntactic parallelism, hyperboles, alliterations, apostrophes, and rhetorical questions. It concludes with rhymed couplets that carry the principle of tidiness in versification almost to the point of bathos:

> What savage monster, not of human kind,
> Hath here been glutted with thy harmless blood,
> And left thy bloody corpse dishonour'd here,
> For me amidst this dark and deathful shades
> To drown thee with an ocean of my tears?
> O heavens, why made you night to cover sin?
> By day this deed of darkness had not been.
> O earth, why didst thou not in time devour
> The vild profaner of this sacred bower?
> O poor Horatio, what hadst thou misdone,
> To leese thy life ere life was new begun?
> O wicked butcher, whatsoe'er thou wert,
> How could thou strangle virtue and desert?

> Ay me most wretched, that have lost my joy,
> In leesing my Horatio, my sweet boy!
>
> (II.v.19–33)[4]

Release of sorrow through the elaborations of eloquence takes yet more extreme forms when Hieronimo lapses into a Latin dirge, a fourteen-line pastiche of tags from Lucretius, Virgil, and Ovid (II.v.67–80), or into his notoriously patterned aria, over fifty lines long, which later dramatists such as Jonson so delighted to travesty:

> O eyes, no eyes, but fountains fraught with tears;
> O life, no life, but lively form of death;
> O world, no world, but mass of public wrongs.
>
> (III.ii.1–3)

Of course the very swollenness of these speeches testifies to the impotence of the characters to find a satisfactory outlet for their feelings, and Hieronimo is very conscious of this impotence. "My grief no heart, my thoughts no tongue can tell" (III.ii.67), he whispers to himself, and later in the peroration of another long soliloquy, he asks, "But wherefore waste I mine unfruitful words, / When naught but blood will satisfy my woes?" (III.vii.67–68). Hieronimo's frustrations about language are partly rooted in the belief that only retaliatory murder can ease his heart and partly in his sense that the heavens are deaf to his cries. Having altered Nature herself with his "ceaseless plaints," having stripped bare the trees by tempestuous speech, "disrob'd the meadows," and "made mountains marsh with spring-tides of [his] tears," he continues to torture himself with the thought that his most fervently articulated sorrows only "Beat at the windows of the brightest heavens, / Soliciting for justice and revenge" in a "place impregnable," a place that will "give [his] words no way" (III.vii.4–18).

Kyd presents hallucination, madness, and nonverbal forms of expression as the inevitable displacements of this frustrated linguistic energy. Emblems and gestures begin to convey what language alone no longer can. Isabella *"runs lunatic"* because she can find no medicine to "purge the heart" (III.viii.3–5), then, as though to make literal her husband's metaphor of grief stripping the trees, she *"cuts down the arbour,"* chopping the "loathsome boughs" (IV.ii.5–6) from which Horatio's body had been suspended. Fantasizing about suicide and Hell, Hieronimo enters with a poniard and rope, the physical tokens of his inexpressible despair, then *"flings"* them away and immediately *"takes them up again"* (III.xii.19–20). He *"draweth out a bloody napkin"* (III.xiii.85), the memento of his son's brutal death, and tears up legal papers with his teeth in a mad attempt to express his rage at the ineffectuality of the law. He searches for objectification of his grief in the experience of others—in the senex Don Bazulto (who also solicits justice for a murdered son), or, if we include the most famous of the 1602 additions, in art (a painter's re-creation of the loss that obsesses him).

Hieronimo's crazed plan to convert art into vengeance, fictional deaths into genuine ones, by staging his *Soliman and Perseda* in four "unknown languages" (IV.i.173) only underscores the breakdown of normal patterns of expression. Yet even these extraordinary forms of emotional release are shown to be unsatisfactory. The ultimate solution to the problem of insupportable grief is, of course, death, and it is notable that both Hieronimo and his wife take their own lives. But Kyd's most radical symbol for the insufficiencies of language is the protagonist's biting out of his own tongue. Although some puzzling textual anomalies are involved, Kyd apparently makes of this desperate act a twofold gesture of defiance—on the one hand, a refusal by Hieronimo to account for the bloody revenge that he has just exacted and, on the other, a despairing acknowledgment of the frustration that has plagued him since his discovery of Horatio's murder, that is, of his failure to find words proportionate to the full depth of his feeling.[5] In the 1602 edition the reviser of the climactic scene makes the protagonist clarify this second point:

> Now do I applaud what I have acted.
> *Nunc iners cadat manus.*
> Now to express the rupture of my part,
> *First take my tongue, and afterward my heart.*
> *He bites out his tongue.*
> (Fifth Addition, ll. 46–48; Edwards, p. 135)

Under the pressures of suffering, Hieronimo has moved from articulated utterance to muteness, from the courtly elegancies of rhetorical invention to their polar opposite, the total eradication of speech. Deprived of the power to match language to his desolation, Hieronimo is first voluble, then crazily oblique, then finally silent; and his ultimate speechlessness implies the complete destruction of his humanity. As the servant Pedro in the 1602 revision phrases it, "extreme grief and cutting sorrow" have "not left in him one inch of man" (Fourth Addition, ll. 14–15; Edwards, p. 127).

The rather prosaic *Alphonus, Emperor of Germany*, a tyrant play crammed with Machiavellian intrigues and counterintrigues that include entrapments, double-crossings, poisonings, stabbings, and sexual violation, is a revenge tragedy in a more diffused sense of the term than Kyd's seminal work. Its novice revenger Alexander, incensed over the murder of his father, is manipulated by the sophisticated murderer Alphonsus (as Laertes is manipulated by Claudius) into becoming a tool in the emperor's plots against an entire coalition of political enemies, so that at one point the objects of Alexander's "vengeance" number no fewer than nine members of the cast. Like Hieronimo, Alexander presides as "Marshall" over "revels" that are intended to result in the deaths of participants; but, unlike Kyd's hero, he possesses no vestige of moral dignity. He resembles Shakespeare's Aaron, upon whom he may have partly been modeled, in his lust, in his restless malice, and in the similarly barbarous mode of his execution—hanging by the heels between two English mastiffs.

Although journeyman writing (including a number of speeches in German) and complexity of plot tend to submerge it, one can again detect in this play a contrast between rhetorically embellished and merely gestic reactions to suffering. The Duke of Saxony, for instance, presents Hedewick, his sexually abused daughter, as a "perfect map of misery" (IV.iii.1),[6] inviting her husband (and of course the theatre audience) to grieve at the piteous "spectacle" while he declaims an "exordium" of some fifty-six lines:

> O, see the hands she elevates to heaven,
> Behold those eyes that whilom were thy joys,
> Uttering dumb eloquence in crystal tears.
> (IV.iii.38–40)

Here the author seems to imitate the famous scene of *Titus Andronicus* in which the floridly tragic father verbalizes the "dumb eloquence" of Lavinia's desolation by addressing her as "thou map of woe, that thus dost talk in signs" (III.ii.12).[7] Admittedly, the opposition between verbal and visual modes of expression is somewhat blurred by the fact that Hedewick actually speaks a few words of German (possibly added, as Thomas Marc Parrott believed, by a Caroline reviser),[8] but the intended effect is nevertheless clear, for the theme surfaces elsewhere in the play. The empress Isabella, torn between loyalty to her husband Alphonsus and her brother Richard of Cornwall, can barely phrase her anxiety:

> O how my joints do shake . . .
> If both should die in these uncertain broils,
> O me, why do I live to think upon 't!
> Bear with my interrupted speeches, lords,
> Tears stop my voice—your wisdoms know my meaning.
>
> (I.ii.59–63)

The Palatine of the Rhine, one of Alphonsus's mortal enemies, announces that his hatred of the emperor "is more than words can testify" (I.ii.106), and Alphonsus is represented as providing (hypocritically, of course) a manual accompaniment to Alexander's lamentations for his poisoned father:

> And I, poor I, am comforted in nothing,
> But that the Emperor laments with me;
> And I exclaim, so he; he wrings his hands,
> And makes me mad to see his Majesty
> Excruciate himself with endless sorrow.
>
> (I.ii.243–247)

Asked for an account of how the emperor came to be slain, Prince Edward is so shocked by the deed that his "faltering tongue / Abhors the utterance," whereupon Alexander glories in an extended recitation of the crimes that led up to the tyrant's death, while the prince remains "silent" (V.i.378–382).

These impressions of half-uttered sorrow or emotion-stifled speech are embedded in a play that affords many instances of the unhampered flow of passion. Naturally enough, the longest and most orotund speeches tend to cluster in the role of the revenger nursing his resentments:

> I must confess, I spend but bootless tears,
> Yet cannot bridle nature: I must weep,
> Or heart will break with burden of my thoughts . . .
> . . . .
> O sacred Emperor, these ears have heard
> What no son's ears can unrevenged hear.
>
> (II.ii.187–195)

O my poor father, wert thou such an eye-sore
That nine the greatest princes of the earth
Must be confederate in thy tragedy?

. . . .

   If that the Pope of Rome himself were one
In this confederacy, undaunted I
Amidst the college of his cardinals
Would press and stab him in St. Peter's chair,
Though clad in all his pontificalibus.
                      (II.ii.256–269)

I am content to suck my sorrows up,
And with dull patience will attend the time,
Gaping for every opportunity
That may present the least occasion,
Although each minute multiply mine anguish,
And to my view present a thousand forms
Of senseless bodies in my father's shape,
Yelling with open throat for just revenge.
                      (II.ii.292–299)

My father's yelling ghost cries for revenge;
His blood within my veins boils for revenge;
O, give me leave, Caesar, to take revenge!
                      (V.i.181–183)

The unmetaphorical author of *Alphonus*, obviously possessed of only meager gifts as a poet, rarely rises about the hyperbole, epistrophe, or static dilation of the examples quoted here; but, although he never manifests the stylistic inventiveness of Kyd or Shakespeare, he seems in a more modest way to have introduced the same tension between the stream of speech and its damming up that the earlier dramatists had employed.

    Marston's *Antonio's Revenge* shows how self-consciously the theme of inexpressible suffering could be adapted to the stylized conventions of the child actors. A prologue introduces the play, welcoming those in the audience who are "nailed to the earth with grief," "pierced through with anguish," or "choked / And stifled with true sense of misery" (Prologue, 22–25):[9] then, like his counterpart in *Henry V,* he reminds them of the gap that separates imagination from performance:

                    O that our power
Could lackey or keep wing with our desires,
That with unusèd peise of style and sense
We might weigh massy in judicious scale.
                  (Prologue, 27–30)

Marston presses the notion of linguistic impotency to its *reductio ad absurdum* in the penultimate scene where conspiratorial masquers "spoil [the] oratory" of the chief villain by extirpating his tongue so that, while his enemies *"triumph over him"* (V.v.33), he can only weep and gesticulate silently when he is forced to confront his son's mangled limbs served up as "a dish to feast [the] father's gorge" (V.v.48).

Between these margins the dramatist reinforces the familiar opposition between oratorical excess and restraint in a number of ways, sometimes associating it, as in the sensational climax, with the idea of forcible repression, verbal collapse, or mime. When the tyrant Piero pours contempt upon his sycophant Strotzo for daring to talk on his own behalf, for "strok[ing] . . . the head / Of infant speech" before "it be fully born," the toady protests he will "not smother [his master's] speech" (I.i.39–42). The courtier Balurdo, a parody of rhetorical affectation obsessed by such words as "retort" and "obtuse" copied into his "tables," contrasts with Maria and Antonio, two victims of bereavement who are scarcely able to digest the news of Andrugio's death into a coherent response:

> *Maria.* O, fatal, disastrous, cursèd, dismal!
>   Choke breath and life. I breathe, I live too long,
>   Andrugio, my lord, I come, I come.   [*Swoons.*]
> *Antonio.* What, whom, whither, which shall I first lament?
>   A dead father, a dishonoured wife? Stand!
>   Methinks I feel the frame of nature shake.
>   Cracks not the joints of earth to hear my woes?
>
>   (I.v.14–33)

Then the playwright modulates this contrast into another between the frenzied Antonio, grieving for his father, and the stoical Pandulpho, who is able to master a parallel grief for his murdered son. The youth can only amplify hyperboles to the point of rant, while the older man rejects such pretentious histrionics:

> *Antonio.*   O boundless woe,
>   If there be any black yet unknown grief,
>   If there be any horror yet unfelt,
>   Unthought of mischief in thy fiendlike power,
>   Dash it upon my miserable head,
>   Make me more wretch, more if thou canst.
>   O, now my fate is more than I could fear,
>   My woes more weighty than my soul can bear.
>
>   (I.v.50–57)
> *Pandulpho.* Wouldst have me cry, run raving up and down
>   For my son's loss? Wouldst have me turn rank mad,
>   Or wring my face with mimic action,
>   Stamp, curse, weep, rage, and then my bosom strike?
>   Away, 'tis apish action, player-like.
>
>   (I.v.76–80)

The limit of Antonio's capacity to articulate his torment—and a turning point in the play—comes when the distraught son prostrates himself upon the paternal tomb and applies its epitaph to his own condition: "*Ne plus ultra.* Ho! / Let none out-woe me, mine's Herculean woe" (II.iii.132–133). The legendary motto from the Pillars of Hercules ("nothing beyond") contains an ironic double meaning, for it refers not merely to the idea of death as the ultimate frontier but suggests also that the mourner may have exhausted his expressive resources. At this point the logical next step for the hero is madness, the total breakdown of verbal coherence; and indeed, Antonio, half feigning, half in truth, reverts to a kind of second childishness symbolized visually by his playing with a toy walnut shell and soap bubbles.

In fact, throughout the tragedy Marston plays off a showy, often tortuous rhetoric against physical gestures and movements that are as grotesque as his vocabulary. The succession of eerie ceremonies, processions, dumbshows, dances, and pantomimic effects, almost balletic in their artifice, makes plain the dramatist's intention to exploit the sophisticated and specialized talents of Paul's Boys. But another of his purposes was surely to italicize the limitations of merely verbal forms of expression. A colloquy between Piero and Mellida, who has been falsely charged with harlotry, reveals how little the heroine trusts words as a means of communicating her plight:

> *Mellida.* Produce the devil; let your Strotzo come.
>   I can defeat his strongest argument
>   Which—
> *Piero.* With what?
> *Mellida.* With tears, with blushes, sighs and claspèd hands,
>   With innocent upreared arms to heaven,
>   With my unnooked [i.e., guileless] simplicity. These,
>   these
>   Must, will, can only quit my heart of guilt.
>   (IV.iii.19–25)

The strangling of Strotzo's entreaties for life "even in [his] jaws" (IV.iii.67) and the plucking out of Piero's tongue, which "Trickl[es] fresh gore about [Antonio's] fist" (V.v.35), represent only the most violent of the play's assaults upon speech as a viable medium.

Inasmuch as *The Spanish Tragedy* and *Titus Andronicus* had made the biting or tearing out of tongues almost a convention of revenge tragedy, it is hardly surprising that in *The Tragedy of Hoffman*, just before the execution of the title character, Chettle should make an outraged survivor of the carnage exclaim, "Cut out the murtherers tongue" (l. 2567; V.iii).[10] *Hoffman*, with its criminal revenger bent upon destroying everyone remotely kin to the Duke of Prussia, who had condemned his father, is unabashedly sensational and melodramatic. Set in a Gothic atmosphere of thunder and lightning, bleak seascapes, caves, sepulchral hermitages, and dismal groves, where cadavers are hung up in chains until their flesh rots off, the play mounts a crescendo of dissimulations and killings that ends only in the final moments when the violence recoils upon Hoffman and his treacherous accomplice Lorrique.

Chettle's indebtedness to earlier plays of the genre is obvious. Recognizable elements from Kyd and his successors include a ritualistic self-dedication to vengeance, deadly disguises, the use of poison, sable clothing, a tomb scene, allusions to Thyestes, Tereus, Philomel, and Niobe, the remains of a dead man secretly hidden, then shockingly revealed, and lovers murderously interrupted in an "arbour." Probably the most striking of the imitations is the character of Lucibella, who goes mad when both her father and her beloved are murdered, who mentions the gathering of flowers by a stream, who sings snatches of old songs, and who nearly drowns herself; but whether Chettle knew Shakespeare's Ophelia or the corresponding figure from the earlier *Hamlet* is unclear.[11] Although emotionally shallow, *Hoffman* has a certain logical neatness and symmetry of structure that lend force to its essential irony. Because the protagonist's father has been executed for piracy by being crowned with searing metal, Hoffman visits the same savage death upon Prince Otho, is crowned ceremoniously as the Duke of Prussia's heir, and is finally trapped by Lorrique and the Duchess Martha, Otho's mother, just as he exults "I am crown'd the King of pleasure" (l. 2554; V.iii) in the mistaken belief that the lady is about to yield to his lust. The tragedy then concludes, as it had begun, with Hoffman himself as the recipient of the burning crown.

Despite some rather aureate writing, *Hoffman* focuses too narrowly on vengeful glee in cunning and stratagem to be much concerned with the psychology of suffering. Unlike Hieronimo, Titus, or Antonio, Chettle's revenger never loses mental control, nor, with death following death so efficiently, does he even feel the customary frustrations of the injustice he imagines he has borne. Such anguish as the play contains is reserved chiefly for victims, but even here there are few obstacles to eloquence. Prince Otho, for example, accompanies his own mortal torture with a descriptive effusion that, from any realistic perspective, approaches the ludicrous:

> I feele an Etna burne
> Within my braines, and all my body else
> Is like a hill of Ice; all these Belgique seas
> That now surround vs cannot quench this flame.
> Death like a tyrant seazeth me vnawares,
> My sinewes shrinke like leaues parcht with the sunne;
> My blood dissolues, nerues and tendons fayle;
> Each part's disioynted, and my breath expires.
> Mount soule to heauen, my body burnes in fire.
> (Ll. 226–234; I.i)

Martha, "the wretched childlesse widdow" (l. 2090; V.i), can elegize conventionally over her dead son, "the soule of [her] delights" (l. 2027; V.i), but then register almost no shock when she discovers his grisly fate as one of Hoffman's "anatomies": "Let them hang a while; / Hope of reuenge in wrath doth make me smile" (ll. 2129–2130; V.i). No character, however extraordinary his situation, is ever portrayed as being at a loss for words. Chettle enlists the major rhetorical forces of the play on the side of Revenge, as Hoffman's lyrical invocation to her illustrates:

> Now scarlet Mistris from thicke sable clouds
> Thrust forth thy blood-staind hands, applaud my plot,
> That giddy wonderers may amazed stand
> While death smytes downe suspectles *Ferdinand*.
> (Ll. 1357–1360; III.ii)

Even the distracted Lucibella recovers her linguistic poise in order to assist in bringing Hoffman to justice.

Rather than contrasting elaborations and attenuations of rhetoric in order to highlight psychic distress, Chettle dramatizes a distinction between the "glib" or "smooth" tongue (l. 2339; V.ii) and the cruel realities that its arts can belie. The purpose, of course, is to underscore active evil. A minor character enunciates the principle when he explains how Martha will trip up Hoffman:

> our Dutchesse hath apparrel'd
> Her speech in a greene liuery;
> She salutes him faire, but her heart
> Like his actions, is attir'd
> In red, and blew, and sable ornaments.
>   (Ll. 2485–2489; V.iii)

Characteristically, heightened language cloaks deceit or serves idiots like Jerome, who writes verses "in prayse of picke-toothes" (ll. 453–454; II.i). That the protagonist-villain, who is contemptuous of "idle words" (l. 394; I.iii) and who is severally referred to by enemies as "two-tongu'd" (l. 1824; IV.ii) or "smooth tongu'd hypocrite" (l. 2578; V.iii), should himself be brought low by a failure to penetrate the lies of an underling's "base tongue" (l. 2323; V.ii) only sharpens the structural irony. *Hoffman* is a revenge play in which the flowers of rhetoric are proved to be dangerously deceptive or ineffectual. As the tragedy gathers to its climax, the young Mathias seems to encapsulate Chettle's attitude toward language: "Cease words, vse deedes; / Reuenge drawes nigh" (ll. 2493–2494; V.iii). The bloody cry for Hoffman's tongue that shortly follows is a brutal but logically consistent emblem of what has gone before.

III

The dramatic technique of playing off speech against silence, begun by Kyd and echoed by Marston, Chettle, and the author of *Alphonsus*, seems to have received its most emphatic reinforcement from *Titus Andronicus*. Indeed Shakespeare, in giving the theme even greater prominence than Kyd, probably did more than any other playwright to establish it as fundamental to revenge drama. But Shakespeare was not merely following in the popular traces of *The Spanish Tragedy*. Clearly the tension was already to be found, whether explicitly or implicitly, in his sources.

The History of Titus Andronicus, the eighteenth-century chapbook that is our closest analogue to the lost narrative from which the tragedy derives, records that "poor Andronicus's Grief for" the rape and mutilation of his daughter "was so great, that no Pen can write or Words express."[12] And Golding in his translation of Ovid's *Metamorphoses* has Philomela, just before her rape and brutal silencing, protest to Tereus: "Yea I my selfe rejecting shame thy doings will bewray. / And if I may have power . . . , them blase I will / . . . or if thou keepe me still / As prisoner . . . , my voyce the verie woods shall fill, / And make the stones to understand."[13] Later, after Progne discovers her sister's terrible fate, we read that "She held hir peace (a wondrous thing it is she should so doe) / But sorrow tide hir tongue, and wordes agreeable unto / Hir great displeasure were not at commaundment."[14] But of course the notion of inexpressible grief is no less Senecan than Ovidian. The *Thyestes*, another obvious influence upon Shakespeare's play, has the protagonist reacting helplessly to the revelation that he has just devoured his sons (in

Jasper Heywood's translation) with "alas I wretch what waylynges may I gyve? / Or what complayntes? what wofull woordes may be enough for mee?"[15] In addition, the epigraph that introduces this essay ("Light troubles speak; the weighty are struck dumb") comes from the same scene of the *Hippolytus* (II.ii) that Shakespeare quotes at IV.i.83–84.[16]

Lavinia, tongueless, handless, and therefore incapable of speaking or writing, is obviously Shakespeare's most extreme emblem of noncommunication; and the paradox of her pathetic gesturing at the center of a play so floridly style-conscious only heightens our sense of the accumulated "wrongs unspeakable" (V.iii.126), to which Marcus in an apt summary phrase alludes. *Titus Andronicus* may be viewed as Shakespeare's most radical exploration of the capacities of theatre to render "miseries [that] are more than may be borne" (III.i.243). When at the nadir of his sufferings Titus receives from Aaron not only the heads of his innocent sons but the severed hand that he had sacrificed to save them, he kneels beside the speechless Lavinia to seek emotional relief in rhetoric so hypertrophic that it totters on the edge of hysteria:

> *Titus.*   with our sighs we'll breathe the welkin dim,
>   And stain the sun with fog, as sometime clouds
>   When they do hug him in their melting bosoms.
> *Marcus.* O brother, speak with possibility,
>   And do not break into these deep extremes.
> *Titus.* Is not my sorrow deep, having no bottom?
>   Then be my passions bottomless with them!
> *Marcus.* But yet let reason govern thy lament.
> *Titus.* If there were reason for these miseries,
>   Then into limits could I bind my woes.
>
>   (III.i.211–220)

This colloquy focuses a double problem that the dramatist faced—first, the difficulty of presenting suffering so intense that the verbal resources of the sufferer are at the point of being stretched beyond rational control, hence imperiling communication between him and the other characters; second (and more difficult), the finding of some dramatic formula, some pattern of words and physical movements, that would serve as "objective correlative" of horrors beyond the experience, almost beyond the comprehension, of the audience. Eliot complained that in *Hamlet* the hero's emotion is "in *excess* of the facts as they appear";[17] *Titus Andronicus* would seem to have confronted Shakespeare with the obverse disproportion—a story whose hideous "facts" were in excess of any human power to match emotion to them.

Marcus's appallingly decorative aria comparing his mangled niece, as she stands bleeding before him, first to a tree "lopp'd and hew'd . . . Of her two branches," then to "a crimson river of warm blood," then to "a bubbling fountain stirr'd with wind," then to "a conduit with three issuing spouts" (II.iv.17–30), has understandably been censured as a revolting lapse of taste. But this speech and those of Titus himself when he first confronts his daughter's martyrdom constitute a nexus of studied effects and techniques that illustrates the young dramatist's keen awareness of the psychological and dramaturgical difficulties inherent in his material. However workable or unworkable we may finally judge his solutions, they at least reflect a clever, even virtuoso, ingenuity.[18]

Lavinia becomes the play's visual embodiment of innocence defiled, of Roman civilization raped, of truth silenced, of individual and corporate humanity gored and dismem-
bered, both physically and psychologically. She almost allegorizes chaos in its moral,
political, and emotional dimensions; and, as Eugene Waith has pointed out in a brilliant
essay, she symbolizes that obliteration of individuality, that numbing dehumanization,
which the most extreme states of emotion can engender and which are implicit in the
urbane style, the distanced treatment of violence, and the transformation into animals of
Ovid's *Metamorphoses*.[19] Marcus's intermixture of animate and inanimate metaphors
may consist with emotion pushed beyond human levels of endurance, but the attempt to
prettify horror that characterizes his painfully elaborate description also dramatizes that
troubling dissociation of sensibility that can result from shock. Naturalistically speaking,
Lavinia needs a surgeon, not a rhetorical display. Marcus totally ignores his niece's
feelings of humiliation and loss, diverting his own emotions into an arabesque of
images that erects a barrier of fanciful language between himself and the object of his
contemplation. The juxtaposition of cumulative artifice with raw barbarity is grotesque
and produces an effect similar to Octave Mirbeau's *Le Jardin des Supplices*—in which
horrifying mutilations are coolly observed from the point of view of a connoisseur—or
Casanova's description of a sexual dalliance during the barbaric quartering of Damiens,
the would-be assassin of Louis XV.[20] The flight from nature into art not only underlines
the cruel reality of Lavinia's plight but also sharpens our awareness of how little we can
bear such realities without reordering them, yet reminding us of how unequal the
inventions of rhetoric are to the task.[21]

The bringing of characters who ingeniously torture language into the presence of
a victim whose genuine tortures have physically incapacitated her for self-expression—
characters who wrestle with their own appropriateness of response or the urge to
articulate, however imperfectly, what she cannot—redoubles the effect of unendurable
frustration that Shakespeare is at pains to dramatize. Poetry and silence are made to
confront each other on the stage and, by their shocking contrast, to suggest an
intensity of emotion that neither could render separately. Moreover, the device of
having Marcus and, later, Titus become mouthpieces for Lavinia weights them with
an overplus of emotion to which any language, however artful, would be less than
sufficient, while imposing unsatisfactory intermediaries between her and us. Therefore,
the technique not only actualizes frustration as a fact of the character relationships
but also involves the audience—and not merely vicariously—in the experience of
that frustration. It is in this context that we must understand Shakespeare's counterpointing of words and gestures throughout the play, a counterpointing that the
frequency of such words as "tongue" (twenty-four instances) and "hand" (seventy-
seven instances) helps to reify.[22] The silent girl becomes a "map of woe," the badge
of her family's verbal impotency in grief, a piece of human heraldry who is partly
the cause and partly the reflection of their own sufferings. Titus speaks not only for
the Andronici but for civilization generally when he fantasizes the metamorphosing
of the entire clan to Lavinia's semihuman state:

> Or shall we cut away our hands, like thine?
> Or shall we bite our tongues, and in dumb shows
> Pass the remainder of our hateful days?
> What shall we do? Let us, that have our tongues,

> Plot some device of further misery,
> To make us wonder'd at in time to come.
>
> (III.i.130–135)

This speech, of course, immediately anticipates the actual chopping off of the hero's hand, consciously an act of self-sacrifice but symbolically of self-destruction (since the act avails nothing) and particularly of the maiming of expressive power with which hands in this drama are repeatedly associated. Titus's frustrations in this respect begin to approach those of his daughter, as he himself recognizes in a speech to his brother, again in her presence:

> Thy niece and I, poor creatures, want our hands,
> And cannot passionate our tenfold grief
> With folded arms. This poor right hand of mine
> Is left to tyrannize upon my breast,
> Who, when my heart, all mad with misery,
> Beats in this hollow prison of my flesh,
> Then thus I thump it down.   [*Beats his breast.*]
>
> (III.ii.5–11)

When there are no more tears to shed and when his pain is no longer compassable in verse, Titus breaks into hysterical laughter, a subverbal form of utterance not far removed from Lavinia's groans or frantic bodily movements. Verbal excess and verbal incapacity thus encroach upon each other almost to the point of identity, and as Titus himself phrases it, this mergence represents "a sympathy of woe . . . As far from help as Limbo is from bliss" (III.i.148–149). As for the hysteria, Shakespeare would seem to give us an earlier version of Edgar's insight that "the worst returns to laughter" (*King Lear*, IV.i.6), for here, as in the later tragedy, "The worst is not / So long as [Titus] can say, 'This is the worst' " (IV.i.27–28).

The action of *Titus Andronicus* from first to last is marked by heavy dependence on gestures and stage movements that contrast with speech. Often these seem designed to give the impression either that words alone are too limited or ineffective to accomplish their purpose or that characters at times of crisis are unable to speak for themselves. The funeral procession in the opening scene, for instance, is pageantlike in its elaborateness (the stage direction fills nine lines in Bevington's text). Titus speaks eloquently, but only after more than a dozen speechless actors have escorted the coffin to the door of the tomb, that symbol of death and "silence" (I.i.93) that dominates the entire first act visually. Then we see Alarbus, one of the silent figures, delivered over to bloody sacrifice without uttering a word of protest or supplication. His mother pleads passionately but unsuccessfully for him, and Demetrius remarks helplessly to Chiron (another silent brother), "Alarbus goes to rest, and we survive / To tremble" (I.i.136–137).

Similarly, Lavinia yields without objection when Saturninus claims her for his wife, even though we learn a moment later that she has already been betrothed to Bassianus. When Mutius speaks up in defense of the wronged couple (a total of only three lines), Titus silences him instantly and forever with his sword. The hero's frustrations mount immediately as the emperor insultingly rejects Lavinia in favor of Tamora, ceremoniously raising Titus's Gothic prisoner rather than his daughter to the empress's throne, and as his own kindred kneel to beg that Mutius be buried honorably in the family vault. A combination of carefully calculated movements thus dramatizes the general's plight and helps show him as torn between adherence to an abstract principle of authority and a dawning recognition that the embodiment of that authority, for whose benefit he has futilely slain his own son, is unworthy of loyalty. The whole first movement of the play thus presents us with a sense of ritualistic formality, supported by public oratory and gesture, at the core of which there is inexpressible pain—a kind of emotional chaos that can only be conveyed indirectly and of which the physical deaths are somehow the outward manifestation.

The remaining acts develop the lead established by the first. We see Titus driven to physical actions that point up the insufficiency of speech.[23] "*Andronicus lieth down*," as the stage direction tells us, "*and the Judges pass by him*" (III.i.11). After losing one of his hands to the chopping block, he lifts the other "up to heaven, / And bow[s] this feeble ruin to the earth" (III.i.206–207). Distractedly, he directs the shooting of arrow-messages to the gods when earthly appeals have failed, and later, on the point of enacting his Thyestean vengeance, he enters "*like a cook, placing the dishes*" (V.iii.25). The most horrible crimes of the play are presented so as to juxtapose the free flow of speech with its contrary. The villains, particularly Aaron and Tamora, are capable of unrestrained eloquence as they plot their monstrous acts (the latter voices the most lyrical praise of nature in the play),[24] but Lavinia must grope uncertainly for animal analogies ("Yet have I heard—O, could I find it now!— / The lion . . . did endure / To have his princely paws pared" [II.iii.150–152]) to argue against her violators. Even as she confronts the rape itself, she admits ironically that "womanhood denies [her] tongue" (II.iii.174) to name it. After her mutilation, we observe her running from her uncle and turning her face away in shame, then sobbing, then comforting her father with a kiss, then trying to communicate through signs—pursuing a schoolboy and turning the leaves of his book with her stumps, lifting her arms in sequence to indicate the number of her assailants, and writing with a stick held in her mouth. Passive victimization is a prominent feature of the dramaturgy. Like Alarbus in the first act, Martius and Quintus, although innocent, are led silently to execution, while their parent vainly implores mercy, the emperor having forbidden them to "speak a word" (II.iii.301) in their own defense. In a balancing scene, Titus orates for thirty-eight lines while the speechless Lavinia holds a basin to catch the ritually spilled blood of Demetrius and Chiron, who, even before their throats are cut, are also silenced: "Stop close their mouths, let them not speak a word" (V.ii.164).

Shakespeare makes the stifling of speech a pervasive motif in the tragedy.[25] Titus stabs Mutius for daring to oppose him, then tries also to silence his other sons for siding with their fatally outspoken brother: "Speak thou no more, if all the rest will speed" (I.i.376). When Lucius and Marcus attempt to excuse their defense of Bassianus, the emperor cries, "Away, and talk not" (I.i.482). Demetrius, bickering with Chiron over precedence, threatens to "thrust" his brother's "reproachful speeches down his throat" (II.i.55). Lavinia begs to be listened to before her rape but is forbidden by Tamora ("I will not hear her speak. Away with her!" [II.iii.137]), whereupon Chiron, with a gruesome pun that implies both kissing and the mutilation to follow, interrupts her curse upon him with "nay, then I'll stop your mouth" (II.iii.185). Aaron murders both the nurse, a "long-tongu'd babbling gossip" (IV.ii.153), and the midwife, either of whom could disclose the secret of his child's parentage; and the Goth who captures him reports how the blackamoor tried to quiet the "brat's" cries to avoid detection (V.i.24–30). Saturninus hangs the innocent clown who delivers a threatening message, and Lucius wants to "stop [Aaron's] mouth" with a gag to curtail the "torment" of his "bitter tongue" (V.i.150–151). Suffering robs two characters of their eloquence in the final scene. Incapable of summarizing the events of the tragedy, an anonymous Roman lord, if we may accept the first quarto's ascription of the lines (some modern editors assign the words to Marcus), urges Lucius to speak for him:

> My heart is not compact of flint nor steel,
> Nor can I utter all our bitter grief,
> But floods of tears will drown my oratory,
> And break my utt'rance.
>
> (V.iii.88–91)

Titus's grandson is similarly overcome: "I cannot speak . . . for weeping; / My tears will choke me, if I ope my mouth" (V.iii.174–175). Characteristically, it is Aaron, inhuman in his callousness, who can remain actively verbal: "Ah, why should wrath be mute, and fury dumb?" (V.iii.184).

The emblematic and near-allegorical techniques of *Titus Andronicus* assist the theme of verbal limitation because they tend to make physical on the stage or give visual form to ideas that are more often reserved for simile or metaphor.[26] Thus Shakespeare actualizes the symbolic Hell into which so many of the characters descend by allowing us to see the body of Bassianus thrown into the pit and then the two sons of Titus successively falling into it. The attack upon family coherence is made grotesquely literal by the mocking return of Titus's severed hand together with the heads of his sons, and later by Lavinia's bearing of the hand in her teeth. Marcus's killing of the fly turns into stage allegory both the idea of murdered innocence and the rage to eliminate the blackest of evils as incarnated in Aaron. The symbolic weapons with their ironic verses from Horace ("*Integer vitae scelerisque purus*") convert the threat of revenge against Tamora's sons into a "conceit" (IV.ii.30) that is at once physical and literary.

Some of the classical allusions (and of course the play is freighted with them) work in the same direction. Lavinia is quite factually a second Philomel, then, secondarily, both a Lucrece and (when her father kills her) a Virginia. Tamora becomes a female Thyestes, consuming the flesh of her own children in full view of the audience. Demetrius, Chiron, and their mother not only personify themselves as Murder, Rape, and Revenge in the play-within-the-play, but also comprise a triangular allegory of moral relationship; as such, they bridge the traditional gap between abstraction and concreteness, between the universality of a concept and its exemplification in a particular form. Indeed, Shakespeare's ostentatious attempt to assimilate so much literary "culture" into the action of the play, quite apart from the youthful display of virtuosity and learning it betokens, points to a restless search for forms of expression emotionally equivalent to a "wilderness of tigers" (III.i.54). Accordingly, the playwright besets his characters with the same quest for "objective correlatives" that defines the aesthetic of his own procedure. Not for nothing does Titus, trying vainly to accommodate unspeakable horror, draw his mute daughter aside to pursue parallels between literature and life:

> Lavinia, go with me.
> I'll to thy closet, and go read with thee

Sad stories chanced in the times of old.
(III.ii.81–83)[27]

It will appear that *Titus Andronicus* represents a most ambitious experiment on the threshold of Shakespeare's tragic career. We may debate whether the thoroughgoing, almost systematic antinaturalism of the play's technique fully realizes its objectives, but the contrasting of overwrought, too highly articulated utterance with gestic and more inchoate kinds of communication can be justified to some extent on psychological and even on aesthetic grounds.

Problems, of course, remain. The static artifices of language, especially when accumulated, can work against dramatic engagement and thus come to resemble the narrative copiousness of *The Rape of Lucrece*, which Shakespeare was indulging himself in about the same time. A ritualistic approach to savagery may serve to canalize and control audience response and hence to push it in the direction of irony or even satire. Moreover, the endless succession of brutalities risks anticlimax. If horror establishes itself as the norm, it may finally desensitize us even as it desensitizes Titus. The obliquities of Shakespeare's technique permit little direct participation in the protagonist's interior conflicts, little opportunity to become involved in any deepening of emotion or expansion of insight. The hero almost never soliloquizes, largely, perhaps, because self-discovery is foreign not only to the character but to the nightmare world of the drama as a whole. Titus's sufferings shrink, rather than enlarge, his sensibilities.

Most damaging of all, the frigidities and elaborations of style to which Shakespeare resorts in *Titus Andronicus* call in question the genuineness of the emotions depicted. Quintillian observed that when an orator "expresses his anger, his sorrow or his entreaties in neat antitheses, balanced cadences and exact correspondences," such ostentation "weakens the impression of emotional sincerity" and provokes the hearer to say that the "truth is not in him."[28] In fact, the charge of insincerity has nearly always informed the most negative assessments of Shakespeare's first tragedy. It was this difficulty, among others, that the dramatist would address so imaginatively in *Hamlet*.

IV

If, at first blush, there might seem to be but few links between *Titus Andronicus* and *Hamlet*, Tom Stoppard in *Rosencrantz and Guildenstern Are Dead* prompts us to reconsider. The title characters of the modern drama wittily hector the itinerant player on a theme as central to the later as to the earlier Elizabethan tragedy:

> *Guildenstern.* Now mind your tongue, or we'll have it out and throw
>   the rest of you away, like a nightingale at a Roman feast.
> *Rosencrantz.* Took the very words out of my mouth.
> *Guildenstern.* You'd be *lost* for words.
> *Rosencrantz.* You'd be tongue-tied.
> *Guildenstern.* Like a mute in a monologue.
> *Rosencrantz.* Like a nightingale at a Roman feast.
> *Guildenstern.* Your diction will go to pieces.
> *Rosencrantz.* Your lines will be cut.
> *Guildenstern.* To dumbshows.

Rosencrantz. And dramatic pauses.
Guildenstern. You'll never *find* your tongue.[29]

This delicious badinage must have been at least partly inspired by the theme of enforced silence and the frustrated attempts to verbalize emotion that almost everywhere inform Shakespeare's most quoted play. That Stoppard should have employed the grim joke of the extirpated tongue, at the same time invoking the image of "a Roman feast," is richly suggestive of *Hamlet*'s less celebrated predecessor on the boards.

We properly think of the Danish prince as the most resourcefully verbal of Shakespeare's heroes. Hamlet comfortably outdistances all other characters of the canon in absolute totals of words, lines, and speeches delivered, as well as all other Shakespearean protagonists in the percentage of words, lines, and speeches within his own play.[30] Yet the margins of his tragic career are bounded mysteriously by silence—by a Ghost at the beginning "dumb" (I.i.171) to all save one, a Ghost who must repeatedly be implored to "speak" (I.i.51), and at the end by the "quiet" (V.i.298) of the grave into which all but a few disappear, leaving the "ears . . . senseless that should give [the English ambassadors] hearing" (V.ii.371) and only Horatio to "speak to th' yet unknowing world" (V.ii.381). Our first impression of Hamlet is of a solitary, mute before the magniloquence of his uncle's rhetoric; our final impression is of a man arrested by "this fell sergeant, Death" from "report[ing himself] and [his] cause aright / To the unsatisfied" (V.ii.338–342).

Hamlet's world, just as importantly as Titus's or Lavinia's, is haunted by terrible secrets and suppressions of the truth. Like these characters, too, Hamlet must search restlessly and often unsatisfactorily for the means to express his feelings. Sorrowing for his father's death and his mother's remarriage, he carries "that within which passes show," a grief to which the "windy suspiration of forc'd breath" (I.ii.79–85) cannot adequately give voice, and, though his heart break, he "must hold [his] tongue" (I.ii.159). After the Ghost's revelation he is bursting to share his dreadful "news" (I.v.118), but he must curb his impulse with "wild and whirling words" (I.v.134) that disguise rather than disclose his heart. We learn that Hamlet appeared to Ophelia looking as though "he had been loosed out of hell / To speak of horrors" (II.i.80–81) but, finding no appropriate language, had to communicate, like Lavinia, exclusively through sighs and gestures. Later we see him misleading Rosencrantz and Guildenstern with a remark that betrays as much emotional constraint as it hides information: "O God, I could be bounded in a nutshell and count myself a king of infinite space, were it not that I have bad dreams" (II.ii.255–257). Hamlet admires the expressive powers of the player, the "broken voice, and his whole function suiting / With forms to his conceit," while he by contrast either "can say nothing" or "Must, like a whore, unpack [his] heart with words / And fall a-cursing, like a very drab" (II.ii.556–587). Again in the nunnery scene, with that complex amalgam of truth and falsehood that so often defines his speeches, the prince confesses his incapacity to give his deepest emotions proper expression: "I am very proud, revengeful, ambitious, with more offenses at my beck than I have thoughts to put them in, imagination to give them shape, or time to act them in" (III.i.125–128).

A certain natural reticence is one of the prince's most understressed traits. Hamlet breaks off his moving praise of Horatio to avoid embarrassing them both ("Something too much of this—" [III.ii.73]), and even after his return from the sea journey when much of the inner tension seems to have been resolved, we are aware of painful silences.

For instance, until he injects himself sensationally into it, Hamlet remains the almost wordless observer of Ophelia's funeral. Although no one in the play rivals Hamlet's eloquence or brilliant powers of articulation—and, paradoxically, this is so even when the prince feigns madness—Shakespeare continually conveys the sense of emotion beyond the reach of language. Hamlet's final words, "the rest is silence" (V.ii.360), sum up this idea poignantly, uniting it to the ultimate experience of inexpressibility—death itself.[31] And in their powerful valedictories the survivors confirm our recognition of linguistic limits. Horatio, deputized by Hamlet with his "dying voice" to "tell [his] story" (V.ii.351–358), will have much "cause to speak"; but, although he takes his authority from a "mouth whose voice will draw on more" (V.ii.393–394), we know that his words must come short of the reality he will seek to verbalize. With equal force Fortinbras, instinctively acknowledging such limitations, invokes "the soldiers' music and the rites of war" to "speak loudly" (V.ii.401–402) for a youth to whom no human eulogist could do justice.

The poetic tone of the final movement of *Hamlet*, then, is such as to call linguistic certitudes into question—to make us rest acceptingly, if sadly, in the stubborn inequality between profound emotions and the rhetorical strategies invented to give them form. In observing to Horatio that "a man's life's no more than to say 'One' " (V.ii.74), the prince seems almost to confess as much, for he reduces the perpetual conflict between human aspiration and the brevity of existence to a monosyllable. With Hamlet we are compelled to become reluctant nominalists, painfully subduing our definitional struggles to the stoic "let be" (V.ii.222) that releases catastrophe even as it somehow lifts our consciousness above it.

Shakespeare supports the impression of experience too deep or too complex for ready formulation by surrounding the prince with characters whose glibness, fluency, or ornateness of speech become symptoms of their shallowness or dishonesty. The conspicuous antitheses and oxymora of Claudius's opening address hint at the doubleness of his inner world before we have corroborating facts. Polonius's comic prolixities that bury tedious "matter" under too much "art" (II.ii.95), his pretentious "windlasses" and "assays of bias" (II.i.62), and his fondness for copybook sententiae all point to moral as well as aesthetic superficiality. The "candied" (III.ii.59) flatteries of Rosencrantz and Guildenstern and the ludicrously "golden words" (V.ii.131) of Osric contribute to the same effect, as do Laertes' crude hyperboles of grief that enrage Hamlet to such passionate mockery:

> 'Swounds, show me what thou't do.
> Woo 't weep? Woo 't fight? Woo 't fast? Woo 't tear thyself?
> Woo 't drink up eisel? Eat a crocodile?
> I'll do 't. Dost thou come here to whine?
> To outface me with leaping in her grave?
> Be buried quick with her, and so will I.
> And, if thou prate of mountains, let them throw
> Millions of acres on us, till our ground,
> Singeing his pate against the burning zone,
> Make Ossa like a wart! Nay, an thou 'lt mouth,
> I'll rant as well as thou.
>
> (V.i.274–284)

Each of these characters, whether consciously or not, is perceived as using rhetoric pervertedly as a public show to screen private feeling. And Hamlet himself is so obsessed with the distinction between sincere and insincere modes of response that he convicts himself and others of falsity even where it does not exist.

At the other end of the scale are figures whose unselfconscious "simplicity" of utterance also suggests the gap between easy speech and hard significance. Ophelia in mental collapse prattles a kind of antic "half sense": she

> hems, and beats her heart,
> Spurns enviously at straws, speaks things in doubt
> That carry but half sense. Her speech is nothing,
> Yet the unshaped use of it doth move
> The hearers to collection; they yawn at it,
> And botch the words up fit to their own thoughts,
> Which, as her winks and nods and gestures yield them,
> Indeed would make one think there might be thought,
> Though nothing sure, yet much unhappily.
>
> (IV.v.5–13)

The complacent digger of graves, contrastingly, speaks so "by the card," reduces words to such an absurd standard of literalness that he fosters a whole range of suggestiveness that paradoxically vitiates his antiequivocal or "absolute" (V.i.137–138) idiom.

Hamlet assumes so many different voices in the play—Christian and pagan, loving and cruel, mad and sane, admiring and condemnatory, hopeful and cynical, cocksure and speculative, self-centered and generous, hate-filled and forgiving, witty and sad— that in some sense he synthesizes and transcends all the other attitudes represented. Regal like his father, devious like his uncle, thoughtful like Horatio, actively courageous like Fortinbras, rash like Laertes, theatrical like the player, he is also the brilliant parodist of Polonius, of Rosencrantz and Guildenstern, of Osric. Yet at the heart of this dazzling ventriloquism stands the soliloquist wrestling heroically and, in a way, *silently* with self-discovery. For, as Charles Lamb noted, Hamlet's "solitary musings," his "transactions between himself and his moral sense," are "light-and-noise-abhorring ruminations, which the tongue scarce dares utter to deaf walls and chambers," and which are "reduced to *words*" only for the sake of stage necessity. Characteristically, of course, Lamb was offended by the convention that required "a gesticulating actor" to "mouth" Hamlet's profoundest sorrows "before an audience, making four hundred people his confidants at once."[32] But we need not assent to Lamb's distaste for Shakespeare staged to grant the idea of almost unutterable privacy that the soliloquies do indeed convey. And we might add, with Hamlet himself, that these verbalized silences represent a tendency to retreat from action, "the native hue of resolution" being "sicklied o'er with the pale cast of thought" (III.i.85–86).

V

For plays so removed from each other in date and tragic effect, *Hamlet* and *Titus* contain a surprising number of elements in common. Some of these, of course, may be accounted for simply as elements endemic to the genre, revenge conventions, which

Shakespeare's two tragedies did much to establish or reinforce. But the continuities go well beyond these obvious features, the most straightforward of which is similarity in plot. Both stories are set against a background of war between nations, and both, too, connect murder with adultery. Both begin with ironic juxtapositions of death and sexual appetite, the burial of Titus's sons and the emperor's espousing of Tamora finding a parallel of sorts in Claudius's balancing of "delight and dole," of "mirth in funeral" and "dirge in marriage" (I.ii.12–13). Both tragedies contrast international conflict with upheaval and corruption at home, Rome and Denmark equally representing advanced stages of moral decay. Both plots also show the purging of this rot my means of alliance with the foreign and originally hostile forces. As Lucius becomes the new emperor of Rome, aided by an army of Goths, the people his father had defeated, so Fortinbras, a Norwegian prince with "some rights of memory" (V.ii.391) in Denmark, becomes the new sovereign of a country that had conquered and slain his father.

Although we expect Machiavellian deception in revenge tragedies and although the source materials of both plays largely account for the fact, the ironic neatness of the trickery in both *Titus* and *Hamlet* is notable. Aaron's return of the severed heads and hand to Titus, for instance, represents a gleefully mortal turning of the tables similar to Hamlet's own practice when he replaces his own death warrant with that for Rosencrantz and Guildenstern. The two tragedies not only make use of the play-within-the-play for purposes of entrapment, they also stress ironic correspondences between the make-believe and the truth. As Tamora and her sons enact Revenge, Murder, and Rape, their genuine roles in the larger action of *Titus Andronicus*, so the actors of *The Murder of Gonzago* represent the principals of both the crime and the revenge in the overall framework of *Hamlet*. We have already noted the elements of mime in Lavinia's attempts to expose her assailants. These, of course, find their counterpart in the formal dumbshow with which the players introduce their conscience-catching performance in *Hamlet*. Even the giving of ominous gifts turns up in both dramas: the weapons presented to Demetrius and Chiron obliquely characterize the violence and portend the death of the two brothers, just as the several flowers that Ophelia distributes to members of the Danish court comment similarly on both the past and future of the recipients.

Curious links between *Titus* and *Hamlet* also appear in aspects of the characterization and in the character relationships. Both dramas depict young heroines (Lavinia and Ophelia) callously rejected by princes (Saturninus and Hamlet) who had intended to marry them.[33] The upright and deserving Bassianus who, contending for the emperorship, loses out to his corrupt brother reminds us of old Hamlet supplanted by Claudius, "Hyperion" opposed by a "satyr"; and of course in both plays the virtuous brother is brutally murdered. In both cases also, the good brother is betrothed or married to a woman for whom the immoral brother becomes a rival. The heroes of both tragedies are shown to be at odds with close relatives—Titus with his brother and sons over Bassianus's claim to Lavinia and Mutius's right to burial, Hamlet with his mother and uncle. In both instances the sense of alienation from their own flesh and blood in addition to the injustices they suffer contributes to the two men's frustration and partly accounts for their retreat into psychic isolation and instability. When the tyrannical emperor of *Titus* prophetically regards the banished Lucius as a threat to his security, he remarks on the great "love" that "the common people" (IV.iv.73) have for the exile. Shakespeare of course repeats this detail when Claudius, on the point of dispatching Hamlet to England, recognizes that his enemy is "lov'd of the distracted multitude" (IV.iii.4).[34] Even the clowns of the two plays are related in the capital they make out of gallows humor. The low comic in *Titus* puns at his first entrance on "Jupiter" and "gibbet-maker" (IV.iii.79–80), then makes his final exit by being condemned to the rope in very truth. His counterparts in *Hamlet* jest in similar fashion on how the "frame" of the "gallows-maker . . . outlives a thousand tenants" (V.i.43–44).

Thematic cross-relations between the two dramas are equally suggestive. Perhaps the most obvious is the careful working out in both plays of the adage that "murder, though it have no tongue, will speak / With most miraculous organ" (*Hamlet*, II.ii.594–595). As we have noted, each tragedy builds psychic tension on the conflict between the impulse to publish terrible truths and the contrary need to internalize them, to "Give [them] an understanding, but no tongue" (*Hamlet*, I.ii.249). The emblem of the tomb or grave takes on a major significance in both plays not merely as a feature of the imagery but as an important device of spatial symbolism. The vault in which the Andronici are ceremonially entombed gives way to the pit where Bassianus's corpse is thrown and into which Martius and Quintus successively fall. Shakespeare gives us a later version of this macabre descent to the dead when Hamlet and Laertes grapple in Ophelia's grave. In both cases, of course, the trap in the stage floor comes to represent the maw of death indiscriminately devouring its victims, reducing human difference to the dust of mortality. Both scenes, also, are proleptic, foreshadowing, as they do, violent deaths that actually occur shortly afterward.

Significant images in *Titus* that strike us with their blatant physicality seem to have been reabsorbed less sensationally into the greater metaphorical complexity of *Hamlet*. Take the sanguinary horror of Lavinia's "bubbling fountain," her "three issuing spouts" of gore (*Titus Andronicus*, II.iv.23–30), or, even more hideously, the physical pouring out into a basin of the blood of Tamora's sons as a "hateful liquor" (V.ii.199). The language horribly decorates the visual reality. Nothing so crude survives in the more mature tragedy, but we can recognize in Hamlet's "Now could I drink hot blood, / And do such bitter business as the day / Would quake to look on" (III.ii.389–391) a remnant of the older tradition adapted to greater psychological subtlety. Shakespeare had learned that the mental image of blood sacrifice was more powerful than its physical representation. Another example is the prince's imaging of his devastated world as "an unweeded garden" wholly possessed by "things rank and gross in nature" (I.ii.135–136). This idea may be regarded as a refinement of the theme of the corrupted or violated garden that so informs the imagery and settings of *Titus*. As Albert H. Tricomi points out: "The metamorphosis of the pastoral forest [in the Roman tragedy] *is* the metamorphosis of Lavinia writ large; the dual transfiguration is part of the same symbolic event."[35] In *Hamlet* also, a symbolic transmutation of nature occurs. Claudius with "juice of cursed hebona" transforms the peaceful "orchard" (I.v.60–63) where his brother took his afternoon rest into a garden of death, and in consequence, he also pollutes the psychic garden of his nephew and indirectly of Ophelia, who, "divided from herself" (IV.v.86), makes "fantastic garlands" (IV.vii.168) of sexually suggestive flowers and is pulled down into the primordial slime.[36]

Even in the use of classical allusion the two plays are significantly linked. *Titus*, of course, deliberately flaunts its Senecan-Ovidian style, whereas *Hamlet* makes less show of being learned or "literary" in effect. Nevertheless, the latter play shares with its precursor references to Aeneas, Dido, Priam, Hecuba, Hyperion, Hymen, Mercury, Vulcan, Mars, Jove, Olympus, and the ancient Greeks. In addition, Lavinia's recourse to Ovid for the literary parallel to her own tragedy finds a remarkable analogy in Hamlet's attraction to the speech, based on Virgil, that describes the murder of King Priam and Hecuba's grief. The need to objectify suffering through formal eloquence is an important ingredient in the psychology of both plays, and Shakespeare in each instance builds the search for objective correlatives—"metadramatically," as it were—into the very staging of the action. In their different ways, then, both *Titus* and *Hamlet* exploit the paradox that art can "cleave the general ear with horrid speech, / Make mad the guilty and appall the free, / Confound the ignorant, and amaze indeed / The very faculties of eyes and ears" (*Hamlet*, II.ii.563–566), while human sufferers must remain inarticulate or silent.

But, of course, to dwell on the links between the apprentice and the riper tragedy is only to become more conscious than ever of the artistic chasm that divides them. Titus is presented as a soldier, single-minded and stubborn, whose rigidities of behavior bespeak his intellectual and emotional limitations. Hamlet, though also a "soldier" (as his funeral rites reaffirm), is an intellectual caught up in the quirks and trickeries of his own mental processes, aware (as Titus never could be) of the puzzling interplay between objective and subjective sides of the truth, torn between the conflicting imperatives of his own complex nature. Susan Snyder suggests that "Hamlet's peculiar tragedy" is "to be flexible where flexibility is a drawback, to see beyond his own convictions," that is, to be intellectually and ironically disengaged in the midst of an enterprise that necessitates singleness of feeling and purpose.[37] Although a number of the Andronici are victims of unspeakable outrage, our observation of their plight remains relatively more distanced and objective. We are encouraged to look upon them in Ovidian fashion as objects of contemplation and wonder, as artifacts of extraordinary woe, and the villains, even Aaron with his special vitality, as totems of evil. But our emotional involvement in *Hamlet*, as everyone knows, extends even to the kingly murderer of the play. As for the hero, we experience *with him*, as though it were our own, the baffling dialectic between Christian and pagan, sensitive and harsh, subjective and objective valuations of a world in which choice seems at once predetermined and free.

In *Hamlet* the soliloquies of both hero and villain become battlegrounds in which the conscious self wrestles with its own divisions. Titus, virtually deprived of soliloquies, feels no anguish for the loss of innocence nor any scruples about purity of motive. For Hamlet delay becomes partly a function of his own sensibility; for Titus it is merely a set of external obstacles. In *Titus* bloodshed, suffering, and revenge circumscribe the ethos and purpose of the play. In *Hamlet* these elements become the means, not the end, the revenge conventions serving chiefly as a medium through which philosophical concerns about the nature of heroism, the limits of the will, and the brevity of life may be profoundly explored. The "madness" of Titus is both a strategy of intrigue and the outward sign of frustrations too great to endure. The melancholy of Hamlet incorporates these features but stretches beyond them to embrace the uncertainties and confusions that lie at the heart of the play's epistemology. Titus changes only in response to external stimuli; Hamlet changes most significantly in response to the probings of his own nature and, as such, marks a brilliant advance in the characterization of revengers. His particular situation is made to universalize the strain between thought and action and, further, to embody the tragic impossibility of fully harmonizing the dissonance that we recognize as fundamental to human nature.

Given such significant differences in scope, we should scarcely be surprised that the two plays should diverge so remarkably in style. The most obvious contrast, naturally, is one of range. Because in *Titus* Shakespeare sought to galvanize his audience with the extravagancy and ingeniousness of his verbal invention, he was as yet less interested than he would later become in subtle adjustments of speech to character and situation. The result is a style fatiguingly rhetorical and monochromatic, as though the characters were perpetually at the rostrum orating tumidly and at the top of their lungs. With the more naturalistic dramaturgy of *Hamlet* came, inevitably, a kaleidoscope of styles and tonalities not only within the play as a whole but also, and especially, within the speeches of the hero. In *Titus*, more or less routinely, we get the tragical equivalent of Berowne's "taffeta phrases," "three-pil'd hyperboles," and "figures pedantical"—artifices of the tongue that fairly teem with "maggot ostentation" (*Love's Labor's Lost*, V.ii.407–410). In *Hamlet* verbal showiness and exuberance are not absent, but Shakespeare tends to reserve such display for speeches like the Ghost's harrowing tale, the player's description of Priam, the queen's elegy on Ophelia, or Laertes' outburst of grief, where a particular contrast in styles is part of the dynamic of the scene.

Hamlet himself, as Maurice Charney has shown, speaks in a multiplicity of voices that include punning, quibbling, logic-chopping, philosophical ruminating, bitter disappointment, cynicism, parody, insult, bawdry, wordiness, and brevity.[38] Capable of the loftiest of passions and the earthiest of revulsions, the prince ranges freely from the most elevated verse to the most colloquial prose, sometimes blending the two with moving effect as in the famous meditation, "What a piece of work is a man!" (II.ii.304–309). Although Hamlet is portrayed as a self-conscious stylist in his own right, directness and simplicity of speech usually characterize his moments of most intense emotion:

> Here hung those lips that I have kiss'd I know not how oft. Where be your gibes now? Your gambols, your songs, your flashes of merriment that were wont to set the table on a roar? Not one now, to mock your own grinning?
>
> (V.i.187–191)

> Not a whit, we defy augury. There is special providence in the fall of a sparrow. If it be now, 'tis not to come; if it be not to come, it will be now; if it be not now, yet it will come. The readiness is all.
>
> (V.ii.217–220)

> If thou didst ever hold me in thy heart,
> Absent thee from felicity awhile,
> And in this harsh world draw thy breath in pain
> To tell my story.
>
> (V.ii.348–351)

Hamlet is as much an actor as the players he instructs, but in the main, he takes his own advice, suiting "the action to the word, the word to the action," being careful (with some purposeful exceptions) to "o'erstep not the modesty of nature" (III.ii.17–19).[39]

VI

We can imagine Dr. Johnson applying to the style of *Titus* what he said of "Lycidas"— that "Where there is leisure for fiction, there is little grief."[40] We can equally imagine him responding favorably to the sense of fact in *Hamlet*, to the emotional genuineness, to the "touches of nature" (as he might have said), and to the stylistic restraints that so often make this verisimilitude possible. The difference is notable even when a decorative flourish adorns the later play. When dawn comes in *Titus*, it comes in a simile of labored and epic pretentiousness:

> As when the golden sun salutes the morn,
> And, having gilt the ocean with his beams,
> Gallops the zodiac in his glistering coach,
> And overlooks the highest-peering hills,
> So Tamora.
>
> (II.i.5–9)

It is perhaps significant that so mannered a comparison should be applied to a villainess, but in *Hamlet* only one of the visiting players could speak so stiffly. In the later tragedy such scenery is transfigured almost unrecognizably into the simpler and much more beautiful

> But, look, the morn, in russet mantle clad,
> Walks o'er the dew of yon high eastward hill.
>
> (I.i.166–167)

Edgar's line, "Speak what we feel, not what we ought to say" (*King Lear*, V.iii.329), conveys some idea of the distance Shakespeare had traversed between his first and his second attempt at revenge tragedy.

But if the circuitous route from *Titus* to *Hamlet* marks an incalculable advance in expressive subtlety, we are nevertheless left in both plays with the recognition that language, even at its most eloquent, can at best only approach or imperfectly represent the tragic passions, doubts, mysteries, and frustrations that are its subject. Man's two possible responses to the deepest kinds of pain—the incapacity to say anything or the impulse to say too much—remain part of the fabric of both plays. All tragedy, of course, depends to some degree upon the ventilation of human agony, for such ventilation reassures us not only that agony is meaningful, but that the meaning can be communicated. And, if it can be communicated, it can in some sense be borne, for "The worst is not / So long as we can say 'This is the worst'." In *Macbeth*, when Macduff receives the shattering news of his family's slaughter, we need to hear him *speak*, not merely to see him "pull [his] hat upon [his] brows"; and we therefore second Malcolm's plea: "Give sorrow words. The grief that does not speak / Whispers the o'er-fraught heart and bids it break" (IV.iii.208–210). But Macduff knows, and we know with him, that his pain, as Goneril says in a very different context, is "more than word can wield the matter" (*King Lear*, I.i.55). Of course he recovers his voice, without which the scene could not continue, but, for the moment, silence is the only truthful possibility. Anything else, in Hamlet's weary phrase, would be merely "words, words, words" (II.ii.193). In the nature of things tragedy tests the limits of expressibility, but *Titus Andronicus* and *Hamlet* in their different ways build that test into the very heart and shape of their meaning.

3

Immediacy and Remoteness in The Taming of the Shrew *and* The Tempest

> the Bard
> Was sober when he wrote
> That this world of fact we love
> Is unsubstantial stuff:
> All the rest is silence
> On the other side of the wall;
> And the silence ripeness,
> And the ripeness all.
> —W. H. Auden, *The Sea and the Mirror*

I

When Shakespeare makes Julio Romano's statue mysteriously descend from its pedestal and live again as Hermione, he does more than dramatize the regenerative theme of *The Winter's Tale*. Tantalizing interplay between art and nature is not merely a perennial concern of pastoral (and therefore of the romances as a group) but a continuing preoccupation in Shakespearean drama, as other chapters in this volume illustrate, from the earliest to the latest plays. But, as G. Wilson Knight among others has noticed,[1] this scene resonates with an otherworldly suggestiveness and bears a visionary emphasis peculiar to the final phase of Shakespeare's dramaturgy. Listen to Paulina:

> As she liv'd peerless,
> So her dead likeness, I do well believe,
> Excels whatever yet you look'd upon
> Or hand of man hath done. Therefore I keep it
> Lonely, apart. But here it is. Prepare
> To see the life as lively mock'd as ever
> Still sleep mock'd death. Behold, and say 'tis well.
> *[Paulina draws a curtain, and discovers]*
> *Hermione [standing] like a statue.*
> I like your silence; it the more shows off

43

Your wonder. But yet speak; first, you, my liege.
Comes it not something near?

. . . .
                                    It is requir'd
You do awake your faith. Then all stand still.

. . . .
                        Music, awake her; strike! [*Music.*]
'Tis time; descend; be stone no more; approach;
Strike all that look upon with marvel. Come,
I'll fill your grave up. Stir, nay, come away,
Bequeath to death your numbness, for from him
Dear life redeems you. You perceive she stirs.
                        [*Hermione comes down.*]
Start not; her actions shall be holy as
You hear my spell is lawful. Do not shun her
Until you see her die again.

                                    (V.iii.14–106)

With a ritualism and solemnity that owe much to the court masque, the dramatist here offers us a theatrical emblem of consciousness expanding, of perception enlarging its context. Identifying first with Leontes' guilt and restricted awareness, then with the amazement of the assembled onlookers, the audience at the Globe or Blackfriars observes a show-within-a-show: Paulina, as presenter, draws a curtain and magically transforms what appears to be stone and paint into flesh and blood. The comparatively remote figure behind the curtain steps forward to join those who had gazed upon her as a thing apart, and as Paulina urges the king and his companions to "awake [their] faith," she speaks past the Sicilians and their guests to stretch the perceptivity of Londoners. Life emerges out of art (a kind of death in Shakespeare's metaphor), but the life in question is "some sixteen years" older than it was, and the reanimation of Hermione is shadowed by the consciousness that all life, which includes art, is subject to limitations of time and physical decay, yet is mysteriously evocative of larger and unseen realities. The rhythm so movingly suggested here—the progression outward from art to life to eternity, from the remoteness of the inert statue through the more immediate and human joy of reunion to the sense of miracle that lies beyond mere sense experience and strangely fuses remoteness with immediacy—may serve as a paradigm for approaching an important aspect of technique and significance in Shakespeare's next play, *The Tempest*.

II

By way of clarifying the poet's procedure in what may well have been his final unaided drama, let us first consider a play that lies at the opposite end of his career, *The Taming of the Shrew*. All the early comedies of Shakespeare, no less than the late plays, are notable for inventive and varied experiments with conventional material; all, too, toy in their different ways with the elusive relativity of the artificial and the natural, the more remote and the more immediate. *The Taming of the Shrew*, however, is an extreme example of this engrossment, most obviously because it is Shakespeare's only play to present itself by means of an induction that is fully dramatic in its own right. In *The*

Taming the playwright conducts his viewers through an elaborate series of gradations or strata that seem peculiarly designed not only to span the gulf between the audience's sense of ordinary life and the farcically simplified world of Katharina and Petruchio but also to call attention to the artistic conventions and processes by which dramatic illusion is achieved. It is as though Shakespeare were asking us with one voice willingly to suspend our disbelief while inviting us with another to admire his professional skills as a technician of the theatre.

The play commences at a level of naturalism not far removed from that of the groundlings. The audience observes Christopher Sly, a drunken tinker, collapse near the door of a tavern from which he has just been expelled by the hostess; too deep in his cups to be more than feebly hostile, he shrugs, "let the world slide" (Induction, i.5), and soon passes out. At this point an anonymous lord and his hunting party enter to the sound of horns and invent an interior comedy into which Sly is to be thrust as the chief focus of attention. Life is to be converted into art. Transported to a country house, dressed in finery, and pampered with luxuries that include paintings, music, and theatrical entertainment, "the beggar" is induced to "forget himself" and mistake "a flatt'ring dream or worthless fancy" (Induction, i.40–43) for reality. To amuse the lord as well as those who have paid their pennies on the Bankside, the actor playing Sly exchanges a more immediate identity for a more remote one, and the tinker's psychological confusion at the sudden shift is explained to him ironically as the effect of a dream; the drunken sleep of a few hours (mere minutes in literal playing time) is fictionalized à la Rip van Winkle into a slumber of fifteen years. The lord supports Sly's illusion and further enriches the comedy by casting his boy page in the role of the victim's wife and by exciting Sly's sexual instincts with pictures of mythological subjects, which, for the sophisticated, represent yet a further degree of remoteness from actuality but for Sly are the immediate enticements of pornography.

After the bibulous tinker has been carried offstage and before he awakens into the illusory world that has been prepared for him, Shakespeare complicates the relationship between drama and life still further by introducing a troupe of itinerant players, one of whom the hospitable lord, like Hamlet in a similar situation, remembers from a former visit. The actor's role on another occasion ("a farmer's eldest son" who "woo'd the gentlewoman so well" [Induction, i.83–84]) is recalled, and the stage-managing lord ironically enlists the visiting players as supporting audience for the deception of Sly. They must be careful not to smile at the absurdity of the peasant's new situation and so break the illusion that is so artfully being constructed around him. Already within the induction Shakespeare involves us in a teasing confrontation of mirror with mirror. A theatre audience watches an actor in the role of a peer assume the function of a dramatist-producer, who imposes his own identity upon an actor, who plays a tinker, who in turn is married to a boy actor playing a page boy dressed as a lady.

Once Sly has settled into the false identity—and he accepts it with minimal protest—the induction defines three levels of engagement (or detachment). As the clever inventor of a complex joke, the lord remains as much as possible on the periphery of the action to observe the comic effects of his handiwork; Sly obtusely occupies the center, unable to preserve any psychological distance from the immediacy of the experience. The page boy mediates between these extremes, being almost equally involved in both: with the aid of an onion he feigns tears of joy for Sly's recovery from protracted sleep, while secretly laughing with his stage-managing master at the gullibility and ignorance of the man he is teaching to address him as "Madam." Moreover, we learn that the actor who plays the tinker-lord is to be solemnly attended by other actors, playing actors, who, from the nobleman's point of view, will be simulating offstage behavior and therefore dealing in illusion, but who, in Sly's distorted vision, will merely appear to be performers who have not yet donned their makeup and costumes.

Having drawn us progressively into this Pirandello-like maze, Shakespeare now extends the process by having the strolling players perform *The Taming of the Shrew* for the benefit of a triple audience—the paying public at the Globe, the members of the lord's household, and Sly himself as a sixteenth-century *bourgeois gentilhomme*. Making himself comfortable to enjoy the show from his position "*aloft*," the beringed tinker unconsciously echoes his own words at the tavern door before succumbing to alcoholic oblivion: "Come, madam wife, sit by my side and let the world slip; we shall ne'er be younger" (Induction, ii.138–139). A flourish of trumpets announces the play even as the horns had signaled the entrance of the lord and his fellow huntsmen. During the first scene of the comedy proper Sly struggles to concentrate on Lucentio's arrival at Padua and Baptista's plan to tie the marriage of his younger daughter to that of his elder. But before long the novice playgoer, heavy with boredom and more drink, is nodding off again. Although a stage direction indicates that Sly and others of his train continue to "*sit and mark*" (I.i.254), at least during part of the succeeding action, the characters of the induction take no further part in the play. It seems clear that these actors soon disappear unobtrusively—probably to reappear below in new roles, as the multiplying complications of the intrigue require. Our last impression of Sly is not unlike our first: as sleep dissolves the reality of the alehouse and enables the lord to supplant it with a manor house, so the reality of the manor house yields to a street in Padua as Sly once again "let[s] the world slip." Since Shakespeare resolutely fails to close the frame so self-consciously erected (a procedure radically different from that of the inferior *Taming of a Shrew*), he would seem to encourage us to look upon the cleverly linked love stories of Bianca and Katharina as coterminous with an elaborate dream—a dream that, in the manner of dreams, combines a sense of strangeness and contrivance with a sense of the natural.

Translated from London to Padua by way of Warwickshire, we discover that the interaction of artifice with naturalness is just commencing. For the sake of exposition, Lucentio and his servant Tranio acquaint us in stiffly mannered verse with what they already know of their own origin, history, and reason for coming to a famous university city; then they stand aside to witness the entrance of Baptista, his daughters, and the suitors who are competing for Bianca's hand—a procession that Tranio describes as "some show to welcome us to town" (I.i.47). Romantically smitten at the first sight of Bianca, Lucentio abandons his role as passive spectator and enters the competition as a participant; but in order to get the better of his rivals, he exchanges clothes with his servant, who now becomes his surrogate, and then assumes the further disguise of Cambio, a tutor to Baptista's daughters, that he may have easier access to the object of his affection. Mask conceals mask; Lucentio plays a role within a role. Here we have the theme of the "supposes," which Shakespeare borrowed from Ariosto (via Gascoigne), and the mistaken identities now proliferate to make a dizzying pattern of complication as the different levels of awareness and ignorance interact. In a remarkable addition to the source story, Hortensio, a second suitor, also masquerades as a tutor, taking the name of Licio; and a wandering pedant is induced under false colors to pose as Lucentio's father, only to cause general consternation when confronted by the real father.

Only after the plot of physical disguises and substitutions has begun does Shakespeare introduce us to Petruchio, so that we reach the earthier and more verisimilar of the contrasting love actions at a more remote point of the narrative sequence. Of course, the taming process itself involves the assumption of a tyrannical role to elicit the genuine good sense and capacity for devotion that lie hidden behind Katharina's unnatural facade of aggression. Petruchio teaches his new spouse to know herself by a distorted reflection of her own willfulness. Until this truth dawns upon her, she understandably thinks of him as a ruthless manipulator of people for theatrical sensation: "Belike you mean to make a puppet of me" (IV.iii.103). Not for nothing is the motif of dress so strenuously emphasized on both sides of the relationship. When Petruchio astonishes the wedding guests by his grotesquely inappropriate apparel ("so unlike yourself" [III.ii.103], in Tranio's phrase), the madcap bridegroom points to the difference between costume and wearer: "To me she's married, not unto my clothes" (III.ii.116). And after Kate has been frustratingly denied the fashionable wardrobe that would support her egotistic self-conception, she must rest content with "honest mean habiliments" and be told that "'tis the mind that makes the body rich" (IV.iii.166–168). When Kate learns to enter into the game of role-playing that Petruchio initiates, when she can symbolically accept fantasy as truth by admitting that the sun is the moon, she demonstrates a new imaginativeness, unselfishness, and humility that fulfill rather than inhibit her deepest longings. The final episode in which Kate wins the wager for her husband and bests her two companion brides in the contest of obedience serves as a dramatic illustration of how role-playing and integrity, wifely submission and independence of spirit, can be harmoniously reconciled in a single personality. Shakespeare has carried the notion of assumed identity from the superficial level of practical jokes in the induction and of narrative intricacy in the "supposes" plot to the deeper plane of character development and psychological self-realization.

The Taming of the Shrew is typical of Shakespeare's early work not only in its obsession with technical virtuosity but also in its buoyant confidence in the capacity of dramatic art to penetrate surfaces and expose truth. The comedy takes us by degrees through a sequence of reflecting mirrors or, to put it another way, into a succession of Chinese boxes that evokes the concept of infinite regression. Shakespeare's layered construction almost suggests analogy with the raked and deeply receding perspective stages of Serlio's description in which the spectator's eye was drawn ever backward toward the vanishing point. Indeed it is not unlikely that Ariosto's *I Suppositi*, the original of Shakespeare's subplot, was actually performed on such a stage in the early 1500s. *The Taming* invites a progressive immersion in illusion, a stepwise movement from comparative realism to comparative artifice, from the more immediate to the more remote, but in a paradoxically circular way that endows the final object of this distancing with the emotional power and immediacy of lived experience. By the end of the play Katharina and Petruchio seem more English than Italian, and when they discard their assumed roles of virago and tamer, yielding to each other with genuine affection ("Why, there's a wench! Come on, and kiss me, Kate." [V.ii.182]), they step forward as the characters nearest to us spatially and psychologically. Such a procedure, a sort of dramatic counterpart to Gerard Manley Hopkins's "inscape," says much about Shakespeare's faith in both the means and validity of mimesis.

III

If *The Taming of the Shrew* directs our attention to the satisfactions of art imitating life, *The Tempest* reverses that perspective. Here the breaking of illusion rather than its creation is Shakespeare's theme, and emergence out of the world of shadows and images is often accompanied by wistfulness or sadness. Even the sordid Caliban, with a melancholy eloquence beyond his normal range, speaks of beautiful dreams that cannot be sustained:

> Sometimes a thousand twangling instruments
> Will hum about mine ears, and sometime voices
> That, if I then had wak'd after long sleep,
> Will make me sleep again; and then, in dreaming,
> The clouds methought would open and show riches
> Ready to drop upon me, that, when I wak'd,
> I cried to dream again.
>
> (III.ii.139–145)

It is no accident that *The Tempest* suggests more links with *King Lear* than with the merry comedies written earlier. Prospero, too, knows about the inadequacy of dreams and illusions. Master dramatist that he is, he grows to an awareness that his "so potent art" is but "rough magic" (V.i.50). He breaks his staff and drowns his book, that he may rejoin common humanity with all its unaesthetic flaws. By forgiving his enemies and freeing Ariel, he frees himself from God-like isolation and the compulsion to order reality in accordance with his own private vision of it. Actual life is more painful and untidy than its image on the stage, but it is also more important. Prospero teaches us to mark this truth and to remember with him that man occupies an uneasy middle ground between the consoling images that he himself creates and those profounder realities beyond his ken of which he himself may be but a crude reflection.

Shakespeare assists our sense of widening perspectives by confining the stage action proper within uncharacteristically classical limits of time and space. Much of what occurs or has occurred offstage must therefore be presented indirectly through narration, a technique that underscores the relation between informant and informer and so, by extension, between audience and play. Prospero fussily peppers the long history of his tribulations, related to his daughter, with such interjections as "Dost thou attend me?" (I.ii.78), "Thou attend'st not!" (I.ii.87), and "Dost thou hear?" (I.ii.106). In tandem with characters inside the play whose worlds are being expanded, our imaginations are invited to range outward from a present and local center to embrace "the dark backward and abysm of time" (I.ii.50) and Claribel's wedding at Tunis, as well as the promise of "calm seas, auspicious gales" (V.i.318) and Miranda's marriage at Naples. The method suggests the movement of concentric circles forming around a disturbance in water.

In contrast to the prolonged opening of *The Taming of the Shrew* with its playfully reflexive sense of overlap between art and nature, *The Tempest* plunges us instantly, *in mediis rebus*, into an illusion of maximal immediacy. The shipwreck scene, with its noise, confusion, and apocalyptic fear, is the most naturalistic of the entire play. With the seamen and their passengers we are made to feel intensely the moments that precede death:

> *Mariners.* All lost! To prayers, to prayers! All lost!
>
> . . . .
>
> (*A confused noise within:*)   "Mercy on us!"
> "We split, we split!"—"Farewell my wife and children!"—
> "Farewell, brother!"—"We split, we split, we split!"
>
> . . . .
>
> *Gonzalo.* Now would I give a thousand furlongs of sea for an
> acre of barren ground, long heath, brown furze, anything.
> The wills above be done! But I would fain die a dry death.
>   (I.i.52–68)

The valedictory note on which the play closes is already present in embryo. But by scene ii, we have discovered with Miranda that our gullible senses have deceived us, and that what we took for reality was in fact only a theatrical illusion created by the necromantic art of a magician: "Be collected. / No more amazement. Tell your piteous heart / There's no harm done" (I.ii.13–15). Almost from the start, then, Shakespeare alerts us to distrust our eyes and ears and to think of life as more mysterious and inclusive than any imitative rendering of it can possibly be, however convincingly presented.

Having instructed us that the tempest was no tempest, Prospero, with the assistance of a metamorphic or invisible Ariel, proceeds to observe the characters under his control as they pursue particular illusions, and to symbolize the nature of these pursuits by various expressions of art—songs, shows, visions, "*glistering apparel*" (IV.i.193), masques, and the like. Whether these illusions attract the guilty or the innocent—whether they involve the desire for power (like Antonio's, Sebastian's, Stephano's, or Caliban's plots to murder and usurp) or misapprehension about survival (like Alonso's and Ferdinand's belief in each other's death) or the contemplation of perfection (like Caliban's "voices" and "sweet airs, that give delight and hurt not" [III.ii.138–140], Gonzalo's "golden age" [II.i.170], or Miranda's "brave new world" [V.i.185])—all are seen to be comically impotent, naïve, or partial. Gilded dreams or distorted fantasies are as little to be relied upon as the "drollery" (III.iii.21) of unnatural shapes that appear and disappear so suddenly or the banquet that Ariel causes to vanish with a clap of his harpy wings, as trivial, in the long run, as the "frippery" (IV.i.227) with which Prospero decoys the drunken butler and his silly mate.

Prospero's most beautiful symbol of illusion is the masque presented to solemnize the betrothal of Ferdinand and Miranda. It is a dramatic form that represented for Elizabethans and Jacobeans not only the ultimate in expensive and ephemeral artifice but also a unique continuity between performer and observer, since, typically, the court masque enlarged its perimeter at the end to embrace members of the audience as participants. Here Shakespeare gathers to a head the ambiguities of nature and art, immediacy and remoteness, that irradiate the entire play and provide that strange sense of new vistas opening out that every student of *The Tempest* has felt. Again the paradoxes of the play-within-the-play are exploited; we return, as Tillyard has noticed,[2] to the principle of infinite regression—Prospero deputizing Ariel to produce a show in which Globe actors, pretending to be spirits, act out the roles of couplet-chanting goddesses, who, in turn, conjure up a still more remote world of "cold nymphs" and "bachelors" (IV.i.66–67), the idealized counterparts of Ferdinand and Miranda.

But in context the dramatic thrust of the masque is less centripetal than centrifugal. Like the statue scene in *The Winter's Tale*, it moves outward from a greater to a lesser remoteness. Iris refers directly to the guests of honor, to "this man and maid" (IV.i.95); Juno speaks of "this twain" (IV.i.104) and then joins Ceres in direct address to the lovers: "Honor, riches, marriage-blessing, / Long continuance, and increasing, / Hourly joys be still upon you!" (IV.i.106–108). Actors playing actors move forward to involve an onstage audience; fictional characters bless relatively less fictional ones. Prospero observes the masque and the couple's reaction to it from a position still further detached, rather as the anonymous lord observes Sly's reception of *The Taming*, but suddenly a more immediate reality shatters the prepared illusion. Thoughts of Caliban's "foul conspiracy" (IV.i.139) rouse Prospero from the pleasures of art and prompt his famous aria on revels ending and spirits melting into thin air. The great showman's comment on the fading of the insubstantial pageant with its reverberant pun on "the great globe itself" (IV.i.153)[3] movingly reinforces the old trope of life as a play, of art appropriating nature by dissolving into it. It is a theme inherent in the very genre of the masque.

The concluding lines of Prospero's great speech bear a double significance, both tragic and comic: "We are such stuff / As dreams are made on, and our little life / Is rounded with a sleep" (IV.i.156–158). In the most obvious sense, the sleep referred to is a metaphor for death, consciousness of which suffuses *The Tempest* in a hundred details from the first until the final scene. In this reading, life is merely the raw material out of which men manufacture their illusions, and death marks the inevitable end of the show. Such a conception recalls Macbeth's despairing image of the "walking shadow, a poor player / That struts and frets his hour upon the stage / And then is heard no more" (*Macbeth*, V.v.24–26). But Hamlet considered a more metaphysical possibility: "For in that sleep of death what dreams may come / When we have shuffled off this mortal coil, / Must give us pause" (*Hamlet*, III.i.67–69). Prospero also seems to glimpse a Christian Neoplatonic continuum, to hint that the stage illusion merely shades into a higher form of itself, behind which simulacrum a transcendent Playwright benevolently observes and superintends his own Creation. As the "baseless fabric" (IV.i.151) of the masque appears to man, so man's "little life" (IV.i.157) may seem to God and those few visionary souls who, like Lear, can "take upon [them] the mystery of things / As if [they] were God's spies" (*King Lear*, V.iii.16–17). Death may be conceived as an end or a beginning, as a final exit or as "a sea-change / Into something rich and strange" (I.ii.403–404). Point of view is all-important. To the unregenerate Antonio a sleeping Alonzo suggests a dead Alonzo. But for the actual sleepers of the play (Alonzo, Gonzalo, Miranda, the Boatswain, even perhaps Caliban), slumber is restorative and life-affirming.

As we have noted already in chapter 1, the view of human existence, *sub specie aeternitatis*, as God's theatre and men as his actors was, of course, a Renaissance commonplace, and Shakespeare fortifies the analogy throughout *The Tempest* by a system of recurrences that implies the Providential Artist as a shaper of events. Miranda's wedding echoes Claribel's; Alonzo and his party relive Prospero's "sea-sorrow" (I.ii.170); the abortive attempt on the King of Naples's life is patterned on a similar conspiracy against the Duke of Milan. To borrow a phrase from Antonio, "what's past is prologue" (II.i.254).

The extraordinary humility that *The Tempest* conveys has much to do with this implied contrast between celestial and human planes of creativity. The expanding sense of reality that the vanishing masque had symbolized now takes place, not as a show, but as a swelling in the hearts of sinful men:

> The charm dissolves apace,
> And as the morning steals upon the night,
> Melting the darkness, so their rising senses
> Begin to chase the ignorant fumes that mantle
> Their clearer reason.
>
> . . . .
> Their understanding
> Begins to swell, and the approaching tide
> Will shortly fill the reasonable shore
> That now lies foul and muddy.
>
> (V.i.64–82)

And Shakespeare completes the rhythm of withdrawal from illusion established in the masque by carrying it a step further in the epilogue. As mythological deities had come forward to join the lovers, so Prospero, having now "discase[d]" (V.i.85) himself, comes forward to join us: "Please you draw near" (V.i.322). The semitropical island melts into thin air, and we are invited to free its most commanding presence from the prison of the stage, even as he has just freed Ariel. The magician becomes a mere duke again, exchanging the robe of the conjurer for rapier and cloak. The demigod, with distant resonances of the Word being made flesh, unites himself to the world that he had held in sway. The artist abandons his contemplative cell to reenter the mainstream of political and social life, his charms "o'erthrown," his strength "most faint" (Epilogue, ll. 1–3), and "Every third thought" his "grave" (V.i.315). As Prospero begs our prayers and applause, we become freshly aware that the Duke of Milan is one of King James's Servants and that, in turn, the actor beneath his splendid costume is but one more specimen of humankind who, like us, needs love and hopes for grace. In the very act of dissolving our illusions Shakespeare poignantly invokes suggestions of a transcendental vision that makes their loss tolerable, even comic. A merely human art must shrink almost to nullity when the frame of reference is dilated to accommodate the artifice of eternity. And we, like Ferdinand as he confronts the disappearing masque, are bidden by the very nature of the enlarged context to "be cheerful" rather than "dismay'd" that "our revels now are ended" (IV.i.147–148).

IV

We must be careful not to overgeneralize or unduly simplify the contrasting attitudes toward illusion that *The Taming of the Shrew* and *The Tempest* so conveniently focus for us. If Shakespeare moved away from a youthful and self-assured embrace of the artist's enterprise in the early comedies toward a riper, more self-abnegating view of it in the romances, the exact route of this journey would be forbiddingly difficult to map. We can think of too many intermediate plays in which the ambiguous relation of truth to illusion not only frustrates our powers of definition but contributes, as nothing else could, to a rich diversity of witty, realistic, romantic, cynical, idealistic, comic, and tragic effects.

The dreamers of *A Midsummer Night's Dream* may awake from a bewildering night in the forest to a reassuring sense of clarified directions and fortified identities, but they do so in a context that suggests that love, like art, cannot breathe in too skeptical or rationalistic a climate; and, significantly, it is the fairies, not the mortals, to whom the playwright assigns the final speeches. *A Midsummer Night's Dream* promulgates the idea that at least in some departments of life what the imagination creates or transfigures may claim a certain priority over mere fact. Yet a chronicle play like *Henry V* can shift this emphasis importantly. The Prologue who attempts eloquently to "work" on our "imaginary forces," transporting us from the "wooden O" of the Globe to the "vasty fields of France," sounds curiously embarrassed about the gulf between theatrical illusion and the historical grandeur it attempts to mirror; and so he grows defensive about the inadequacies of his medium, depreciating the actors as "crooked figure[s]," "ciphers to this great account," or "flat unraised spirits that hath dar'd / On this unworthy scaffold to bring forth / So great an object" (*Henry V*, Prologue, ll. 9–18). And the epilogue to *All's Well That Ends Well* also highlights the disjunction between a dramatic character and the player who has just enacted him, for only seconds on the stage separate the King of France's offer to dower Diana's marriage from his plea to the audience for applause: "The king's a beggar, now the play is done. / All is well ended, if this suit be won, / That you express content" (Epilogue, ll. 1–3).

Various degrees of aesthetic engagement and disengagement are common in Shakespeare, and his plays encourage us to remark the difference.[4] The brittle sophisticates of *Love's Labor's Lost* maliciously relish the failure of theatrical illusion to sustain itself in the pageant of the Nine Worthies; and the mockery is easy enough when a timid curate such as Sir Nathaniel tries to re-create Alexander the Great, or when the diminutive Moth takes on the role of Hercules. But here the satire is aimed at artistic pretension in a play that stresses assumed postures as impediments to emotional honesty; nor have Berowne and his companions yet learned the magnanimity and need for empathy that Duke Theseus in a parallel situation enjoins upon Hippolyta: "The best in this kind are but shadows; and the worst are no worse, if imagination amend them" (*A Midsummer Night's Dream*, V.i.210–211). Shakespeare's Claudius cannot afford such aloofness as the snobbish young critics of *Love's Labor's Lost* express. For that guilt-ridden regicide, theatrical performance has the devastating impact of a confrontation with the inner self; Hamlet's *Murder of Gonzago*, an ingeniously double illusion that reenacts the crime at the same time that it adumbrates the punishment, becomes unbearable to the King of Denmark for reasons precisely contrary to those that make *The Nine Worthies* unacceptable to the King of Navarre.

The composite figure who bids us farewell at the end of *The Tempest*—a magician, a duke, an actor, and finally just a man—seems to gather together some of these earlier perspectives and symbolizes for the audience both commitment to, and disengagement from, theatrical art. The unassuming plainness, the almost painful intimacy of the epilogue's tetrameter couplets, stylistically so different from Prospero's more symphonic utterances, suggests a fresh identity, as though the subject of a portrait had stepped from its own frame and had to some extent appropriated the persona of the painter. And yet the speaker is not merely an actor who has shed his role nor wholly a surrogate for Shakespeare, for he continues to speak of Naples and of his Milanese dukedom. One foot, so to say, remains inside the frame. After expanding our whole concept of illusion and reality to take in metaphysical horizons, the dramatist deliberately blurs or fuses the trata discriminated earlier and thereby produces an effect that is intensely personal, human, and specific at the same time that it is profoundly general and philosophic. Somewhat as Chaucer's Parson at the end of *The Canterbury Tales* raises the level of discourse from that of a particular English journey to that of the pilgrimage of the soul, so Shakespeare's Prospero, at a like juncture, directs our attention away from the dramas that playwrights make to the universal drama in which all men have their exits and their entrances. As the Parson's words shade into Chaucer's, preparing us, as it were, for the Retraction, so Prospero's words shade into Shakespeare's, preparing us for the dramatic silence that was soon to follow. Inevitably the new emphasis brings a shift in tone. We move from a concern with aesthetic problems to a sense of life whose very inclusiveness reorders priorities, and orients us away from the sophistications of art toward the deepest of simplicities. The mood is one that mingles nostalgia and love for what is being abandoned with a quickened awareness of the peace that passeth all understanding.

   The Tempest thus raises once more the issue debated so charmingly in *The Winter's Tale* on the relation of art to nature. Prospero (and the dramatist behind him) understands well enough the doctrine of Polixenes as illustrated in the discussion of horticultural grafting. He knows how "art . . . does mend nature," how indeed, in one view of the matter, "art itself is nature" (*The Winter's Tale*, IV.iv.96–97).[5] Had Shakespeare lost faith in the mimetic power and importance of drama, he could hardly have gone on to write *Henry VIII* and possibly *The Two Noble Kinsmen*. Nevertheless, in the final phase of his career, he was breaking away from the kind of stage illusion that has allowed A. C. Bradley and many others to treat Hamlet, Othello, Macbeth, and King Lear almost as if they were living persons. And the effect that Prospero's epilogue seems designed to evoke is emotionally closer to Perdita's innocent distrust of art than to Polixenes' more sophisticated embracement of it. A rereading of *The Taming of the Shrew* in conjunction with *The Tempest* may serve to remind us that as Shakespeare approached the end of his highly experimental and successful career as an illusionist, he came finally to prefer simplicity before Heaven to virtuosity before men.

4

Wit, Wisdom, and Theatricality in
The Book of Sir Thomas More

I

Ever since Richard Simpson suggested over a century ago that two scenes of the manuscript play *Sir Thomas More* (c. 1596–1600) are in Shakespeare's handwriting, the twin issues of the play's authorship and date have aroused the interest, and occasionally the spleen, of numerous scholars.[1] Paleographers, textual specialists, and theatre historians have tried for years to pluck out the heart of the play's authorial mystery, while, for the most part, literary critics, perhaps suspicious of the artistic integrity of an "unfinished" manuscript play that bears the marks of seven different hands,[2] have tended to avoid discussion of its merits. The neglect is unfortunate, for not only does *Sir Thomas More* contain some of the best verse (even excluding those passages ascribed to Shakespeare) in all the plays of its biographical type,[3] it also possesses, despite its apparently garbled state and multiple authorship, a coherence of design uncommon among such plays.[4]

Scott McMillin, one of the few scholars to approach the work from an aesthetic-theatrical point of view, makes this point persuasively.[5] He notices that the manuscript of the play reflects a carefully wrought dramaturgy built around a pattern of "visual repetitions" and "visual contrasts" ("Theatrical View," pp. 22–23). The drama presents a series of "interior scenes," all set indoors, which by their simple "contrast in stage furnishings give a visual delineation to the *de casibus* theme of the play" (p. 22). McMillin explains: "The objects [of scenery] change in accordance with More's disgrace. . . . More's achievement in the play is entirely personal, a retaining of spiritual integrity in the condition of public disgrace, and as the interior scenes increase the sense of withdrawal in the action, they also give visual unity to the dramatization of More's personal consistency in the face of outward change" (p. 22). In addition to these "interior scenes," however, the play also includes two major "public" episodes that likewise invite similar comparison and contrast. McMillin suggests convincingly that the very place at which More ascends the scaffold to meet his death in act V is the same stage space as

---

Originally written in collaboration with Joseph Candido and reprinted here (in revised form) with his permission.

that from which he quells the May Day insurrection in act II, an event that triggers his sudden rise to power. These two episodes thus serve as distinctly visual "moments of public action which define the rise and fall pattern of the play" (p. 22) and, when taken in conjunction with the "interior scenes," emerge as significant evidence of "an intentional and coherent design in stagecraft" (p. 23).

The structural unity of *Sir Thomas More*, however, is not confined to matters of stagecraft alone. It is a curious irony indeed that among all the critics who have discovered verbal or ideological patterns in the play that correspond to similar patterns in Shakespeare, none has noted with what striking consistency such patterns recur in the play itself. It is the thesis of this discussion that the same kind of "intentional and coherent design" that McMillin notices in the dramaturgy of the play also manifests itself—for explicitly thematic purposes—in its language and ideas. And when we consider that the work was either written or revised by at least four different playwrights (Munday, Chettle, Heywood, and Dekker—not to mention Shakespeare), this structural consistency becomes even more remarkable. Clearly, the dramatists who collaborated on *Sir Thomas More* were moving toward a unique kind of stage biography, far more analogous in aesthetic and organizational technique to prose models like Roper's *More* or Cavendish's *Wolsey* than to more loosely constructed dramatic ones such as *Captain Thomas Stukeley* (c. 1596), *Sir John Oldcastle* (1599), and *Thomas Lord Cromwell* (c. 1600) roughly contemporaneous with it. The real misfortune regarding the compositional history of the play, therefore, is not that scholars have been unable for over a hundred years to identify "Hand D" positively as Shakespeare's but rather that the marginalia of the play's censor, Sir Edmund Tilney ("Hand T"), seem—at least initially—to have forestalled performance.

Notwithstanding the somewhat fluid state of its text, *Sir Thomas More* remains the most fascinating and revealing stage biography of its time. No other Elizabethan play in the biographical mode strives more assiduously to reveal the interior life of its hero at the expense of political or religious concerns. Historical events sweep by in a hazy background, providing us with fleeting glimpses of various stages in More's public career from his activities as Sheriff of London to his death for high treason. The play, however, focuses consistently upon those special features of More's mind and personality that set him apart from ordinary men rather than upon the political or religious significance of his life and actions.

Perhaps the episode that best reflects this emphasis on the private man—one that seems to lie at the thematic and structural heart of the play—is that in which More entertains the Mayor of London at his house in Chelsea. This scene is one of many that takes place entirely behind closed doors, its setting emblematic of the inner life it seeks to represent. It opens with More, in typically domestic fashion, seeing that all preparations are in order for the evening's festivities. Suddenly a troupe of actors appears, prompting the Lord Chancellor to suggest that they favor his guests with a play from their "divers" repertory. Among the titles mentioned by the spokesman for the company, More chooses one that seems particularly appropriate to the situation at hand:

> *The Marriage of Wit and Wisdom?* That my lads,
> I'll none but that. The theme is very good,
> And may maintain a liberal argument.
> To marry wit to wisdom asks some cunning.

Many have wit that may come short of wisdom.
We'll see how Master Poet plays his part,
And whether wit or wisdom grace his art.
(III.iii.43–49)[6]

It would be a dull spectator indeed who failed to see the relevance of these words to More's life and times; yet this oblique and passing reference to the political world outside the walls of the great house is as close as the dramatists in this scene ever come to a statement on "history."[7] What follows is an informal chat between More and the player on the practical difficulties of performing a theatre piece with an undersized cast, and a Theseus-like admonition by More to his guests: "if art fail, we'll inch [the play] out with love" (III.iii.115).[8] And inch it out they must; for the interlude begins with one of the major actors gone "to Ogle's for a long beard for young Wit" (III.iii.123–124) and unfortunately not able to arrive back in time to play his own allegorical role, that of Good Counsel. Only moments earlier we have observed More's spontaneous and creative wit when, ostensibly talking about the context of the play and punning on the name of the vice (Inclination), he actually delivers a series of trenchant comments on the nature of life in general, comments such as "Wit's inclination may gallop so fast that he will outstrip wisdom and fall to folly" (III.iii.138–139). Sir Thomas's ability to intersect art and life, however, is never more in evidence than at the moment when Luggins, the actor who plays Good Counsel, fails to enter the stage on cue. Speaking with a self-conscious duality of reference that embraces the real world and the play world at the same time, More asserts: "We'll not have our play marred for lack of a little good counsel. Till your fellow come I'll give him [i.e., Wit] the best counsel that I can" (III.iii.242–244).

Thus More, counselor to the king, enters *The Marriage of Wit and Wisdom* as Good Counsel and proceeds to utter a statement whose theme reverberates repeatedly throughout the language, thought, and action of *Sir Thomas More*:

Wit, judge not things by the outward show;
The eye oft mistakes, right well you do know.
Good Counsel assures thee upon his honesty
That this is not Wisdom, but Lady Vanity.
(III.iii.260–263)

On the one hand More's speech has the effect of reducing all human action, including his own, to the level of a mere play; yet on the other hand it also defines an important aspect of his personality in symbolic terms, thus heightening its reality through art. More *does* play the part of Good Counsel, both in the interlude and in the actual world, although he harbors no illusions about his effectiveness in either sphere. In a statement strangely evocative of More's own metaphor in *The History of Richard III*, the title character of the drama says of himself, "Thus fools oft-times do help to mar the play" (III.iii.275).[9] On this fittingly dualistic note, referring ironically to his role in both the interlude and in real life, More leads his guests away from the illusory world of theatre into the banqueting room where they may enjoy their dinner.

The episode is important as biography in several respects. One notices almost immediately, for instance, the debt to William Roper's prose life of More. It will be remembered that Roper opens his account of his father-in-law with the now-famous vignette of More as a boy dazzling guests in Cardinal Morton's household by spontaneously entering a play before their eyes and creating for himself "a part of his own."[10] What concerns us most about the way in which the authors of *Sir Thomas More* adapt this incident to their own uses, however, are the significant changes they make. Obviously in a play that deals exclusively with the adult life of its hero, it would be impossible to stage the scene *exactly* as Roper describes it; but the issue of More's age in the play-acting episode is not so easily dismissed. Why, we may ask, do not the dramatists simply ignore the vignette entirely, since it occurs during a period of More's life with which their play has nothing to do? The answer to this question seems to lie in a small peculiarity of the text that critics have often noted with interest but have never been able to explain.

It has been known for some time that although the interlude performed by the actors before More and his guests is entitled *The Marriage of Wit and Wisdom*, the play-within-the-play is actually an adaptation of an extant interlude known as *Lusty Juventus*. The substitution would not be so important in itself were it not that *Lusty Juventus* is one of the pieces that the spokesman for the players lists as part of the troupe's repertory when More chooses *Wit and Wisdom* instead. Since the collaborating dramatists obviously intended all along to use *Lusty Juventus* for their incorporated interlude, why do they go to such lengths to designate it inaccurately as *The Marriage of Wit and Wisdom*? Clearly the change of title is more than mere accident—and its implications, when examined more thoughtfully than previous commentators have cared to do, are explicitly biographical.

The title of the renamed interlude, *The Marriage of Wit and Wisdom*—it is repeated several times for emphasis (III.iii.41–43, 68, 113, 162)—serves as a kind of descriptive shorthand for More's personality both in this scene and in the play as a whole. More enters the interlude, in a rush of dramatic creativity, to preserve Wit from Vanity and to marry him to Wisdom—an activity that he reenacts time and time again in actual life. Indeed the tripartite association of wit, wisdom, and theatricality lies at the very heart of More's complex personality, manifesting itself at various times throughout his colorful career, always suggesting the intimate connection between the world of fact and the world of fancy. More himself reinforces the analogy with his prophetic comment, "fools oft-time do help to mar the play," a notion echoed by the actor who exclaims that the Lord Chancellor would "make a rare player" (III.iii.281–282). And indeed More does, for it is the protagonist's witty and wise theatricality in the public world that reveals most poignantly the character of the private man.

II

Wit and wisdom theatrically joined as the unique features of the hero's personality manifest themselves from the very outset of the play proper. More makes his first appearance onstage as Sheriff of London, sitting in Sessions with the Lord Mayor and other officers of the court, ready to "give ear to petty felonies" (I.ii.2). The scene, in an even broader sense than McMillin suggests, is an "interior" one, for it allows us to enter both the enclosure of the court and the private life of Sheriff More. But even before More speaks his first words, our attention is directed to the misadventures of one Lifter, an insolent but adroit cutpurse, who has been haled into court by Justice Suresby for laboring, Falstaff-like, in "his profession" (I.ii.11). But the sententious and moralistic Suresby is not content merely to prosecute Lifter alone; absurdly, he would also cast his litigious net wide enough to enmesh the victim of the theft. Addressing the plaintiff Master Smart, he argues:

> I tell thee plain, it is a shame for thee
> With such a sum to tempt necessity.
> No less than ten pounds sir will serve your turn,
> To carry in your purse about with ye,
> To crack and brag in taverns of your money.
> I promise ye, a man that goes abroad
> With an intent of truth, meeting such a booty,
> May be provoked to that he never meant.
> What makes so many pilferers and felons
> But such fond baits that foolish people lay
> To tempt the needy miserable wretch?
> Ten pounds odd money, this is a pretty sum
> To bear about, which were more safe at home.
> 'Fore God 'twere well to fine ye as much more,
> To the relief of the poor prisoners,
> To teach ye be more careful of your own.
>   (I.ii.25–40)

Here More sees an opportunity for the creative theatrics that are the hallmark of his personality. He calls Lifter to his side and assures him that if he will but contrive some means to "pick or cut [Suresby's] purse" (I.ii.59) in the courtroom, he need no longer fear the penalty of the law. Indeed, More even volunteers to direct the little scene:

>   I'll be thy setter.
> I'll send him hither to thee presently,
> Under the colour of thine own request,
> Of private matters to acquaint him with.
>   (I.ii.81–84)

Suresby of course walks into the trap that More "sets" for him, and Lifter relieves him of his purse. When the credulous justice later realizes that he has somehow been robbed of "seven pounds odd money" (I.ii.172), More comes in on cue with an ingenious burst of mimicry. He draws his own little morality play to a close by using Suresby's own words wittily against him:

> Seven pounds odd money? What, were you so mad,
> Being a wise man and a magistrate,
> To trust your purse with such a liberal sum?
> Seven pounds odd money? 'Fore God it is a shame
> With such a sum to tempt necessity.
> I promise ye, a man that goes abroad
> With an intent of truth, meeting such a booty,
> May be provoked to that he never thought.
> What makes so many pilferers and felons,

But these fond baits that foolish people lay
To tempt the needy miserable wretch?
Should he be taken, now, that has your purse,
I'd stand to't, you are guilty of his death;
For questionless, he would be cast by law.
'Twere a good deed to fine ye as much more,
To the relief of the poor prisoners,
To teach ye lock your money up at home.

(I.ii.173–189)

More's point is made with unmistakable clarity; yet it is also made with the wit, wisdom, and self-conscious dramatic flair that centrally define his character. There is a moral purpose to the Sheriff's "merry jest" (I.ii.76) or, to put it another way, a wisdom to his wit; and this simultaneous attraction to the frivolous and the grave, so indelibly a part of More's psychology, is here, as elsewhere, forged into a coherent and edifying whole by his creative impulse toward drama.

This same juxtaposition of wit, wisdom, and theatricality in the major figure surfaces soon afterward in an even more explicit fashion. The scene in question is another "interior" one, set in the privacy of More's chamber at court; and as it opens we see "*A table covered with a green carpet, a state cushion on it, and the purse and mace lying thereon*" (III.i.1). These, of course, are the symbolic trappings of More's new position as Lord Chancellor; yet rather than puffing him up with vanity (as they did Wolsey, his tragic predecessor), they inspire in him a deepening awareness of the transience of earthly fame. More opens the scene with a moving soliloquy in which he deprecates "honour, office, wealth and calling" (III.i.15) with a terse yet expressive maxim that fully reflects the creative agility of his mind: "to be great / Is, when the thread of hazard is once spun, / A bottom great wound up, greatly undone" (III.i.19–21). But lest we assume that such gravity represents a new emphasis in the characterization of More, in walks his unsophisticated servant Randall, attired in the Lord Chancellor's clothes, to receive instructions from his master for yet another "playful" enterprise.

Sir Thomas is preparing to meet Erasmus, and the manner of his reception bears an unmistakably "Morean" stamp. Randall is to "act [More's] part" (III.i.46) in an attempt to deceive the learned visitor from Rotterdam, but this newest of More's plays is more than mere playfulness. As with his other dramatic creations, this one, too, clothes a serious didactic purpose in external levity. More says to his servant:

> beware
> You talk not overmuch, for 'twill betray thee.
> Who prates not much *seems wise*, his *wit* few scan;
> While the tongue blabs tales of the imperfect man.
> I'll see if great Erasmus can distinguish
> Merit and outward ceremony.

(III.i.36–41; emphasis added)

Again More creates a short dramatic homily the purpose of which is to marry wit to wisdom rather than to vanity. The problem is obviously an intensely personal one for the Lord Chancellor, who only moments earlier, while contemplating his freshly acquired honor and power, expressed fear that "these things, / Not physicked by respect, might turn our blood / To much corruption" (III.i.12–14). Just as he did at Chelsea and in the court of law, More again vivifies and heightens his own psychological tensions by translating them into creative play. Life becomes art. And although More repeatedly insists that his feats of dramatic creativity are no more than "slight" jests resulting from his inherently jovial nature (III.i.187), we recognize them for what they really are— mimetic extensions of the private thoughts and fears of the man who creates them. It is in this sense that they serve a distinctly "biographical" function, for behind them we see the workings of a brilliant, active, yet troubled personality, struggling constantly to resolve the stresses that define his "interior" life.

At no time are these stresses more apparent than in the episodes that follow More's refusal to sign the mysterious "articles" (IV.iv.146) sent to him by the king. Hardly a scene goes by without some verbal echo of precisely those thematic notes already sounded in More's earlier dramatic homilies, and especially in *The Marriage of Wit and Wisdom*. Back home in Chelsea, for instance, the former Lord Chancellor offers his immediate family "*low stools*"; he makes a point of placing his wife "upon an humble seat," since the "cricket and high throne [are] alike near heaven" (IV.iv.2–5). Then he suggests ironically:

> Perchance the King,
> Seeing the Court is full of vanity,
> Has pity lest our souls should be misled,
> And sends us to a life contemplative.
> O happy banishment from worldly pride,
> When souls by private life are sanctified.
>   (IV.iv.81–86)

Incidentally, the episode balances an earlier one (III.iii) in which Lady More as hostess of the banquet, clearly reflecting her husband's values, refuses to sit higher than her guest, the Lady Mayoress. More's preoccupation with "vanity" and "worldly pride" never absorbs him more deeply than during his period of decline. He depreciates utterly "this poor painted cloth, / This outside of the earth" that covers up his flesh (IV.iv.96– 97). And when he learns moments later that the earls of Surrey and Shrewsbury have come at last to remove him to the Tower, he greets the news of their arrival epigrammatically on a note of *contemptus mundi* more reminiscent of John Webster's alienated and embattled characters than of the good-natured statesman we know him to be: "Here let me live estranged from great men's looks: / They are like golden flies on leaden hooks" (IV.iv.135–136).

But More's period of "melancholy" (IV.iv.56)—we might almost call it his dark night of the soul—is remarkably short-lived. He soon regains his accustomed jocosity, and uniting it once again to the creative theatricality that never seems to desert him, he prepares for his final dramatic scene. The episode in question, of course, is his death on the block, which both in subject matter and in tone owes much to Roper's account. Here we have the familiar incidents of More's comforting words to the Lieutenant of the Tower, his witty remarks to the executioner, the reference to the weak scaffold, and the like. Yet Shakespeare, Munday, and their collaborators are also careful to include along with these some unmistakable analogies to More's earlier theatrical inventions. The fallen statesman applies his ironic wit once again to the question of vanity: he jokes that if anyone should come an hour or two hence to see him, "I shall be so proud I will not speak" (V.iv.24); and then warming to the theatrical possibilities inherent in his situation, he begins his last play in earnest. Taking the hands of Surrey and Shrewsbury, he establishes his physical connection with them and, by extension, with all other members of the assembly, as he both delights them with his wit and underscores once more the idea of life as a drama:

> Ye see, though it pleaseth the King to raise me thus high, yet I am not proud; for the higher I mount, the better I can see my friends about me. . . . [*He walks along the scaffold.*] Truly here's a most sweet gallery; I like the air of it better than my garden at Chelsea. By your patience good people, that have pressed thus into my bedchamber. If you'll not trouble me, I'll take a sound sleep here.
>
> (V.iv.56–68)
>
> I confess his Majesty hath been ever good to me, and my offense to his Highness makes me of a state pleader a stage player—though I am old and have a bad voice—to act this last scene of my tragedy.
>
> (V.iv.72–76)

Again the dramatic trope has the effect of reducing More's tribulations to the level of a mere play, albeit a "tragedy," at the same time that it heightens them by calling attention to his self-conscious artistry. And as before, this playfulness serves explicitly didactic ends. More draws attention to the artistic quality of his life, captivating the hearers with his wit, precisely that he may show them the vanity of overvaluing such earthly shadows. For More, as for other creators of drama from Shakespeare to Calderón, life finally *is* a dream; and like Prospero,[11] he steps forth moments before he bids farewell to his art to place it in its proper cosmic perspective:

> Here More forsakes all mirth, good reason why.
> The fool of flesh must with her frail life die.
> No eye salute my trunk with a sad tear.
> Our birth to heaven should be thus—void of fear.
>
> (V.iv.122–125)

With this final dramatic performance More resolves the tensions that have so constantly troubled his "interior" life and served as the subject of his earlier artistic creations. Like Prospero, who uses his art to reorder life and then abandons his magic for the new and more hopeful world he has created through it, More teaches his audience, through art, the ultimate value of putting such insubstantial vanities aside for the life beyond the grave. It is a final irony superbly fitted to the extroverted yet deeply humble and inward personality of Sir Thomas More that his most intense and self-conscious dramatic scene is the one through which he expresses his farewell to art and his "birth to heaven."

III

By repeatedly underlining the thematic triad of wit, wisdom, and theatricality, the collaborating authors of *Sir Thomas More* pull the discursive episodes of their play into tighter structural relationship. But the association of these ideas also bears significantly upon the lessons of self-discovery and self-knowledge that the play as a whole is at pains to enforce. As we have seen, More is envisioned as a role-player, a self-fashioner, an actor on the world's stage, whose performance fulfills the traditional literary requirement of being pleasurable (witty) and instructive (wise). In the course of his performance, however, More not only comes to a deeper sense of his true self but also is able to stimulate such growth in others. Elizabethan tragedies familiarly stress theatrical posturing, or role-playing, as a means of communicating tragic divisions within a character (we think immediately of *Richard II* and of course of *Hamlet*, discussed in chapter 1); but in *Sir Thomas More*, despite the poignant death of the hero, the theme bears an essentially Christian and therefore comic emphasis. Role-playing and its relation to self-discovery permeate the play in a way that helps dramatize More's inner growth as well as his salutary and exemplary effect upon others less witty and wise than he.

Sir Thomas's quest for true identity, for the genuine and authentic self in a world of false appearances and distorted priorities, marks his career at every stage.[12] Knighted for his masterful role in pacifying the May Day riot and appointed to the king's Privy Council, where his wit and wisdom can again serve the state, More accepts his new honors graciously but with concern lest his duties sever old loyalties and friendships:

> Though I depart for Court my love shall rest. . . .
> I now must sleep in Court, sound sleeps forbear.
> The chamberlain to state is public care.
> Yet in this rising of my private blood
> My studious thoughts shall tend the City's good.
> (II.iii.235–239)

The potential conflict between public responsibility and private value, between political and spiritual commitments, is already implicit; but More is ready to play the role assigned him, partly out of devotion to public service and partly also as a means of testing his own integrity, of discovering the extent to which his obligations to his king and to God are congruent. He enters upon the new role as minister of state, then, knowing that he owes his advancement in large measure to a powerful and public exposition of the doctrine that the two obligations are in theoretical harmony:

> For to the king God hath His office lent
> Of dread, of justice, power and command;
> . . . .
> He hath not only lent the king His figure,
> His throne and sword, but given him His own name,
> Calls him a god on earth.
> (II.iii.110–116)

But what serves to calm a mutiny of tradesmen and apprentices will hardly answer to the deeper anxieties of a thinker like More who cannot forget the transience of earthly success and the dangerous mutability of politics: "New days beget new tides. / Life whirls 'bout fate, then to a grave it slides" (II.iii.249–250).

Again, upon becoming Lord Chancellor, More is troubled by the lengthening gap between his high worldly estate and the needful humility of a Christian soul. Aware of the dangers of power, he embroiders the traditional contrast between human appearances and divine realities with a view to clarifying the essential self and distinguishing it from its temporal context. This involves a rejection of the conventional notion, so popular in biographical and chronicle plays, that man is but the plaything of Fortune and her endlessly revolving wheel. Instead he asseverates the providence of God:

> It is in heaven that I am thus and thus,
> And that which we profanely term our fortunes
> Is the provision of the power above,
> Fitted and shaped just to that strength of nature
> Which we are born withal. Good God, good God
> That I, from such an humble bench of birth,
> Should step as 'twere up to my country's head,
> And give the law out there: I, in my father's life,
> To take prerogative and tithe of knees
> From elder kinsmen, and him bind by my place
> To give the smooth and dexter way to me,
> That owe it him by nature. Sure, these things,
> Not physicked by respect, might turn our blood
> To much corruption. But More, the more thou hast,
> Either of honour, office, wealth and calling,
> Which might accite thee to embrace and hug them,
> The more do thou in serpents' natures think them,
> Fear their gay skins with thought of their sharp state.
> (III.i.1–18)

Welcoming the Lord Mayor and the aldermen of the city to his table, More brushes aside a compliment to his political and social eminence ("My Lord, you set a gloss on London's fame, / And make it happy ever by your name" [III.iii.80–81]). Rather, he stresses his origin and identity as a fellow Londoner:

> once I was your brother,
> And so am still in heart. It is not state
> That can our love from London separate.
> . . . .
> But they that cast an eye still whence they came,
> Know how they rose, and how to use the same.
> (III.iii.73–79)

Enjoining Christian humility as they do, such speeches are obviously choric in nature, but they also represent More's admonitions to himself and so dramatize by implication the politician's struggle to assert religious priorities in the face of increasing secular pressure. The Lord Chancellor's active participation as Good Counsel in the allegorical interlude discloses the same self-defining, self-educative impulse, for the host-turned-actor addresses not only the leading man of the entertainment and the double audience on and offstage but, most importantly, himself: "Wit, judge not things by the outward show . . . this is not Wisdom, but Lady Vanity" (III.iii.260–263). Increasingly More becomes an autodidact.

When Sir Thomas Palmer presents the Act of Supremacy for signature to the Privy Councillors (the document is referred to with studied vagueness as simply "these articles enclosed" [IV.i.70]), the acid test of More's character is at hand. The Lord Chancellor instantly perceives the agonizing dilemma that the required signature thrusts upon him, but before resolving the issue finally in his own mind, he waits to see how Bishop Fisher will respond:

> Subscribe these articles? Stay, let us pause.
> Our conscience first shall parley with our laws.
> My lord of Rochester, view you the paper.
>   (IV.i.73–75)

Even after Rochester, shunning the role of "hypocrite" (IV.i.79), boldly refuses to assent, More temporizes, "entreat[ing] / Some time for to bethink me of this task" (IV.i.87–88); then he resigns his office in the hope of avoiding the necessity to choose between God and king. It is only when More returns home, now a private citizen once more, that we observe how he has satisfied his conscience. Paradoxically the symptom of his spiritual freedom, of his newfound wholeness, is the characteristic adoption of a role in which wit and wisdom, artifice and sincerity, double entendre and singleness of purpose are perfectly at one:

> As seamen, having passed a troubled storm,
> Dance on the pleasant shore, so I—
> O, I could speak now like a poet. Now afore God I am passing light. Wife, give me kind welcome. [*Kisses her.*] Thou wast wont to blame my kissing when my beard was in the stubble, but I have been trimmed of late. I have had a smooth Court shaving, in good faith I have.
>   (IV.ii.50–57)

The former statesman, who even now anticipates his execution (as shown by his choice of metaphors), enjoys the drama of revealing his new and plainer identity to his slightly obtuse wife. Roper notices that "he bears himself most strangely":

> *Lady More.* Will your lordship in?
> *More.* Lordship? No wife, that's gone.
>   The ground was slight that we did lean upon.
> *Lady More.* Lord, that your honour ne'er will leave these jests.
>   In faith it ill becomes ye.
> *More.*   O good wife,
>   Honour and jest are both together fled.
>   The merriest councillor of England's dead.
> *Lady More.* Who's that my lord?
> *More.* Still lord? The Lord Chancellor wife.
> *Lady More.* That's you.
> *More.*   Certain, but I have changed my life.

> Am I not leaner than I was before?
> The fat is gone: my title's only More.
> Contented with one style, I'll live at rest.
> They that have many names are not still best.
> I have resigned mine office. Count'st me not wise?
>
> (IV.ii.61–75)

The comment on the false security of titles is replete with irony, for it seems deliberately to recall Shrewsbury's words before dubbing More a knight: "Your name is yet too short" (II.iii.217). The writers of the play seem to build into More's language with its grimly pointed allusions to increasing "leanness," "shortness," and the "merriest councillor of England's" being "dead," a kind of anticipatory foreshortening of life that functions on a deeper plane as the psychological equivalent of beheading.

As earthly doom closes in upon him, More preserves his "constancy of mind" and "peace of conscience"—indeed he fortifies them—by facetiously dramatizing to family, servants, and state officials alike that "the world and I / Are at a little odds" (V.iii.8–13). He cannot resist, for instance, one final small charade with Lady More and Roper when they beg him to submit to the king's wishes:

> The world, my lord, hath ever held you wise,
> And 't shall be no distaste unto your wisdom
> To yield to the opinion of the state.
>
> (V.iii.91–93)

More's witty response to this argument is briefly to mislead them by playing an assumed role:

> I have deceived myself, I must acknowledge.
> And as you say son Roper, to confess the same,
> It will be no disparagement at all.
>
> (V.iii.94–96)

Only when his wife "*offers to depart*" (V.iii.97) in her haste to inform the king that her husband has recanted does More disabuse her: he has indeed "deceived" himself, not about spiritual priorities, but about the need of a man who faces the headsman's axe to trouble with the services of a barber.

The self-dramatizing aspects of More's behavior throughout the play thus amount to something like a spiritual discipline, a means of living and loving in the world while distancing himself through irony from its superficialities and impermanences. As More becomes increasingly involved in the world of public affairs, he comes more and more to value the interior life. And the nearly perpetual merriment that so frustrates his less complicated wife is not merely evidence of his Christian cheerfulness but the outward manifestation of a psychological program for developing and preserving moral balance in the slipperiest of environments. More's role-playing, then, may be viewed as a way of keeping equipoise between social and spiritual imperatives, and his attraction to the players—even to the extent of participating in their craft—has much to do, as in Hamlet's case, with their simultaneous reflection of, and detachment from, the confusing tangles of diurnal experience. Writing some three centuries later in his journal, William Butler Yeats endorsed the very principle that appears to govern Sir Thomas's behavior in the drama:

> There is a relation between discipline and the theatrical sense. If we cannot imagine ourselves as different from what we are and try to assume that second self, we cannot impose a discipline upon ourselves, though we may accept one from others. Active virtue as distinguished from the passive acceptance of a current code is therefore theatrical, consciously dramatic, the wearing of a mask. It is the condition of arduous full life. One constantly notices in very active natures a tendency to pose, or a preoccupation with the effect they are producing if the pose has become a second self.[13]

IV

If *Sir Thomas More* focuses centrally upon the hero's own deepening realization of who he is and what he must be, the play also buttresses this concern by touching upon the theme of moral identity at other points. Thus More's nurturing of conscience, his continuing assessment of responsibility, is seen not only as an inward process but one that extends outward to touch and influence others. The drama opens ominously by showing native Londoners threatened as to their very selfhood and existence by Lombards, who seize their wives and steal their food under the protection of diplomatic immunity. As alien outrage breeds English insurrection, we see Doll Williamson, one of the wives who has been violated, march across the stage "*in a shirt of mail, a headpiece, sword and buckler*" (II.i.1). As with Shakespeare's Jack Cade scenes in *2 Henry VI*, the effect is seriocomic, but the monstrous shift from female to male role is emblematic of the social and moral anarchy that is already spreading dangerously. More prevents civil disaster, not by trying to persuade his fellow Londoners that their grievances are without substance, but by teaching them that in proceeding violently they actually attack themselves:

> by this pattern
> Not one of you should live an aged man:
> For other ruffians, as their fancies wrought,
> With selfsame hand, self reasons, and self right,
> Would shark on you; and men like ravenous fishes
> Would feed on one another.
>
> (II.iii.92–97)

More's lesson, like Menenius's under similar circumstances, is to enlarge perspectives and correct priorities. The citizens must consider more deeply who and what they are. Though grossly wronged, they must nevertheless recognize that they are not simply individuals but part of a larger system of laws and obligations whose earthly authority is vested in the sovereign. Except for the ringleader John Lincoln, whose pardon ironically arrives too late, the expanded awareness saves them from the gallows and presumably brings redress as well.

Even the comic episodes tend to reinforce the importance of self-knowledge. At

More's behest Lifter teaches Suresby what it feels like, when one has been robbed, to be the recipient of the smug moralizing on temptation that he has just dispensed to Smart. And here the dramatist (probably Munday at this point) enriches the irony of Suresby's blindness to self by making the thief inform upon a fictional double at the very moment he steals the justice's money:

> *Suresby.* Th'art an honest knave.
>   Tell me what are they, where they may be caught.
>   Ay, those are they I look for.
> *Lifter.* You talk of me sir—
>   Alas, I am a puny. There's one indeed
>   Goes by my name, he puts down all for purses.
>   (I.ii.118–123)

Sir Thomas administers a parallel lesson in self-awareness to Faulkner, the hirsute servant of the Bishop of Winchester's secretary, who has been summoned before the bar on a charge of public brawling. More permits the cheeky ruffian, who has refused the offices of a barber for three years on the strength of an ill-considered pledge, to choose between three years in Newgate Prison *with* his untidy locks and one month there *without* them. At first the prisoner insists stubbornly that he will "not lose a hair to be Lord Chancellor of Europe" (III.i.126), then, upon reflection, changes his mind and reenters "a new man," not only in appearance but in common sense. More playfully pretends not to recognize the altered Faulkner, is reassured ("I am he in faith my lord, I am ipse" [III.i.236–237]), then releases him, averring that the significance of the change is more than tonsorial:

> Because I see some grace in thee, go free.
> . . . .
> Thy head is for thy shoulders now more fit:
> Thou hast less hair upon it but more wit.
>   (III.i.246–249)

Incidentally, the motif of hair as a clue to attitude, or state of mind, recurs several times—another symptom of the play's conceptual unity. In the interlude Wit, played by a young actor, feels at a loss without his long stage beard, prompting More to comment, "Why man, he may be without a beard till he come to marriage, for wit goes not all by the hair" (III.iii.125–127). A little later he remarks, "I'd lend him mine but that it is too thin" (III.iii.152). Both episodes curiously anticipate More's jests about his beard when he resigns ("I have been trimmed . . . I have had a smooth Court shaving" [IV.ii.55–57]) and when he faces execution ("I thought to have had a barber for my beard. . . . The headsman now shall cut off head and all" [V.iii.99–101]). In all these instances the jests on hair point up the ironic relationship between outward form and inward awareness.

The dressing of Randall in More's garments and gold chain puts Erasmus in the position of having to distinguish the true humanist, the genuine man of learning, from his unlettered surrogate or "Painted barbarism" (III.i.180), as More calls him. When Randall fails to respond in Latin to Erasmus, the Dutch visitor instantly smells a rat ("Is this Sir Thomas More?" [III.i.168]), and again the discovery of truth is linked to the theme of identity. More's motive in fostering this momentary deception is perhaps less to demonstrate to an internationally famous writer the obvious verity that scholarship and prepossessing appearance are frequently at odds than to remind himself of the dangers of pretension and pomposity when two such savants greet each other for the first time:

> Pardon thou reverent German, I have mixed
> So slight a jest to the fair entertainment
> Of thy most worthy self. For know, Erasmus,
> Mirth wrinkles up my face, and I still crave,
> When that forsakes me, I may hug my grave.
>
> (III.i.186–190)

V

No one can claim that *Sir Thomas More* is a dramatic masterpiece, despite the probable involvement of Shakespeare in its composition and the magnetic characterization of its subject. The writing is impressive in places, but it is admittedly uneven, and it sinks on occasion to a pedestrian clumsiness that argues both haste and intermittent failure of inspiration. Nevertheless it should be clear that E. M. W. Tillyard's statement that the play "is not well plotted," that "it has no formal unity,"[14] is totally misleading. Although the play may never have come upon the boards (to have complied with Tilney's directives for revision could have eviscerated it beyond saving),[15] it is nevertheless evident that the collaborators did at least strive to produce a drama with thematic and structural coherence. Their solution was to unify a number of incidents in the legendary rise and fall of a popular national and folk hero around two of his best-remembered and most revered qualities—his wit and his wisdom—and to present the unusual combination of levity and seriousness in a personality that not only was self-dramatizing but also implied connections between theatrical behavior and interior growth.

Doubtless the attractiveness and charm of the historical More as transmitted to Elizabethans through Roper and other sources accounted in large measure for this procedure. But the dramatic ambiguity inherent in the conception of More as a player of roles must have seemed especially advantageous to a group of Protestant dramatists who were seeking to stage the life of a Catholic martyr with sympathy. Whatever their own sentiments (and we know that Munday in particular was virulently antipapalist), they had to address an audience loyally committed to the daughter of Henry VIII who had stabilized the Anglican settlement.[16] The tact required to negotiate these treacherous waters is such as to make us wonder that the subject was even attempted. It goes without saying that the playwrights had to suppress entirely the religious beliefs for which More died (the play never mentions his Catholicism or the king's "great matter") and to vindicate explicitly the authority of the state. This they did, most baldly in Surrey's summary at the end: "A very learned worthy gentleman / Seals error with his blood" (V.iv.126–127). But they also tried to suggest the development in More himself of an increasingly profound allegiance to private conscience, to the irrefragable mandate of the soul. For this dual purpose a concentration on the interrelationship of wit, wisdom, and theatricality had its obvious utility.

Part II

The Green World

2. Emblem of the garden, from Henry Hawkins's *Parthenia Sacra: Or the Mysterious and Deliciovs Garden of the Sacred Parthenes* (Rouen, 1633), sig. A vi verso

5

"All the World's a Stage":
Multiple Perspectives in Arden

The make-believe action and perfunctory exposition of *As You Like It*, notoriously attenuated,[1] are obviously designed to throw the emphasis of the comedy on the rural setting and on the variety of characters and attitudes that can meet, converse, and interact in the forest of Arden. The haste with which Shakespeare maneuvers his figures into the woods may suggest the escapist impulse that underlies much pastoral literature, but Shakespeare's play, as has often been observed, is anything but an evasion of reality. What the dramatist gives us in addition to the contrivances of fairy tale and the richly varied characters, ranging from dukes to country bumpkins, is a subtle web of contrasting attitudes and values that comprise the real interest and substance of the play. The apparent simplifications of pastoral become devices for isolating certain kinds of complexity and focusing them with the precision of a finely ground lens. Arden, then, is a carefully prepared context in which multiple perspectives or points of view may compete for our interest and attention and can modify each other through contact, intersection, and reciprocating patterns of stimulus and response. Like most pastoral settings, it is conceived mainly as a place of temporary rather than permanent residence, the literal geography being less important than the emotions, stances, or verities for which it becomes the symbolic backdrop. Shakespeare makes his green world a place of growth—ethical, psychological, and spiritual as well as merely vegetative—but he is more interested in how the human heart may internalize this landscape than in the landscape for its own sake.

The assured yet delicate equipoise of *As You Like It* may be illustrated with reference to four sets of contrasting, complementary, but sometimes overlapping perspectives that emerge from an overview of the comedy. These may be expressed under the headings Nature versus Grace, Life versus Art (or naturalness versus artificiality), Time versus Timelessness, and Subjectivity versus Objectivity. In combination all are symptoms of the thematic fullness and intricacy of the play, and they point to a comprehensiveness of vision characteristic of Shakespeare's mature art, a comprehensiveness to which Norman Rabkin has applied the term "complementarity."[2] Indeed inclusiveness appears to be one of the several significances embedded in the play's rather casual title—a signal, so to say, of the recognition that there are many ways to look at experience and that no single attitude can contain the whole truth.

In a well-known essay on Spenser, A. S. P. Woodhouse pointed out some years ago that Elizabethans were accustomed to thinking about reality in terms of the double order of nature and grace, distinguishing the human from the divine, the corrupt from the perfect, the finite from the infinite, and the fallen world of creation from the unfallen world of the Creator. Some thinkers such as Calvin stressed the divergence of the two orders, exalting grace as nearly beyond man's ken and depreciating nature on account of original sin and innate human depravity. Others such as Hooker, emphasizing the unity of all creation, tended to see the two orders as the poles of a continuum. Thus conceived, "the order of grace was the superstructure whose foundations were securely laid in nature," and nature might therefore be understood as "an ascending scale, at whose successive levels are added, first, life, then consciousness, then rationality and a moral sense, and finally religious feeling, which last marks the transition to the order of grace."[3] Certainly *As You Like It*, especially in the first act, acknowledges the fallen condition of the world, and even the forest, however idyllically or invitingly presented, is not wholly free from selfishness, inconvenience, or danger. Nevertheless, Shakespeare's concept of physical nature in the comedies is much closer to Hooker's than to Calvin's. It is a conception that allows us to see the green world as a mirror of grace while yet retaining some consciousness of the barriers that separate us from it.

This duality, of course, is one of the traditional advantages of pastoral settings, and it might be said that the playwright in this instance simply exploits its possibilities. In any case, it is clear that in Shakespeare's hands, Arden becomes a highly idealized place, a *locus amoenus* defined in large measure by an ethos of relaxation, art, romantic love, and pastoral *otium*. The banished duke lives there with his followers in a state of contentment, abundance, good fellowship, and loving generosity to strangers. He enjoys peace; he has beautiful music and the pleasures of the hunt for entertainment, and the harmonies of God's handiwork to contemplate in earth, in water, and in sky. Compared with the hateful and envious court from which he has been exiled, the woods are reasonably "free from peril" (II.i.4), and he can discover "tongues in trees, books in the running brooks, / Sermons in stones, and good in everything" (II.i.16–17).

Arden is both self-contained and self-sufficient, it knows no malice or politics, and it is a setting "exempt from public haunt" that can "feelingly persuade" (II.i.11–15) the dispossessed duke to cultivate a profounder knowledge of himself. The Robin Hood style of his sylvan court is such that "many young gentlemen flock to him every day" to live "carelessly, as they did in the golden world" (I.i.112–114). Not surprisingly, the errant princesses think of the forest as "liberty" rather than "banishment" (I.iii.136). It is a place where starving travelers like Orlando's old servant are "providently cater[ed] for" (II.iii.44) by the same God who feeds the ravens and the sparrows, where men, remembering the "holy bell" of the church, share their feasts "in gentleness" and wipe from their eyes the tears "that sacred pity hath engend'red" (II.vii.120–123). The forest, then, is partly a reflection of divinity, a second Book of Revelation (as the Elizabethans liked to conceive of nature), and when characters enter it, they seem to change for the better. Orlando's wicked brother is converted from hate to love almost instantly, as if by magic, as soon as he crosses the border. And with like speed, the worldly Frederick abandons both his usurped throne and his fratricidal hostility for the monastic cell of a "convertite" (V.iv.183) upon reaching "the skirts of this wild wood" (V.iv.158). One thinks of Marvell's equally unspoiled landscape, "Where willing Nature does to all dispence / A wild and fragrant Innocence."[4] Hymen's lyrics at the quadruple marriage suggest the numinous possibilities of the forest glade, the pervasiveness of Deity, and the sense in which nature may become the fictive coordinate or physical prefigurement of paradise itself: "Then is there mirth in heaven, / When earthly things made even / Atone together" (V.iv.107–109).

But if Shakespeare associates the greenwood both with Eden and with the golden world of classical tradition, he does not equate it with them. Arden is far from being prelapsarian. As such, it represents not only the world as one could wish it—as we like it—but also the world in its more negative aspect. The deer are slaughtered there so that the exiles may banquet on venison, and the duke worries about usurping the rights of the animals even as his own rights have been usurped. The winter winds blow bitterly under a freezing sky; a lioness, a snake, and the "venomous" toad (II.i.13) may threaten life; and Orlando at first speaks of the place as "this uncouth forest" (II.vi.6) and "this desert inaccessible" (II.vii.109). To some the forest may be merry; to others its boughs are "melancholy" (II.vii.110). Arden does not eliminate weariness, old age, or the possibility of sudden death. Adam nearly expires from hunger; Oliver and Orlando have brushes with a nature red in tooth and claw. Even the virtuous duke must capitalize on "the uses of adversity" (II.i.12), must *translate* the stubbornness of fortune" by means of inner adjustment to the quietness and sweetness of his Arden "style" (II.i.19–20; emphasis added). Some of the natives are self-seeking—Corin's churlish master, for instance, and the cruelly proud Phebe. An ignorant priest, Sir Oliver Martext, wanders about only too willing to marry any persons of opposite gender "as they join wainscot" (III.iii.79–80), and sluttishness and stupidity appear in the persons of Audrey and William.

The forest symbolizes both the fallen world, where seasonal change—"the penalty of Adam" (II.i.5)—still reminds men of their imperfection, and the Edenic world of innocence and charity that we half remember from the prehistory of myth and look forward to as the reward of our salvation. The biblical name and character of Orlando's faithful servant—a role Shakespeare is said to have played himself—crystallize the bifocal attitude toward nature that the play encourages. In his age and physical weakness, old Adam may be an archetype of human limitation and transience, but his saintly virtues also identify him with the lost innocence for which man is perennially nostalgic: "O good old man, how well in thee appears / The constant service of the antique world" (II.iii.56–57).

Although *As You Like It* has religious overtones without being explicitly doctrinal, it is also a very literary and style-conscious play. Conversational spontaneity jostles set speeches or "arias" of studied rhetorical artifice. As Jaques carefully divides man's advance from infancy to decrepitude into "seven ages" (II.vii.142), so Touchstone distinguishes the seven steps of quarreling from "the Quip Modest" to "the Lie Direct" (V.iv.75–81). Anaphora, chiasmus, antithesis, parison, and other euphuistic embellishments are deliberately imported into the dialogue to suggest the civilizing—and sometimes overcivilizing—effects of nurture upon nature. Prose and verse encroach upon each other. The woods reverberate with rhymes, classical allusions, aphorisms, and witty juxtapositions. Such effects exploit the delightful interplay between the artificiality of familiar pastoral conventions and the gentle mockery of these same conventions. Some features of Arden can exist only by poetic license—a climate that accommodates both the tropical palm and the English holly, a weeping deer whose tears augment the water level of the stream by which he stands, a lover who festoons every tree in sight with amorous verses to a supposedly absent lady, a shepherd and shepherdess whose sole reason for being is to woo and be wooed in highly patterned iambic pentameter. Silvius undergoes a thousand humiliations and emotional deaths for a cold nymph whom he compares with Petrarchan exuberance to an executioner, a tyrant, a butcher, and a murderer, because she stubbornly refuses to return his affection. A classical god appears out of nowhere to join four couples in the ceremonial dancing of a court masque, the most elaborately contrived of all Elizabethan art forms, in the middle of the forest.

Of course Shakespeare continually undercuts the literary and artificial postures with satirical deflation of the romantic clichés and a sense of life's actuality. Touchstone, who at one point insists that "the truest poetry is the most feigning" (III.iii.17–18), is forever parodying the Platonic love poems by reducing the high-flown rhetoric of romance to mere animal sexuality and bawdry:

> If a hart do lack a hind,
> Let him seek out Rosalind.
> If the cat will after kind,
> So be sure will Rosalind.
> Wint'red garments must be lin'd,
> So must slender Rosalind.
> They that reap must sheaf and bind;
> Then to cart with Rosalind.
> Sweetest nut hath sourest rind,
> Such a nut is Rosalind.
> He that sweetest rose will find
> Must find love's prick and Rosalind.
>   (III.ii.99–110)

The sacramental unity of marriage can be compared irreverently to the sudden "fight of two rams" whose locked horns "clubs cannot part" (V.ii.29–40). Irrefutably Touchstone points out that at one level, at least, mating is primarily a matter of mere instinct: "As the ox hath his bow, sir, the horse his curb, and the falcon her bells, so man hath his desires; and as pigeons bill, so wedlock would be nibbling" (III.iii.73–75). Rosalind, though she is in love herself, understands the difference between romantic literature and life. The tragic love stories of Troilus and Leander are mere "lies," constructs of pure fiction: "Men have died from time to time, and worms have eaten them, but not for love" (IV.i.101–102). Thus, by taking a lofty view of amorous dedication and by voicing the Platonic doctrine that poets are liars, Rosalind can function both as idealist and realist at once. The comedy celebrates romance, but it also makes us aware of how ridiculously lovers behave when they adopt literary poses.

Jaques thinks it asinine for a man to leave "wealth and ease" (II.v.48) for rustic playacting, enabling us to smile at the duke in Lincoln green rather as we smile at Marie Antoinette at the *Petit Trianon* for affecting the exquisite ruralities of a Fragonard shepherdess. Corin and Touchstone debate the age-old question of sophistication versus simplicity, and the clown, making nonsense of the subject by reducing it to a medley of logical contradiction and tautology, travesties a dialectic on the precise value of pastoral retreat that informs the comedy as a whole:

Truly, shepherd, in respect of itself, it is a good life; but in respect that it is a shepherd's life, it is naught. In respect that it is solitary, I like it very well; but in respect that it is private, it is a very vile life. Now, in respect it is in the fields, it pleaseth me well; but in respect it is not in the court, it is tedious. As it is a spare life, look you, it fits my humor well; but as there is no more plenty in it, it goes much against my stomach. Hast any philosophy in thee, shepherd?

(III.ii.13–21)

Audrey keeps smelly goats, not the freshly laundered sheep of literary convention, and the word "poetical" (III.iii.15) is not in her vocabulary. Corin knows about real sheep, how greasy they are and how they actually reproduce themselves. Still, his emphasis on the biology of the shepherd's trade and Touchstone's witty censure of a calling that subsists on "the copulation of cattle," on "be[ing] bawd to a bell-wether" (III.ii.78–79), in no way wrecks the pastoral idealization of Arden. Much of the sophisticated pleasure in *As You Like It* derives from appreciating the many ways in which art and life cut athwart, without annihilating, each other.

When Rosalind asks at one point, "I pray you, what is 't o'clock?" and Orlando replies that "there's no clock in the forest" (III.ii.295–297), Shakespeare calls attention to another set of contrary perspectives in the play. Logically, the opposition of time to timelessness is one aspect of the polarity between the temporal and the eternal, between nature and grace, but by virtue of its prominence, the play elevates this concern almost to the status of a separate theme.[5] Rosalind rebukes Orlando for being an hour late for his appointment with her and then retires to "sigh till he come" (IV.i.209) again. Defining a lover (partly on the basis of her own feelings) as someone who "sigh[s] every minute and groan[s] every hour" (III.ii.299), she goes on wittily to anatomize the "divers paces" (ambling, trotting, galloping, etc.) in which Time may travel, depending upon a person's state of mind (III.ii.303-327). She herself has been forced to quit the court within "ten days" (I.iii.41) and, as prime mover of the comic action, is necessarily aware of time and its importunities. Touchstone, the literal timekeeper in the forest, looks at his dial "with lack-luster eye" to note how "from hour to hour, we ripe and ripe, / And then, from hour to hour, we rot and rot; / And thereby hangs a tale" (II.vii.21-28). Jaques too is very conscious of transience, seeing all life as a depressing progress from "the infant, / Mewling and puking in the nurse's arms" to "second childishness and mere oblivion, / Sans teeth, sans eyes, sans taste, sans everything" (II.vii.142-165).

The forest may echo with the *carpe diem* lyricism of a song like "It was a lover and his lass" (V.iii.15); it may contain Rosalind's urgency of love, Audrey's impatience to be wed, or Jaques' and Touchstone's pessimistic comments on death and dissolution. But Arden also represents a state of contentment and holiday freedom emancipated from the constraints of the clock and the calendar. The banished duke "fleet[s] the time carelessly" (I.i.113-114); he "lose[s] and neglect[s] the creeping hours of time" (II.vii.111), not worrying about when he will be able to retrieve his usurped throne. Orlando, having complained of enforced idleness at home, wanders dreamily through the greenwood with no thought of obtaining justice from his wicked brother. Rosalind does not trouble to seek out her exiled father even though he is in the immediate vicinity, and Celia announces after arriving in Arden, "I like this place, / And willingly could waste my time in it" (II.iv.90-91). Life in the forest is untrammeled by chores or routines, and even eating and sleeping are apparently casual and unregulated. One of the lessons of the forest is that the holiness of the heart's affections, the world of selflessness and joy truly experienced, may liberate us from thinking in terms of yesterday or tomorrow and put us in touch with what is timeless. It is not always necessary or desirable to conceive of time chronometrically; one may regard it with Walton or Thoreau as simply a "stream" to "go a-fishing in."[6]

The paradoxical view of time that pastoral and antipastoral attitudes in combination may promulgate is symbolized by both the songs of the play and its numerous references to seasonal change. Although by definition music is sequential and performed in obedience to time, it may nevertheless evoke a sense of the timeless by transporting the listener or performer to a higher emotional state, thus freeing him from merely quotidian preoccupations. Moreover, its recurrences suggest changelessness through the very processes of change. A chorus such as "Then heigh-ho, the holly! / This life is most jolly" (II.vii.181–182) must produce some such effect. Similarly the regularity of seasonal rhythms, the inevitability by which "winter and rough weather" (II.v.8) yield to "spring time, the only pretty ring time" (V.iii.18), can give rise to a concept of transcendent permanence. In Spenser's "Mutabilitie Cantos," Nature articulates a Christian Neoplatonic philosophy of time that, while not explicitly stated in *As You Like It*, is nevertheless consistent with the strain of pastoral idealism in the play:

> I well consider all that ye haue sayd,
>   And find that all things stedfastnes doe hate
>   And changed be: yet being rightly wayd
>   They are not changed from their first estate;
>   But by their change their being doe dilate:
>   And turning to themselues at length againe,
>   Do worke their owne perfection so by fate:
>   Then ouer them Change doth not rule and raigne;
> But they raigne ouer change, and doe their states maintaine.
>   (*The Faerie Queene*, VII.vii.58)[7]

The final pair of opposites—objectivity and subjectivity—is as much a part of Shakespeare's theme in *As You Like It* as the others I have mentioned, chiefly because romance is one thing for those whose emotions are deeply engaged in it and something quite different to those who merely look on from a position of detachment.[8] It has been wisely said that there is only one thing sillier than being in love, and that is thinking that love itself is silly. Shakespeare allows us as his audience to take both positions at once—to see love through the eyes of both the lover and the skeptic. Therefore we have the double privilege of laughing *with* the characters at the same time that we laugh *at* them. To the lovesick Silvius, Phebe is a goddess of love, a paragon of celestial beauty, but we know that he re-creates her in the image of his own ideal because of the emotion he feels. Phebe in turn thinks that she loves Rosalind in the same way that Silvius loves her because she cannot penetrate the male disguise of the person to whom she is superficially attracted. But Rosalind can be brutally objective about Phebe's distinctly limited charms:

> mistress, know yourself. Down on your knees,
> And thank heaven, fasting, for a good man's love;
> For I must tell you friendly in your ear,

Sell when you can, you are not for all markets.

(III.v.57–60)

We can see that Audrey is taking a fool (and probably a libertine as well) for her husband when she accepts Touchstone so uncritically, but love does not see with the eyes of reason or practicality, nor do we desire that it should.

Touchstone, the professional fool, rudely hails Corin as "you clown!" (II.iv.62) because he can see on first meeting that the old rustic prefers the country to the court; but we soon learn that the pot is calling the kettle black, or rather that a shallow kind of wit is rebuking the wisdom born of age and experience. To the fool, wisdom may look like folly, and yet we are permitted to enjoy the fun of Touchstone's mistake without being solemnly judicial or moralistic about it. Some men, like the duke and his companion foresters, are inclined to see a deer as the natural source of sport and food, while more earnest observers, like Jaques, may be moved to look upon the same animal as an emblem of human suffering. *As You Like It* not only shows up the limitation of both points of view but also enables us to recognize how dreary the world would be if it were composed exclusively of archery enthusiasts, connoisseurs of venison, solicitors for the SPCA, or fanatic vegetarians. One of the important lessons of Arden is that to a great extent truth is relative, and that beauty, especially in the case of lovers, resides in the eye of the beholder.

Amidst this welter of attitudes and perspectives, how, we might ask, does Shakespeare unify his play? One way, I would suggest, is to make us more or less continuously aware of his own medium—the theatre—during the progress of the comedy. Of course we enter Arden with the hero and heroine, participating imaginatively and sympathetically in their experience. But at the same time, we keep our distance from the stage because Shakespeare is forever calling our attention to the conventions and artificialities that make the theatrical illusion distinct from life. One of the more amusing instances of this *Verfremdungseffekt* is Jaques' hasty departure from the stage when Orlando greets Rosalind decasyllabically in the midst of a prose scene: "Nay, then, God buy you, an you talk in blank verse!" (IV.i.29). The discrepant awareness keeps us responding to the experience of the play on two separate planes of reality. It is one of the techniques Shakespeare uses to habituate us to holding contrary perspectives or attitudes in equilibrium. Jaques' famous speech, "All the world's a stage, / And all the men and women merely players" (II.vii.138–139), is the most obvious example of this self-consciousness, but other characters also use the same ancient metaphor. The duke speaks of life as "this wide and universal theatre" (II.vii.136), Corin refers to the wooing of Phebe as "a pageant truly play'd / Between the pale complexion of true love / And the red glow of scorn and proud disdain" (III.iv.50–52), and Rosalind "prove[s] a busy actor in their play" (III.iv.57). "All the world's a stage" was, after all, an idea very close to Shakespeare's heart, for (as already noted in chapter 1) his own playhouse, newly constructed in 1599, was called the Globe, and the words of Jaques just quoted are a translation of the theatre's motto: *Totus mundus agit histrionem* ("All the world practices stage-playing").

The world of theatre is both like life and different from it at the same time. Not only do human actors play the roles of Touchstone and Jaques and the exiled duke; inside the play proper these characters all play roles to each other, showing different sides of themselves, striking different postures in different situations and relationships. Touchstone, for instance, plays the critic of courtly values while he is still at court, but when he is talking to a country swain in Arden, he pretends to be the spokesman for courtly elegance and sophistication. Jaques adopts melancholia as a conscious stance to impress others, claiming that he rails satirically against the world to cure it of its pride and folly. But he himself is the most prideful and egotistical of all the characters, and his steadfast refusal to participate in the happiness of others is a kind of foolishness that makes all his vaunted travel and experience nearly worthless. It may be true that babies vomit, that lovers sigh like furnaces, that some old men turn into senile vegetables, but to pretend that these images define infancy, adolescence, or old age is an absurd falsification of what everyone knows. Shakespeare makes the hollowness of Jaques' melancholic role obvious by bringing the dignified and lovable old man Adam onstage immediately after the facile generalizations on the toothless senility of the aged. The banished duke may take on the role of Robin Hood for a time, but he abandons it quickly enough when the opportunity comes to regain his dukedom.

The character of Rosalind, a beautiful girl who is disguised as a boy for most of the play (and who of course was acted by a boy in Shakespeare's theatre), focuses the tension between the play world and the real world most creatively and variously for us. She is a role-player of the richest humor and complexity, for she pretends to give disinterested lessons in wooing to the very man she wants to woo her. Her first words at the beginning of the comedy set the characteristic tone of her utterance: "Dear Celia, I show more mirth than I am mistress of" (I.ii.2–3). We watch her playing a theatrical game that combines pretense with sincerity, that involves both detachment and engagement at the same time, that mediates between an acerbic, intelligent wittiness and the pathos of longing. She sets up, and acts in, a joyous and theatrically contrived comedy-within-a-comedy that merges with what we accept as a deeply felt reality. When Rosalind (in her disguise as Ganymede) faints at the sight of the bloody napkin, the evidence of Orlando's injury, and then pretends that she only "counterfeited" (IV.iii.167) shock as part of the wooing game, Shakespeare gives us a wonderfully effective example of humor and pathos fusing. And Rosalind's serious yet playful role-playing is intimately related to that deepening self-awareness that seems always to be concomitant with Shakespeare's celebration of romantic love.[9]

George Bernard Shaw remarked that the role of Rosalind "is to the actress what Hamlet is to the actor"—a part so intrinsically varied and fascinating that, with any competence at all, the performer who undertakes it can scarcely fail.[10] Much of this fascination and variety lies in the multiple perspectives of the play that converge so charmingly in her. She is both natural and gracious, strong and frail, virtuous and full of mischief, divinely beautiful and humanly earthy all at once. She is conscious of time at the very moment that she seems to occupy and irradiate a world of timeless contentment. She is an activist without being too crudely or obviously aggressive. She is both a lover and a mocker of love, by turns both a subjectivist and an objectivist. As soulful and sensitive princess, as clever teacher and manipulator, as actor-actress, as stage manager, and finally as epilogue to her own play (a function that gives fresh meaning to Jaques' proverb on life's exits and entrances), she makes it possible for us to share more fully than do any of the more limited characters the unique matrix of perspectives that is Shakespeare's comic art. Rosalind is the very symbol of theatre as they liked it at the Globe in 1599, and as we continue still to like it.

6

Shakespeare's Chronicle Plays as Historical-Pastoral

> The best actors in the world, either for tragedy, comedy,
> history, pastoral, pastoral-comical, historical-pastoral, trag-
> ical historical, tragical-comical-historical-pastoral.
>
> —*Hamlet*

I

The critic who invokes the failing mental powers of Polonius in matters of literary terminology no doubts risks impaling himself upon the point of his own irony. Neverthe-less, the risk is worth taking, for there is a sense in which the old counselor's words go beyond their immediate context to describe the modes of Shakespeare's own artistic practice. Elizabethan drama is nearly always "impure art,"[1] and Polonius's final category is more applicable than has generally been recognized to Shakespeare's ten plays on English kings from *1 Henry VI* to *Henry VIII*. It is the "pastoral" element in these histories that I want specifically to discuss in this chapter, but perhaps, by way of laying the necessary foundation, I may be permitted a few general comments on the unity of the history plays as a group and the generic principles that appear to inform that unity.[2]

Although the individual plays have their own dramatic unity and have been acted independently ever since they were first presented at the Globe,[3] it is obvious from the arrangement in the Folio, where they are grouped according to the chronology of reigns, that their plots and characters are related and that they share common thematic and political interests. All the plays are crowded with action, compose a more or less continuous drama covering roughly a century and a half of political and military history, and therefore project an image of great temporal and spatial extent. Because the emphasis is political, they usually present ambiguous conflicts between characters or groups of characters who represent opposed systems of value, partial or complementary mixtures of good and evil, so that our moral sympathies necessarily hover between the different sides of an issue. In all the plays, too, Shakespeare raises the complex question of order in both its political and metaphysical aspects.

The so-called Tudor myth with its orthodox teleological and providential assumptions about the movement of history might support the idealistic position that political order was ultimately an aspect of divine order. Tillyard (although we now recognize his interpretation to be misleadingly overschematic) has shown how importantly that essentially medieval tradition influenced Shakespeare. Yet the equally forceful and more modern notion that man might, in some sense, be the shaper of his own destiny, that political goods and evils could and *did* result from the strength or weakness of individual leaders, cut precisely the other way; it seemed to suggest, with disturbing Machiavellian import, that the two orders had little practical connection and might in fact conflict. The struggle between Richard and Bolingbroke in *Richard II* obviously owes something to both attitudes.

It has been common ever since A. W. Schlegel's *Lectures on Dramatic Art and Literature* (delivered in 1808) to take the plays together as composing a national epic in dramatic form, a great panorama involving some two hundred different characters from both high and low life, a great patriotic celebration (despite the prominence of tragic unhappiness depicted) of "this happy breed of men; . . . This blessed plot, this earth, this realm, this England" (*Richard II*, II.i.45–50).[4] Although the epic qualities of the series have generally been granted, critics on the whole have been somewhat vague in their use of the term. One might begin the search for a clearer definition by noting that Tasso's summary of epic requirements (although of course the Italian poet was thinking not of drama but of the romantic-heroic poem in the tradition of Ariosto) fits Shakespeare's histories surprisingly well in a general way. The essentials for Tasso, apart from the orthodox classical purpose of inspiring admiration in the audience and delighting it through instruction were: "The authority of history, truth of religion [i.e., specifically Christian values], the license of fiction, suitability of period [i.e., an epoch neither so remote as to appear uncivilized by contemporary standards nor so close to the present as to hamper unduly the poet's freedom of invention], and grandeur and mobility in the incidents."[5]

The plays include, of course, elements of both comedy and tragedy, but taken as a cycle,[6] they define the ideal leader, the public man, the English hero in peace as well as war. There could not be, of course, as in classical epic, one central hero, and Tillyard, in fact, has tellingly restated the old notion that Shakespeare's real hero was the nation itself. In a general sense this is undeniable, but it is surely possible, without contradicting him, to say that Shakespeare builds up through the ten plays, as Spenser does in *The Faerie Queene*, a kind of composite hero through examples both negative and positive. Richard III and Henry V may represent the most obvious extremes, but the plays present us with a succession of heroic types, some of them very limited and hardly any unflawed, who nevertheless embody some of the qualities desirable in a public man—physical valor, patriotism, honesty, wisdom, generosity, loyalty, responsibility, justice, humility, as well as other qualities that Shakespeare numbered among the "king-becoming graces."[7] The constant allusion to the heroes of classical epic as well as to such illustrious native figures as Richard the Lion-Hearted, Edward III, and the Black Prince (the legendary King Arthur receives occasional mention as well) has the effect of heightening the heroic tone. The great profusion of stirring exhortations of troops, formal challenges flung back and forth, and speeches of diplomatic exchange have a similar effect. With the succession of heroic types goes a whole chain of anti-heroes, many of whom are very moving or humorous in their weaknesses. Shakespeare's interest in the histories, then, is not limited to the figure of the ideal king, but includes the loyal public servant, the wise counselor, the brave soldier, and the righteous churchman as well. It might be added that the medium of blank verse was ideally suited to such epic celebration, for it had been first used in English, after all, by the Earl of Surrey, himself a courtier and man of action, for his famous translation of Virgil's *Aeneid*.

But Shakespeare found it necessary to show the personal and private side of his public men, not only for the sense of depth and wholeness that would be missing without it, but in order to capitalize upon the tension between epic generality, monumentality, and detachment on the one hand and comic or tragic involvement on the other—in other words to reconcile epic with dramatic requirements. Shakespeare's two most tragic kings in the cycle, Henry VI and Richard II, are tragic because they are temperamentally unsuited to bear public responsibility, and his most comic king, Richard III, is even more unsuited to bear it because he turns the acquisition of power into a monstrous private joke.

The tension between public and private worlds in the histories relates to another contrast fundamental to the series—that between order and chaos; for this conflict too may be seen in terms of an epic or idealized conception of order violated by comic or tragic disruptions. Almost all the important thematic contrasts of the history cycle—Peace against War, Love against Hate, Rise against Fall, Divine against Human Power, Legitimacy against Illegitimacy, Strength against Weakness, Pleasure against Duty, Ceremony against Informality, Innocence against Guilt—may be subsumed under the two principal contrasts already mentioned: Order versus Chaos and Public versus Private Life.

The subtle and complex dramatic form that the greatest Elizabethan plays exemplify is based not on unity of action (in the Aristotelian sense) but on multiple actions related to each other, as musical themes are related, by repetition and variation—by a system of ironic contrasts and parallels. This principle of organization, although of course Shakespeare uses it elsewhere, was perhaps especially significant to him in the history plays because of the special problems of ordering in dramatic compass the epic sweep and multitudinousness of the chronicle source material.

What I propose to argue in this chapter is that Shakespeare often found it convenient to organize his system of contrasts and parallels in the histories with reference to another traditional literary dichotomy—one exploited almost contemporaneously by Tasso in *Jerusalem Delivered*, Spenser in *The Faerie Queene*, and Sidney in the *Arcadia*—that between epic and pastoral. I must warn readers at the outset that I am using the term "pastoral" very elastically (in the fashion of Empson), for to the formal pastoral drama of Tasso and Guarini, the drama that Jonson and Fletcher were later to imitate in England, Shakespeare owed comparatively little. His tradition was rather the rustic, spontaneous, and popular pastoralism of his native country—the tradition to which the medieval nativity plays, the popular romances, the Robin Hood ballads, and other folklore contributed much, and in which the word "shepherd" could suggest a various world of lovers, poets, holiday humor, nobles disguised as peasants, and Christian simplicity. The familiar Renaissance contrasts of court versus country and art versus nature—contrasts already touched upon in the preceding discussion of *As You Like It*—lie very close to its heart. My central point is that by drawing upon this pastoral tradition directly and also indirectly by making the audience aware of nature and the natural world through language, character, action, and setting, Shakespeare was able to dramatize more effectively some of the ironic contrasts between public and private life and between order and chaos that give the history plays their special richness.

II

Shakespeare introduces the pastoral tradition most schematically in the earliest plays—those that make up the *Henry VI* trilogy. Probably the most obvious and familiar example occurs in the third part where "Holy Harry of Lancaster" (as he was sometimes called in the sixteenth century) contemplates the advantages of the shepherd's life as the battle of Towton rages around him. He sits upon a molehill that reminds us ironically of another molehill earlier in the play upon which the ambitious York aspirant to the crown, Richard Plantagenet, has been ritually mocked, crowned with paper, and savagely murdered. As the king sits, meditative and withdrawn, wishing he had only sheep to tend instead of warring subjects, he watches an emblematic little morality play on the unnaturalness of civil war in which a son kills his father unwittingly and a father kills his son:

> This battle fares like to the morning's war,
> When dying clouds contend with growing light,
> What time the shepherd, blowing of his nails,
> Can neither call it perfect day nor night.
> . . . .
> Here on this molehill will I sit me down.
> To whom God will, there be the victory!
> . . . .
> Would I were dead, if God's good will were so!
> For what is in this world but grief and woe?
> O God! Methinks it were a happy life
> To be no better than a homely swain,
> To sit upon a hill, as I do now,
> To carve out dials quaintly, point by point,
> Thereby to see the minutes how they run:
> How many makes the hour full complete,
> How many hours brings about the day,
> How many days will finish up the year,
> How many years a mortal man may live.
> . . . .
> So minutes, hours, days, months, and years,
> Pass'd over to the end they were created,
> Would bring white hairs unto a quiet grave.
> Ah, what a life were this, how sweet, how lovely!
> Gives not the hawthorn bush a sweeter shade
> To shepherds looking on their silly sheep
> Than doth a rich embroider'd canopy
> To kings that fear their subjects' treachery?
> O, yes, it doth, a thousandfold it doth.
> And to conclude, the shepherd's homely curds,
> His cold thin drink out of his leather bottle,
> His wonted sleep under a fresh tree's shade,
> All which secure and sweetly he enjoys,

Is far beyond a prince's delicates—
His viands sparkling in a golden cup,
His body couched in a curious bed—
When care, mistrust, and treason waits on him.

(3 Henry VI, II.v.1–54)

Shakespeare is dramatizing several ideas in this scene. Henry represents the timorous warrior and incompetent king who retreats from the harsh realities of his reign into an imaginary golden world where "the lion fawns upon the lamb" (*3 Henry VI*, IV.viii.49). But the king's pastoral daydream characterizes him also as a kind of Holy Idiot (like Dostoevsky's Prince Myshkin). The molehill is an emblem of his humility (just as the contrasting molehill was a bitter mock of his Yorkist rival's reaching at mountains). His meditation throws the unnatural savagery of the civil war into vivid relief, and Shakespeare forges a symbolic link between the golden world of pastoral and the eternal world of Henry's religious commitment. A few scenes later, King Henry, now unsuccessfully disguised, becomes a deer in his own deer park and is taken prisoner by two of his own gamekeepers to be delivered over to the new York claimant, Edward IV. He is only too willing to make a spiritual kingdom of his cell, where he may be a king, as he says, "in mind":

My crown is in my heart, not on my head;
Not deck'd with diamonds and Indian stones,
Nor to be seen. My crown is call'd content;
A crown it is that seldom kings enjoy.

(III.i.62–65)

The pastoral motif here betokens Shakespeare's concern with the conflict between private and public values and their relation to order in the universe, the state, and the individual soul. Henry's golden world, his crown of "content," contrasts finely with Richard of Gloucester's idea of a golden world. For him, as for Tamburlaine, perfect bliss and sole felicity is the sweet fruition of an *earthly* crown ("the golden time I look for" [*3 Henry VI*, III.ii.127]), and, "like one lost in a thorny wood," he will "hew" his way to it "with a bloody axe" (III.ii.174–181). In the penultimate scene of *3 Henry VI* the worlds of force and spirit are effectively juxtaposed through metaphor: Richard murders Henry in the Tower of London, and Shakespeare transforms the pastoral associations used earlier into ritual sacrifice. The protective jailer, suddenly dismissed from the room, becomes the timorous shepherd driven from his charge, and Henry, "the harmless sheep," "yield[s] his fleece" (V.vi.8) and "makes[s] a bloody supper" (V.v.85) for the ravenous wolf. Such imagery becomes nearly automatic throughout the early tetralogy.[8] Peace, order, and innocence are repeatedly thought of in terms of the shepherd with his sheep; and the ruthless forces of power that turn the pastoral landscape into a scene of slaughter are imaged in terms of preying wolves and foxes.

The idea of the king as shepherd is very old. Northrop Frye tells us it can be traced to ancient Egypt;[9] but for European writers it derives mainly, of course, from biblical tradition, for Christ was the prototype of the good shepherd (the *bonus pastor*) who was also king of the universe. To Elizabethan audiences, who were used to being told that kings were a sort of gods on earth—deputies elected by the Lord, anointed, crowned, planted many years, the analogy would not have seemed in the least strange. Furthermore, it was useful to poets and dramatists because, by enshrining a paradox, it focused upon a fundamental conflict in the nature of kingship—the conflict between power and humility. Hall's *Chronicle* (1548) calls so warlike a king as Henry V "a shepherde whom his flocke loued and louyngly obeyed";[10] nor is it surprising to find the figure employed in history plays by Shakespeare's contemporaries. In Greene's *James IV* (c. 1589–92) Douglas laments the king's defection from responsibility ("O, hapless flock, whereas the guide is blind!" [II.ii.2],[11] and Robert of Artois in *Edward III* (c. 1592–95) refers to his sovereign as "the true shepherd of our commonwealth" (I.i.41).[12] James Shirley elaborates the idea in one of his early plays, *The School of Compliment* (1624):

> A shepherd is a king, whose throne
> Is a mossy mountain, on
> Whose top we sit, our crook in hand,
> Like a sceptre of command.
> Our subjects, sheep grazing below,
> Wanton, frisking to and fro.
>
> (IV.ii)[13]

Shakespeare gradually modifies this idea in the later history plays until the rather artificial and conventional image of the shepherd disappears, but the pastoral longing for escape from public duty to a quieter, simpler, more anonymous and contemplative world, continues throughout the histories until it merges with the potentially tragic concept of kingly isolation.

Prince Arthur, the rightful heir to England's crown but a helpless pawn in the game of international power-politics, dreams of the pastoral life in *King John*:

> By my christendom
> So I were out of prison and kept sheep,
> I should be as merry as the day is long.
>
> (IV.i.16–18)

The Lady Constance bemoans her lost hopes for him, sitting, like the shepherds of pastoral elegy, upon "*a grassy knoll*":[14]

> my grief's so great
> That no supporter but the huge firm earth
> Can hold it up. Here I and sorrows sit;
> Here is my throne, bid kings come bow to it.
>
> (III.i.71–74)

Even when Shakespeare drops the pastoral imagery and puts the longing for humble anonymity in more realistic and varied terms, he seems repeatedly to have his royal characters express attitudes that may be called "pastoral" in the sense of anti-heroic—when they imagine themselves as monks, beggars, and commoners or indulge themselves in escapist roles such as that of poet or tavern roisterer. Crookback Richard, who describes himself as "a plain man" of "simple truth" (*Richard III*, I.iii.51–52), and who is forever glancing heavenward with such utterances as "I thank my God for my humility" (II.i.73), parodies Henry VI's desire for the contemplative life with mordant irony (the wry glance at his own deformity creates a certain "camp" effect) as he woos the London citizens:

> Alas, why would you *heap* this care on me?
> I am unfit for state and majesty.
> I do beseech you, take it not amiss;
> I cannot nor I will not yield to you.
> > (III.vii.204–207; emphasis added)

This is the man of whom Buckingham has just said with such comic unction:

> When holy and devout religious men
> Are at their beads, 'tis much to draw them thence,
> So sweet is zealous contemplation.
> > (III.vii.92–94)

Richard II, Shakespeare's first study in depth of a man caught tragically between his ceremonial image of himself and his own private emotions, lapses periodically into a kind of sentimental pastoral role. Returning from Ireland, he stoops to pat the gentle earth of his kingdom in affectionate greeting while his active fantasy conjures up a poetic landscape in which nettles, adders, and toads annoy the feet of Bolingbroke's invading army; he threatens to exchange his scepter for a palmer's walking staff and his gorgeous palace for a hermitage. Or, again, he half welcomes "worldly loss":

> Say, is my kingdom lost? Why, 'twas my care;
> And what loss is it to be rid of care?
> > (*Richard II*, III.ii.95–96)

For a moment, he recognizes, like Wolsey, "the blessedness of being little" (*Henry VIII*, IV.ii.66). Becoming a spectator at his own tragedy, he sits upon the ground (like a shepherd) to tell sad stories of the death of kings, he muses on the theme of time (as Henry VI does on his molehill) and comes at last, unlike Henry, to the perception that he has played "in one person many people, / And none contented" (*Richard II*, V.v.31–32):

> Sometimes am I king;
> Then treasons make me wish myself a beggar,
> And so I am. Then crushing penury
> Persuades me I was better when a king;
> Then am I king'd again, and by and by
> Think that I am unking'd by Bolingbroke,
> And straight am nothing.
> > (V.v.32–38)

In *Richard II*, the pastoral idea of escape from responsibility is connected with Richard's feeling for the beauty of his emerald isle and his love of words and artificial postures. For the role-playing king, as for Duke Senior in the most pastoral of Shakespeare's comedies, "Sweet are the uses of adversity" (*As You Like It*, II.i.12).

The insomniac Henry IV expresses a familiar pastoral attitude when, weighed down under a crown that has become a "polish'd perturbation," a "golden care" (*2 Henry IV*, IV.v.22), he wishes for the uncomplicated life of an ordinary subject—for the condition of those fortunate enough to lie "in smoky cribs, / Upon uneasy pallets" rather than "in the perfum'd chambers of the great" (III.i.9–12). And his son takes up the same theme when, wandering incognito among his soldiers in the dark hours before Agincourt, he ruminates half enviously upon the "lackey" who "all night / Sleeps in Elysium" (*Henry V*, IV.i.269–271). "Uneasy lies the head that wears a crown" (*2 Henry IV*, III.i.31) captures a sentiment that Shakespeare's own sovereign probably appreciated, for Walton in his idyllic treatise on fishing records the story "that our good Queen *Elizabeth* did . . . often wish her self a Milkmaid all the month of *May*, because they are not troubled with fears and cares, but sing sweetly all the day, and sleep securely all the night."[15]

In the last play of the ten, Shakespeare returns to the more conventional symbolism of pastoral. There we see Henry VIII, not as a second Bluebeard or the heavy, brooding figure of Holbein's familiar portrait, but as a monarch young and buoyantly romantic. He interrupts Wolsey's festive banquet in the masquing costume of a French shepherd and, temporarily forgetting matters of state, loses his heart to pretty Anne Bullen. For Shakespeare, then, in the history plays, the worlds of pleasure, naturalness, contemplation, carelessness (in the root sense), art, and romance may all be seen as versions of pastoral. They remind us of that "infinite heart's-ease" (*Henry V*, IV.i.233) that all too often kings must neglect and private men may enjoy.

But pastoral symbolism may also serve ironically to emphasize disorder and unnaturalness. Since pastoral values typically suggest some sort of peaceful, civilized social norm, the abandonment or perversion of these values usually signifies anarchy. It is as though Shakespeare were reminding us that particular historical disorders may be rooted in some fundamental crime against Nature herself, in a violation of natural law. Some such purpose seems to lie behind Shakespeare's portrayal of Joan of Arc, whose dark character in Holinshed he manages to blacken further. Although she is "by birth a shepherd's daughter" who "waited on . . . tender lambs" (*1 Henry VI*, I.ii.72–76), she repudiates the pastoral world that is her lot and, assisted by hellish powers, helps to turn a peaceful land into a battlefield. Shakespeare makes her into a sort of female Tamburlaine (who was also a shepherd to begin with)—a conqueror not only of the English but of her own sovereign. The Dauphin inverts traditional order in one scene by acknowledging her his vanquisher:

> Thou art an Amazon
> And fightest with the sword of Deborah.
> . . . .
> My heart and hands thou hast at once subdu'd.
> Excellent Pucelle, if thy name be so,
> Let me thy servant and not sovereign be.
>   (*1 Henry VI*, I.ii.104–111)

At the end of the play she is revealed to be not only a witch but also a lascivious hypocrite arrogant enough to claim that royal blood runs in her veins. Shakespeare makes the moral contrast between order and disorder unmistakable when her own father, a humble shepherd content with his lot, curses Joan as unnatural and reflects that it would have better if "some ravenous wolf had eaten thee" "when thou didst keep my lambs a-field" (V.iv.30–31).

Jack Cade, "born under a hedge" (*2 Henry VI*, IV.ii.50), is another of Shakespeare's falsely aspiring and misplaced rustics. His rebellious energies create the very chaos that Henry VI's inept rule has courted and portend the even greater chaos that the rising house of York already threatens. Cade, like Joan, claims royal descent with a bogus tale of mixed-up twins that might come straight out of some pastoral romance. His watchwords are ignorance and brute force, and he sits upon London Stone, a kind of surrogate king, and imagines a silly communist utopia where exercise of reason in any form is a hanging offense and where "the pissing-conduit" shall "run nothing but claret wine this first year of our reign" (IV.vi.3–4). The frightening commonwealth that Cade dreams of is a sort of peasant's brave new world, a parody version of the legendary golden world that Gonzalo later imagines in *The Tempest* (II.i.149–170) and that Shakespeare partly derived from the fifteenth book of Ovid's *Metamorphoses* and Montaigne's delightful essay on cannibals. But Cade's imaginary order is really the very opposite of Gonzalo's idyllic primitivism. Cade's idea of the state of nature, because it is uncultivated by art or learning, is savage and unnatural. Dick Butcher cries out in his enthusiasm for reform, "let's kill all the lawyers" (*2 Henry VI*, IV.ii.74); and Cade says to his rabble army, "then are we in order when we are most out of order" (IV.ii.185–186).

The priestly function in medieval and Renaissance life was traditionally idealized, of course, as the Christian pastor's cure of souls, his selfless responsibility for the spiritual health of his flock. If this standard could be met by such lowly men as Chaucer's country parson ("He was a shepherde" able to "drawen folk to hevene by fairnesse" and "good ensample" who "waited after no pompe and reverence" [*The Canterbury Tales*, General Prologue, ll. 514–525]), how much more was it to be enjoined upon the great prelates of the church whose very symbol of episcopal authority was the crosier, or shepherd's crook. The mere presence of the lords spiritual in the histories reminds us of the historic pastoral commitment to be *in* the world without quite being *of* it; but of course many of Shakespeare's ambitious clerics fall very short of this ideal and behave in fact like lords temporal. Malicious or worldly churchmen like Cardinal Beaufort in *1* and *2 Henry VI*, Cardinal Pandulph in *King John*, the Archbishop of York in *1* and *2 Henry IV*, or Wolsey in *Henry VIII* dramatize the great gulf between an order based upon Christian grace and charity (the order of the Good Shepherd) and the perverted greed for riches, power, and privilege that makes a mockery of their pastoral calling. Such are the corrupt clergy that Milton was later to attack through Saint Peter's words in "Lycidas"—those who "for their bellies' sake, / Creep and intrude, and climb into the fold," or "scramble at the shearers' feast / And shove away the worthy bidden guest" (ll. 114–118). Prince John of Lancaster strongly, if somewhat smugly, rebukes Archbishop Scroop's perversion of his pastoral function:

> My Lord of York, it better show'd with you
> When that your flock, assembled by the bell,
> Encircled you to hear with reverence

> Your exposition on the holy text
> Than now to see you here an iron man,
> Cheering a rout of rebels with your drum,
> Turning the word to sword, and life to death.
>   (*2 Henry IV*, IV.ii.4–10)

We see the true standard of Christian behavior when Henry VI, more a priest than a king, prays for the soul of Cardinal Beaufort, who has served him so treacherously, or when Wolsey moralizes on his own fate:

> O Cromwell, Cromwell!
> Had I but serv'd my God with half the zeal
> I serv'd my King, he would not in mine age
> Have left me naked to mine enemies.
>
> ·
>   Farewell
> The hopes of court! My hopes in heaven do dwell.
>   (*Henry VIII*, III.ii.454–459)

When Shakespeare is not reinforcing the various aspects of the pastoral theme by contrasts in action and characterization, he often seems to do so obliquely by evoking a sense of ideal landscape through imagery and setting. One cannot read the histories consecutively without being struck by the constant prevalence of natural imagery. As early as *Titus Andronicus* Shakespeare had begun, in Milton's phrase, to "warble his native wood-notes wild" ("L'Allegro," l. 134), and indeed we are usually not far from the out-of-doors throughout Shakespeare's poetry. But in the history plays especially, landscape is often evocative of moral attitude rather than merely decorative or atmospheric. The dramatist shares with Wordsworth that pastoral impulse that makes poets turn to the countryside for reflections on man's experience in the bustling world, that looks to Nature as a teacher. Certain stock metaphors constantly recur. Health and unhealth in the body politic are regularly imaged by figures drawn from husbandry. Commonwealths as well as individual fortunes bud, ripen, and wither.[16] Another of Wolsey's speeches—even if it was written by Fletcher (as some believe) rather than by Shakespeare—illustrates the typical practice:

> Farewell? A long farewell to all my greatness!
> This is the state of man: today he puts forth
> The tender leaves of hopes; tomorrow blossoms,
> And bears his blushing honors thick upon him;
> The third day comes a frost, a killing frost,
> And when he thinks, good easy man, full surely
> His greatness is a-ripening, nips his root,
> And then he falls, as I do.
>   (III.ii.351–358)

Weeds in gardens, caterpillars eating leaves, and cankers in roses stand, of course, for various evils. Genealogical relationships are traditionally associated with trees or vines, and one gets in the histories the constant linking of blood with growth and vegetation. Bolingbroke, at the end of *Richard II*, sees himself as a plant watered by the scarlet rain of his rival's murder:

> Lords, I protest, my soul is full of woe,
> That blood should sprinkle me to make me grow.
> (V.vi.45–46)

The landscape mirrors the values of peace and war, so that, typically, "cedar[s]" (like Warwick) yield "to the axe's edge" (*3 Henry VI*, V.ii.11), "branch[es]" (like Rutland) are "lopp'd" when their "leaves put forth" (*3 Henry VI*, II.vi.47–48), and "sweet . . . plant[s]" (like Prince Edward) are "untimely cropp'd" (*3 Henry VI*, V.v.62). The "soil" of England "daub[s] her lips with her own children's blood," "trenching war channel[s] her fields" and "bruise[s] her flow'rets with . . . armed hoofs" (*1 Henry IV*, I.i.5–8), soldiers "Make boot upon the summer's velvet buds" (*Henry V*, I.ii.194), a "crimson tempest . . . bedrench[es] / The fresh green lap of fair King Richard's land" (*Richard II*, III.iii.46–47), or a dynastic crisis "ill become[s] the flower of England's face," changing the "complexion of her maid-pale peace / To scarlet indignation and bedew[-ing] / Her pastures' grass" with blood (*Richard II*, III.iii.97–100). If Shakespeare had liked Stendhalian titles, he might have called the entire cycle "The Red and the Green."

Seasonal imagery of course is vital to the pastoral tradition (*The Shepheards Calendar* springs instantly to mind), and accordingly, in the history plays, glorious summers succeed winters of discontent. But sometimes, as in *Richard III*, what ought to be a rebirth turns out to be a hideous storm of terror. In *Richard II*, the Duchess of York, referring to the new king's favorites, asks her son Aumerle, "Who are the violets now / That strew the green lap of the new-come spring?" York warns him sagely, "Well, bear you well in this new spring of time, / Lest you be cropp'd before you come to prime" (V.ii.46–51). Political mutability has its familiar analogue in the cycles of nature, and Shakespeare puts it to eloquent use.

Security, coolness, ease, and natural order are traditionally associated with the country-side, but for Shakespeare ideal landscapes are populated, controlled by human beings, methodized (as Pope might say) so as to analogize natural law. Behind this symbolism, of course, lies the Christian Neoplatonic habit of regarding nature as a second Book of Revelation—that way of thinking, already noticed in the previous chapter, that allows Duke Senior, "exempt from public haunt," to find "tongues in trees, books in the running brooks, / Sermons in stones, and good in everything" (*As You Like It*, II.i.15–17). There was also the possibility of analogy, often ironically employed, between the green landscape of England and the biblical garden of Paradise. Shakespeare exploits this parallel in the famous allegorical garden scene of *Richard II* in which a pair of gardeners, following the pastoral tradition that goes back to Virgil, discuss their betters and moralize at length upon the misgovernment of the nation in the language of pruning, weeding, and the propping up of limbs. The land that Gaunt earlier described as "this other Eden, demi-paradise" (II.i.42) has fallen from its prelapsarian state to the condition of a mere "pelting farm" (II.i.60). Under Richard's slovenly care, as the names of his sycophants Bushy and Green (despite their derivation from Holinshed) may help to symbolize, it has become an unweeded garden. Things rank and gross in nature possess it merely.

The Duke of Burgundy in one of the loveliest speeches of *Henry V* sees the disordered countryside of "fertile France," that "best garden of the world" (V.ii.36–37), in the same terms:

> all her husbandry doth lie on heaps,
> Corrupting in it own fertility.
> Her vine, the merry cheerer of the heart,
> Unpruned dies; her hedges even-pleach'd,
> Like prisoners wildly overgrown with hair,
> Put forth disorder'd twigs; her fallow leas
> The darnel, hemlock, and rank fumitory
> Doth root upon, while that the coulter rusts
> That should deracinate such savagery.
> The even mead, that erst brought sweetly forth
> The freckled cowslip, burnet, and green clover,
> Wanting the scythe, all uncorrected, rank,
> Conceives by idleness, and nothing teems
> But hateful docks, rough thistles, kecksies, burrs,
> Losing both beauty and utility.
> And all our vineyards, fallows, meads, and hedges,
> Defective in their natures, grow to wildness.
>
> (V.ii.39–55)

War has its heroic side in *Henry V*, but here it is seen as a violation of natural law revealed in a landscape that forfeits "both beauty and utility."

So often in Shakespeare a scene is placed in a garden or forest[17] not for the sake of realistic background or local color but for ethical or thematic suggestiveness.[18] This partly explains why often—indeed ordinarily—we get no detailed or specific impression of place in the verse beyond a stereotyped or generic locale.

One of the most illuminating examples of Shakespeare's use of emblematic setting occurs in the famous Temple Garden scene of *1 Henry VI*, where with ingenious wit and ceremonial rhetoric the playwright dramatizes the growing factionalism between the red rose of Lancaster and the white rose of York. The whole episode is an extended metaphysical conceit in dramatic form. The plucking of the red and white roses with its accompanying verbal quarrel constitutes both a prophecy and a pastoral reduction of the fratricidal war to follow. In this sense it serves as an analogue to the Fall. The garden setting, in fact, establishes a whole complex of interrelated ironies. As in *Richard II*, it is a foil to set off the sickness and chaos in the state against the health and order in nature. Indeed, this contrast becomes the more emphatic because the garden adjoins an ancient school of law. Moreover, the garden is rich in connotations that go back to medieval literary tradition. We recall the gardens of Chaucer's *Troilus* and *Canterbury Tales* that often mingle the erotic associations of *The Romance of the Rose* with the idea of gardens as types of Eden and therefore allegories of sacred order, divine love, and human charity.[19] The birth of a national blood feud therefore takes place in a setting that normally connotes love, whether secular or religious. In the great chain of being, the rose was traditionally at the top of the floral hierarchy and hence analogous to royalty. This idea became associated in medieval religious tradition with the symbolism of martyrology,[20] and Shakespeare seems to draw upon this association again in later plays when he causes Tyrrel to describe the kissing lips of the little princes in the Tower as "four red roses on a stalk" (*Richard III*, IV.iii.12) and has the queen call Richard II "my fair rose" (*Richard II*, V.i.8) or Hotspur refer nostalgically to the same monarch after his murder as "that sweet lovely rose" (*1 Henry IV*, I.iii.175). The color contrast is symbolic too: Shakespeare exploits its ironic possibilities when he makes the traditional heraldry of white for innocence and red for love prefigure pale fear and gory death:

> *Plantagenet.* Now, Somerset, where is your argument?
> *Somerset.* Here in my scabbard, meditating that
>   Shall dye your white rose in a bloody red.
> *Plantagenet.* Meantime your cheeks do counterfeit our roses;
>   For pale they look with fear, as witnessing
>   The truth on our side.
> *Somerset.*   No, Plantagenet,
>   'Tis not for fear, but anger, that thy cheeks
>   Blush for pure shame to counterfeit our roses,
>   And yet thy tongue will not confess thy error.
> *Plantagenet.* Hath not thy rose a canker, Somerset?
> *Somerset.* Hath not thy rose a thorn, Plantagenet?
>   (*1 Henry VI*, II.iv.59–69)

The plucking of the roses, then, becomes the emblem of natural law violated. It expresses in iconographic form the same sentiment that one of the remorseful murderers in *Richard III* is reported as having uttered:

>   We smothered
>   The most replenished sweet work of nature
>   That from the prime creation e'er she framed.
>   (IV.iii.17–19)

King Henry, sitting on his molehill, later notices "the red rose and the white . . . The fatal colors of our striving houses" (*3 Henry VI*, II.v.97–98) on the mangled face of the boy slain by his father at Towton.

Gardens, orchards, parks, and forests keep reappearing in the history plays. In her husband's garden the Duchess of Gloucester (*2 Henry VI*, I.iv) dabbles in black magic by involving herself with the notorious witch Margery Jourdain and two sinister priests.[21] There by blasphemous invocations and other occult ceremonies—to the accompaniment of thunder and lightning—they raise "a spirit" who, in riddling fashion, foretells the deposition of the king and the deaths of York, Somerset, and Suffolk. Richard Plantagenet allies himself with Warwick the kingmaker in another garden scene (*2 Henry VI*, II.ii). Strolling together in a "close walk" (II.ii.3), later described as "this private plot" (II.ii.60), they plan to root up the red rose and plant the white, biding their time until their enemies "have snar'd the shepherd of the flock / That virtuous prince, the good Duke Humphrey" and the hour be ripe to stain their swords "with heart-blood of the house of Lancaster" (II.ii.66–74). The walled garden or *hortus conclusus* (as it was called in the Middle Ages) is traditionally the place for quiet contemplation and retirement. Yet here the contemplation runs on political murder—as it does later for Brutus in still another garden. The ordered gardens become ironic settings in which to mirror impending chaos, to commune with evil forces, to sow seeds of destruction, to contemplate (with un-Marvellian ferocity) the annihilation of all that's made with green thoughts in a green shade. Shakespeare gives us a comic scene of ambitious contemplation later on when Falstaff, informed of Prince Hal's accession to the throne, tells Shallow in the latter's "arbor" within an "orchard" (*2 Henry IV*, V.iii.1–2) that "the laws of England are at my commandment" (V.iii.138).

In Shakespeare, as in Spenser (compare the episodes in book VI of *The Faerie Queene* where Serena is nearly devoured by cannibals or in which Pastorella is kidnapped by brigands and her father murdered), violence and savagery seem constantly to menace the idyllic aspects of the green world. In *2 Henry VI*, Alexander Iden (one can scarcely overlook the symbolic overtones of a name spelled "Eden" in the 1587 edition of Holinshed) contemplates his own garden in a typically pastoral vein:

> Lord, who would live turmoiled in the court,
> And may enjoy such quiet walks as these?
> This small inheritance my father left me
> Contenteth me, and worth a monarchy.
> I seek not to wax great by others' waning,
> Or gather wealth, I care not with what envy.
> Sufficeth that I have maintains my state
> And sends the poor well pleased from my gate.
>   (IV.x.16–23)

When Jack Cade leaps the garden wall in order to steal food (see IV.x.6–9), we have chaos breaking in upon order, and Iden has to kill him in order to reestablish the natural equilibrium. Perhaps Shakespeare suggests in this scene, as he does later in *As You Like It*, that the separation between the world of affairs and the pastoral world can never be complete or more than temporary.

Of course all the Shallow scenes in *2 Henry IV* with their delightful local color serve to underscore the traditional pastoral contrast of court and country. The rambling chatter about grafting pippins, sowing the headland with red wheat, settling debts with "pigeons" and "a couple of short-legg'd hens" (V.i.25–26), and selling "a score of ewes" (III.ii.50) or "a good yoke of bullocks at Stamford fair" (III.ii.39) dramatizes a world removed from civil war and indicates that the distance between Gloucestershire and Westminster Palace, where the king lies stricken, is more than a matter of miles. The point, incidentally, has not been lost on producers of the play. Sir Frank Benson in 1864 brought out the country quality of the scenes at Shallow's "through the visible and vocal presence of sheep, pigeons, and fowls," and subtler modifications of his idea have marked more recent productions.[22]

Richard of Gloucester sends the Bishop of Ely to order strawberries from a garden in order to break up a council meeting and suddenly change the atmosphere from one of natural amity and established law into a little reign of terror. The contrast between the strawberry garden outside and Richard's shrunken arm inside, "like a blasted sapling, wither'd up" (*Richard III*, III.iv.69), points one of the morals Shakespeare desires us to draw from the scene. Indeed, the strawberry itself, as Lawrence J. Ross has shown in a significant article, was emblematic of both "the good or uncorrupted man" and "the seemingly good man, the hypocrite."[23] Ross traces the symbolism of the strawberry as an apparent good that conceals evil to a passage in Virgil's *Eclogues* (III, 92–93), and also points out the idyllic connotations of the fruit in classical and Christian literature and art. For instance, in Ovid's *Metamorphoses* (I, 104), the strawberry typifies the food of the pastoral Golden Age; and, as signifying the fruit of the spirit, it traditionally "appears near the blessed or in the Eden of unfallen Adam and Eve in representations of the celestial or earthly paradise."[24] King John dies in an "orchard" whither he has been brought in the hope that "the open air . . . would allay the burning quality / Of that fell poison which assaileth him" (*King John*, V.vii.7–10). The fresh air of the orchard cannot restore his health, but the shift of the final action to a natural setting does foreshadow the cure of England's ills and the restoration of natural order to the state. In both plays, details of setting with "pastoral" or green-world overtones help to define moral contrasts that are significant in the total structure.

Natural settings sometimes seem to agree with actions in the later plays too. The rebels of *2 Henry IV* are betrayed into dispersing their forces at a place in Yorkshire called Gaultree Forest. Holinshed's spelling ("Galtree") with its built-in suggestion of the Crucifixion again brings out more clearly the ironic connotations of the name. Queen Katharine's lady-in-waiting in *Henry VIII* tries to cheer her mistress's heavy heart by singing a pastoral lyric in which Orpheus creates a poetic landscape as different as might be from the dolor of her palace apartment:

> Orpheus with his lute made trees,
> And the mountain tops that freeze,
>   Bow themselves when he did sing.
> To his music plants and flowers
> Ever sprung, as sun and showers
>   There had made a lasting spring.
>   (III.i.3–8)

But a little later in the scene the queen seems to identify herself with the flower of a poetic landscape, indulging in the pathetic fallacy that is so marked a feature of the song:

> Like the lily,
> That once was mistress of the field and flourish'd,
> I'll hang my head and perish.
>   (III.i.151–153)

The reverse symbolism appears in Cranmer's great prophecy in which Shakespeare compliments James I by identifying him with a cedar of Lebanon with its obvious biblical overtones:

> He shall flourish,
> And, like a mountain cedar, reach his branches
> To all the plains about him. Our children's children
> Shall see this and bless heaven.
>   (V.v.53–56)[25]

Symbolic weather is an adjunct of natural setting, and Shakespeare frequently employs it in the same way—that is, to point up how the actions of men are reflected or prophesied in physical nature. Richard III notices that the sun "disdains to shine" on Bosworth Field and draws the ironic inference: "A black day will it be to somebody" (*Richard III*, V.iii.278–280). The bloody sun appearing "above yon busky hill" (*1 Henry IV*, V.i.2) at Shrewsbury foretells the "dread correction" (V.i.111) that waits upon the rebel forces in *1 Henry IV*: "The southern wind / Doth play the trumpet . . . / And by his hollow whistling in the leaves / Foretells a tempest and a blust'ring day" (V.i.3–6). The blasted "bay trees" in *Richard II* are obviously related to the same literary technique, for Shakespeare includes them among the portentous and unnatural "signs" that "forerun the death or fall of kings" (II.iv.8–15).

III

To summarize then, Shakespeare uses the pastoral motif and its extension into details of landscape, imagery, and setting both to mirror and to challenge ideas or order and disorder in the great world of affairs. The green world becomes for Shakespeare what Northrop Frye has called a "complex variable," a kind of archetypal symbol that functions in such a way as to express a continuing tension between the ideal and the actual as it affects both the individual and the state. The "pastoral" emphasis shows us, as it were, the underside of epic. It permits points of rest between the excursions and alarums. By allowing for reflection—sometimes choric reflection—upon the action, it helps to evoke what is timeless in the context of speeding time. The contrast partly enables Shakespeare to dramatize history in both long and short perspective at once—and in a way that ultimately humanizes the grand as well as the trivial in the lives of men and nations. To put it another way, the complementary relationship of epic and pastoral in the history plays illustrates afresh the truth of Dryden's wise and splendid words about Shakespeare: "He was the man who of all modern, and perhaps ancient poets, had the largest and most comprehensive soul. *All* the images of Nature were still [i.e., ever] present to him" (emphasis added).[26]

As Shakespeare's dramatic powers matured, he relied less and less exclusively on traditional and iconographic devices and was able more and more to realize contrasts between the private and the public, between order and chaos, with greater psychological subtlety—that is to say, through the creation of richly contrasting and complementary characters. Time and time again throughout the history plays, comic or semicomic actions and characters are used to parody the heroic and tragic aspects of the story and thereby to qualify simplistic attitudes. By this means, orthodox political and moral notions that a less humane poet might accept uncritically are constantly reexamined and submitted to new tests of validity. Pistol's nearly meaningless bombast, a tissue of shreds and patches from theatrical rant, does not cancel the stirring effect of Henry V's great martial speeches, but it does force us to reconsider them in a new light. Faulconbridge's wiseacre remarks, interjected while international diplomacy is being conducted, make us aware of the pretension and hypocrisy that public utterances so often cloak. The two *Henry IV* plays, as C. L. Barber's influential discussion has persuaded most of us,[27] constitute Shakespeare's greatest achievement in this way. There we watch Prince Hal grow up by experiencing what is best and worst in the divided but linked worlds of tavern and court, the two kingdoms of Falstaff and Bolingbroke. The point, of course, is that each of the two kingdoms deepens and qualifies our understanding of the other by virtue of the dramatic interaction between them. William Empson, in fact, has suggested that structures of this kind are built upon a version of pastoral;[28] but the element of parody in the histories is a subject in itself and deserves full discussion in a separate essay.

The reflection of order and disorder through pastoral and through the evocation of physical nature in the history plays raises but does not answer some of the great metaphysical questions of the Renaissance. Nature in one of its aspects suggests the possibility of an ordered and harmonious cosmos in Hooker's terms—a great universal garden, created, tended, and brought to ultimate fruition by a supreme and loving Gardener. This is the kind of order that the more conservative critics have usually seen as lying behind Shakespeare's histories. But the plays, although they have their moments of peace, are never very far removed from war, which, if it involves heroism, also involves butchery of the innocent. The brutish realities of dynastic struggle, of power conflicts, of the human ego asserting itself politically, do not permit us to forget that, in its other aspect, nature is Hobbesian—red in tooth and claw.

Many of the characters in the histories, from Henry VI to Katharine of Aragon, die patiently confident of a Christian heaven; yet the total dramatic action of the plays in which these characters appear, as well as of the other histories written in between, puts more emphasis upon the vanity of human wishes than upon man's eternal hopes. In *Henry VIII*, to be sure, Queen Katharine is vouchsafed a supernal vision. Figures in a sort of pastoral ballet hold a garland of bays above her head in an action clearly meant to symbolize spiritual victory. But Shakespeare wrote that play only three years before his death, and in any case, many scholars still think Fletcher's hand was stronger in it than his own. The earlier plays are concerned more with Nature and less with Grace, and they are not so affirmative in tone. To some degree, they do contain that which points forward to the half-sunny world of the forest of Arden and beyond it to the pastoral sweetness of *Cymbeline* and the "great creating nature" of Perdita's flower garden (*The Winter's Tale*, IV.iv.88). But the histories also anticipate a view of nature in which Ophelia, driven mad by disorders she cannot comprehend, can drown beneath a willow in a weeping brook—in which Lear can stagger about a heath, "Crown'd with rank fumiter," with "hardocks, hemlock, nettles, cuckoo flow'rs, / Darnel, and . . . all the idle weeds that grow / In our sustaining corn" (*King Lear*, IV.iv.3–6).

When we learn from Hostess Quickly that Falstaff died babbling "of green fields" (*Henry V*, II.iii.16–17),[29] it is moving to think of that lovable reprobate departing this world with that most pastoral of psalms, the twenty-third, on his lips. Despite Falstaff's clear association with the Vice tradition of the medieval moralities, we should like to think that at the end, at least, the Lord is his shepherd and that he comes at last to lie down in green pastures. But Nell Quickly, who is outrageously sentimental and no theologian, probably misses the point. Surely it is not without significance that she mistakes Abraham's bosom for Arthur's. There is much in the history plays that looks forward to the great tragedies—those profound dramas in which man's hopes about universal order are so terribly shaken. Shakespeare does not let us forget that in *this* world—the world of history—we fear evil even as we create it, and that we walk through the valley of the shadow of death.

7

The Green Underworld of
Early Shakespearean Tragedy

I

To speak of greenery or vegetation as a significant component of Shakespeare's tragic ethos may seem at first bizarre, then, on soberer reflection, merely strained or farfetched. Mention of the dramatist's green world inevitably calls up the settings of romantic comedy—Valentine's sylvan retreat, Navarre's park, Robin Goodfellow's fairy playground, Jessica and Lorenzo's moonlit bank, Orlando's verse-bedecked forest, or Perdita's rustic but unspoiled Bohemia.[1] Alternatively, we may think of the English histories (discussed in the preceding chapter) with their deer parks, woods, and symbolic gardens—the Temple Garden of *1 Henry VI*, where the bitter factionalism of the red and white rose has its emblematic inception; Iden's walled garden, where the anarchic Cade meets death; the scrupulously tended *hortus conclusus* at the ironic center of Richard II's disordered kingdom; or Henry V's France, that "best garden of the world" *(Henry V, V.ii.36)*, whose husbandry, neglected as a consequence of war, Burgundy describes so evocatively.[2] But Shakespeare does not exclude touches of the green world even from his darkest plays, however tangentially or unemphatically he may employ them. Details of foliage and landscape—especially the benign evidence of nature's environment—may appear less prominently in the tragedies than in the rest of the canon; but such details, cumulatively understood, may be said to compose a suggestive if comparatively inconspicuous underside of a world characterized chiefly by evil, suffering, and devastation. Inherent in any Renaissance concern with the vegetative realm are riddling questions about the relation of nature to nurture, about the elusive coordinates that link God's creation with man's cultivation or perversion of it. Doubts about the true shape of reality necessarily lie at the heart of any tragic vision. It is therefore hardly surprising that the green world—the manifestation of nature that most readily symbolizes the cycle of growth and decay, of birth and death, that adumbrates but cannot fully reveal the mysterious interchange between immediate and final causes—should find a place in Shakespeare's tragic universe.

The reciprocity, or complementarity, of genres is now recognized as an established principle in Shakespearean dramaturgy.[3] As a group, the histories tend to interweave comic with tragic, private with public, meditative with active strands in a richly variegated tapestry. Green tones, quieter, cooler, more pacific than their accompanying red ones, sometimes mute or distance, sometimes cast into bold relief the royal splendor and savage violence of political power and conflict. As we have seen already, Holy Harry of Lancaster, Shakespeare's shepherd-king, muses upon "sleep under a fresh tree's shade" (*3 Henry VI*, II.v.49) at the battle of Towton even as a father unwittingly slaughters his son and a son his father. In a related way, the comedies and tragedies bespeak, if they do not actually subsume, attitudes or values contrary to those that their happy or unhappy endings define. As such critics as Northrop Frye, C. L. Barber, and Thomas McFarland have noted or implied, Shakespearean comedy, in celebrating marriage, social cohesion, and the perpetuity of the race, earns its affirmation in part by temporarily silencing, averting, or absorbing the menace of death.[4] Hermia faces possible execution at the opening of *A Midsummer Night's Dream* if she should refuse to give up her beloved Lysander in favor of Demetrius. But the fanciful and comic confusions of the forest (where anything can happen) supervene; the true lovers, though puzzled, emerge from their verdant maze united and unharmed, and death is robbed of its sting. In concert with the multiple pairs of lovers, we may relax in the assurance that a tragic possibility has been transposed to the mode of burlesque—the staged hilarity of Bottom and Flute unconsciously parodying the cruel fates of Pyramus and Thisbe.

Romeo and Juliet, a play whose situation, structure, and character types are all potentially comic, shows us the obverse of this interdependence. Like Hermia, Juliet knows the frustration of having an authoritarian and antiromantic father. Romeo's infatuation with Rosaline and Mercutio's mockery of it dramatize romance as a familiar species of adolescent folly. But when Juliet suddenly displaces Rosaline in Romeo's affection, the emotional realignment amounts to more than the temporary effect of a fairy's flower. Passion grows intense, the stars become increasingly inimical, maturity deepens understanding, and the pain and pathos of the Pyramus and Thisbe plight engage our hearts. The characters cease to be merely archetypal. We are constrained finally to reject the Mercutian attitude toward love—love as frivolity, love as dream engendered by the mischievous Queen Mab—and embrace its reality, with the lovers themselves, as compelling, ineluctable, agonizing, and ultimately sacrificial.

II

The green world functions significantly in both plays. In the comedy, appropriately enough, it serves as the stage for nearly all of the action—indeed, for everything that happens between the framing scenes in Athens that open and close the drama. Love, imagination, and magic must work their diverting miracles if there is to be any play at all, and the moon-drenched forest, set apart from the more rationalistic city, is their proper domain. *Romeo and Juliet*, by contrast, is an urban play whose action takes place principally in the hot streets of Verona and Mantua, in citizens' houses, in church buildings, and finally in the tomb. The play's green world, associated chiefly with the privacy of romantic emotion, comes into view only tenuously and intermittently and is notable for its protracted absences. This is precisely what we should expect in an environment so given over to family hatreds, bourgeois materialism, insensitivity, sexual cynicism, and a general hostility to romance that seems to enlist in its service even heavenly bodies and an epidemic of plague. Romeo takes solitary walks "underneath the grove of sycamore" and steals "into the covert of the wood" (I.i.121–125) near Verona to sigh, to attitudinize about Rosaline, to indulge his emotions in Petrarchan clichés, but his father compares his unhealthy state to a "bud bit with an envious worm" before it "can spread his sweet leaves to the air / Or dedicate his beauty to the sun" (I.i.151–153). Death has already entered this Arcadia. The important green settings of the play are Capulet's enclosed orchard, where genuine love flowers so briefly, and Friar Laurence's monastery garden, where the priest gathers herbs, among which are those that he hopes will preserve the threatened marriage of the newlyweds. But Death is also resident in both these places.

The two nocturnal scenes in the orchard—the only scenes that permit the lovers to realize untrammeled intimacy—are bathed in a kind of gracious enchantment. Romeo swears eternal love "by yonder blessed moon" that "tips with silver all these fruit-tree tops" (II.ii.107–108). Such a detail would not be out of place in the kingdom of Oberon and Titania. But Juliet instantly reminds her lover and us that the moon is "inconstant" and "monthly changes in her circled orb" (II.ii.110), a consideration that introduces melancholy thoughts of flux and the pressures of injurious time. These are attitudes that would inappropriately dampen the festive spirit of *A Midsummer Night's Dream*.[5] The orchard walls, which Romeo refers to as "stony limits," are "high and hard to climb" despite the "light wings" of love with which he has "o'erperch[ed]" them (II.ii.63–67). However much these walls may be felt to shelter the rapture of first love, they also encircle the "place" of "death" (II.ii.64) if he should be discovered.

In the later balancing scene of poignant separation, when "Night's candles are burnt out, and jocund day / Stands tiptoe on the misty mountain tops" (III.v.9–10), when the "pale reflex of Cynthia's brow" (III.v.20) yields to the "severing" (III.v.8) reality of dawn, the lovers affectionately dispute whether it is the nightingale "on yond pomegranate-tree" (III.v.4) or the lark that makes their "sweet division" (III.v.29). Juliet's window "let[s] day in, and let[s] life out" (III.v.41), so that when Romeo descends from the heaven of Juliet's arms to the cold ground from which he had climbed (the stage movement is emotional as well as physical) the beautiful garden has metamorphosed with prophetic effect into a graveyard:

> Methinks I see thee, now thou art so low,
> As one dead in the bottom of a tomb.
>   (III.v.55–56)

Capulet's orchard gives the paradox of love and death in which the tragedy is rhetorically and psychologically rooted a spatial dimension. Like the tomb with which Juliet associates it, the enclosed garden becomes a geographic oxymoron, a place of union and of separation, of ecstasy and of sorrow. By the final scene the "yew trees" (V.iii.3) of the churchyard, where the Capulet vault is located, have supplanted the fruit-bearing trees outside Juliet's bedchamber.

The extensive imagery of flowers and fruits supports this pattern of union in antithesis. Shakespeare conveys the extreme youth of the lovers by comparing them to buds. Romeo, as we have seen, is likened to a cankered bud when he is mooning over Rosaline, a remote and unattainable beauty who never appears onstage and whose symbolic name constitutes her entire identity. Juliet too, like the other "fresh fennel buds" (I.ii.29) whom Capulet invites to his ball, is scarcely "ripe" enough "to be a bride" (I.ii.11), although in the heady atmosphere of the orchard she expresses to Romeo her hope that "This bud of love, by summer's ripening breath, / May prove a beauteous flow'r when next we meet" (II.ii.121–122). Juliet wishes Romeo could "deny [his] father and refuse [his] name" (II.ii.34), since "a rose / By any other word would smell as sweet" (II.ii.43–44). Such metaphors are conventional in love poetry, for, in addition to their connotations of freshness, softness, and fragility, they suggest as well the possibility of growth and fruition.

But Shakespeare builds a sense of mortality into his vegetative imagery that keeps us aware of love's enemies and reinforces the idea of a romance too perfect and intense for survival—"too rich for use, for earth too dear" (I.v.48). The summer heat that ripens love so speedily is the same heat that shortens tempers, intensifies hatreds, promotes street brawls, and increases the danger of plague. Before Romeo approaches Juliet's window for the first time, he hides among the fruit trees below, while Benvolio pokes fun at his unsociable behavior in the mistaken belief that he still dotes on Rosaline: "Blind is his love and best befits the dark" (II.i.33). This remark triggers an explosion of sexual puns from Mercutio on medlars and poperin pears. The coarseness of the bawdry only augments our sense of Romeo's innocent idealism. Nevertheless, his jocular companions speak truer than they know. Darkness of a tragic rather than a sexual kind is already half in prospect, and blindness in the form of stupid animosities and critical ignorances will increasingly beset the lovers. Moreover, the mention of the medlar, a fruit proverbially ripe only when it is rotten, reinforces the thematic fusion of happiness and destruction, of fulfillment and loss. Nor is it accidental that Paris, Romeo's unwitting rival, also figures significantly in the floral symbolism. Lady Capulet extols the young nobleman to her daughter, insisting that "Verona's summer hath not such a flower," and the nurse mindlessly reiterates, "Nay, he's a flower, in faith, a very flower" (I.iii.78–79). If Romeo and Juliet are both identified with blossoms, so too is the courtly outsider whose intrusion on their secret love forces the heroine to simulate death. In a further twist of irony Paris brings to Juliet's tomb the flowers intended to adorn their marriage and is wantonly killed by Romeo for his pains. The grave unites not only Romeo and Juliet in its embrace but also Paris, Mercutio, and Tybalt—the *jeunesse dorée* of Verona—whom circumstances had so ironically separated in life.

Juliet's nurse teases her youthful charge by commending Romeo's physique ("his leg excels all men's") while dispraising his social polish, doubtless with Paris in mind ("He is not the flower of courtesy" [II.v.40–43]). Later, in hasty reaction to the shedding of her cousin's blood, Juliet must try to reconcile the apparent contradiction of her husband's "serpent heart, hid with a flow'ring face" (III.ii.73):

> O nature, what hadst thou to do in hell
> When thou didst bower the spirit of a fiend
> In mortal paradise of such sweet flesh?
>   (III.ii.80–82)

When Capulet laments that "Our bridal flowers serve for a buried corse, / And all things change them to the contrary" (IV.v.89–90), he articulates not only a central irony of the tragedy but a double one as well; for, of course, Juliet really lives. As the friar knew they would, "The roses in [her] lips and cheeks . . . fade / To wanny ashes" (IV.i.99–100), and, in her father's lyrical phrase, "Death lies on her like an untimely frost / Upon the sweetest flower of all the field" (IV.v.28–29). Paris, taking up the motif, plays off the literal sense against the metaphoric with elegiac wit: "Sweet flower, with flowers thy bridal bed I strew—" (V.iii.12). In a more grotesque double entendre Capulet conceptualizes Death as his "son-in-law" and "heir": "There she lies, / Flower as she was, deflowered by him" (IV.v.36–38). Life that wears but the appearance of death is a potentially comic device (as in *Much Ado about Nothing*), but Shakespeare converts the error to truth by making actual deaths contingent upon the feigned one. The temporary suspension of life changes to a final denial of it. Surface image and underlying substance unite, and growth has realized its mutable perfection almost in its beginning. The world of summer flowers goes underground; Tybalt's is not the only corpse "but green in earth" (IV.iii.42).

The hopeful and pessimistic possibilities of the green world reveal themselves most explicitly in the friar's herb-gathering soliloquy, spoken, like the orchard dialogue when the lovers part, in the symbolic half light of dawn—when "the grey-ey'd morn smiles on the frowning night" (II.iii.1). Here the mysterious contrarieties of nature are made emblematic in the "baleful weeds and precious-juiced flowers" that the holy man collects in his "osier cage" (II.iii.7–8). Although this speech is perfectly in character, it is also choric, expressing, as it does, a philosophy of man's relation to the landscape that not only is fundamental to *Romeo and Juliet* but also permeates the corpus of Shakespeare's Elizabethan works:

> The earth that's nature's mother is her tomb;
> What is her burying grave, that is her womb;
> And from her womb children of divers kind
> We sucking on her natural bosom find,
> Many for many virtues excellent,
> None but for some, and yet all different.
> O, mickle is the powerful grace that lies
> In plants, herbs, stones, and their true qualities.
> For nought so vile that on the earth doth live
> But to the earth some special good doth give;
> Nor aught so good but, strain'd from that fair use,
> Revolts from true birth, stumbling on abuse.
> Virtue itself turns vice, being misapplied,
> And vice sometime by action dignified.
>
> *Enter Romeo.*
>
> Within the infant rind of this weak flower
> Poison hath residence and medicine power:
> For this, being smelt, with that part cheers each part;
> Being tasted, stays all senses with the heart.
> Two such opposed kings encamp them still
> In man as well as herbs, grace and rude will;
> And where the worser is predominant,
> Full soon the canker death eats up that plant.
>
> (II.iii.9–30)

The birth-death or womb-tomb paradox that we have already noted elsewhere in the action and verbal texture of the tragedy obviously resurfaces here, but now Shakespeare (through the friar) is at pains to place it in the larger context of natural law. Life and death may intersect cruelly and bafflingly for lovers, but the green world confers a comforting king of intelligibility on such contradictions by relating them to the governing cycle of all existence, to the age-old rhythms of the earth by which living things come into being, are nourished, suspire, and finally return to their origins. Moreover, the same "weak flower" by virtue of its different properties may bring both sadness and joy, poison and healing. In this perspective, nature, though fallen, shadows forth through its foison, or plenitude, the beneficence of its divine Creator, and so may transmit to mankind a taste or smell of the infinite within the realm of the finite. Because the order of nature mirrors the order of grace, nature must necessarily be good; and although man may misuse or pervert its gifts ("Virtue itself turns vice, being misapplied"), all human action is to be measured against the moral standard it implies. Varieties of plants, like varieties of persons, all have "some special good" to bestow because they were created by and in the image of a loving God. The infinite diversity of the many, be they flowers or persons, refers us ultimately to the all-generating One.

But the plants also symbolize the conflict between good and evil that rages in the postlapsarian hearts of human beings. "Grace and rude will," impulses to love and to sinful egoism, are the "opposed kings" who perpetually "encamp" themselves in herbs as in men. Romeo is both a lover and a killer in Shakespeare's play, a boy who not only is identified with flowers in his role as an amorist but can also use the mortal liquor distilled from "simples" (V.i.40) self-destructively. It is probably not fortuitous that the dramatist fixes Romeo's entrance to Friar Laurence in this scene at the very moment that the churchman mentions the double power ("poison" and "medicine") of the flower he holds in his hand. But we should remember also that earlier in the play Romeo had bitterly minimized the curative powers of plants. When Benvolio in act I suggests that his friend's debilitating frustration over Rosaline is a "poison" that only "some new infection to the eye" can drive out, Romeo sarcastically implies that the standard remedy for a bruised shin is worse than useless for a broken heart: "Your plaintain leaf is excellent for that" (I.ii.49–51). Romeo, at least in his more obsessive moments, cannot accept his ghostly father's cooler, more comprehensive view of the green world.

Clearly the friar's regenerative concept of life with its reverence for nature as theo-phanic or quasi-sacramental owes much to Christian Neoplatonism and is essentially comic in its optimism. Such asssumptions familiarly pervade Shakespearean comedy. Lorenzo, sitting romantically beneath the stars among the trees of Portia's Belmont, senses harmonic continuities between "this muddy vesture of decay" and "the young-ey'd cherubins" above, between the moonlight of his sublunary "bank" and the "floor of heaven . . . thick inlaid with patens of bright gold" (*The Merchant of Venice*, V.i.54–64). *As You Like It*, as already indicated in an earlier chapter, provides a more thoroughgoing example. The forest of Arden, a highly idealized place, free from politics, flattery, and malice, succors love and can awaken even deep-dyed sinners such as Orlando's wicked brother and the usurper Frederick to virtue. Its ambience of charity, relaxation, and good humor is intended to evoke nostalgia for the Golden Age of classical myth and the Sherwood Forest of Robin Hood, both of which are mentioned in the text. The banished duke finds his enforced exile under the greenwood tree morally and religiously improving. The forest, serving him as both church and library, offers "tongues in trees, books in the running brooks, / Sermons in stones, and good in every thing (*As You Like It*, II.i.16–17). But despite this idealism Arden is far from being perfect. Age, weariness, and cold, melancholy, grossness, and stupidity—even death (at least for the deer)—are not excluded from its precincts, and in Shakespeare's hand the forest becomes a setting for satire on naïve, self-deceptive, or overindulgent attitudes toward pastoralism as much as a place of celestial immanence.[6] Arden invites a mixed response to nature, a response already implicit in the poisonous and health-giving herbs that grow near Friar Laurence's cell and in the happiness and pain, the love and death, that characterize the atmosphere of Capulet's orchard.

A bifocal or divided view of the green world—of nature as fallen yet adumbrative of paradise—is as applicable to *As You Like It* as to *Romeo and Juliet*. Differences between the two plays are profound, but these lie less in the philosophical formulations or assumptions that undergird both than in all-important shifts of tone and emphasis. In the comedies love triumphs over mortality in a way that subordinates our awareness of suffering and of human limits to the joyous confirmation of our hopes, to our belief in growth, personal fulfillment, and continuity. In these plays the green world stands principally for a universe morally, emotionally, socially, and even metaphysically in tune with its Maker—or at least potentially in tune with Him. But in tragedy the stress necessarily falls elsewhere. *Romeo and Juliet* does not portray the happy solutions of *The Merchant of Venice* and *As You Like It* as impossible, nor does it absolutely contradict the friar's beneficent and transcendental understanding of nature. Rather, the play encourages a more negative reading of nature's book by pointing to the remoteness and inauspiciousness of the stars, by underscoring the brevity of happiness, the alarming speed and violence with which the cycle of life and death may revolve, and by compelling us to acknowledge the canker in the bud. These are the tragic lessons that the green world can teach with the same force and validity as its more usual comic ones.

The green world may signify timelessness or time in Shakespeare, depending on mood. It may cheer us by a focus on spring and the myth of eternal return. It may also evoke the imminence of winter and the pathos of evanescence. In Arden (except for Jaques with his misanthropic insistence on man's seven ages and Rosalind with her sense of urgency about Orlando's punctuality) the importunities of clock and calendar may be largely ignored or forgotten. In Verona, days, even hours, make all the difference between life and death, hope and despair. If the friar's sense of time governed the Capulets and Montagues, all might end well. The priest belongs to a life removed, to a monastic world where time is carefully measured, regularized, adjusted to the perception of supernal rhythms: "Wisely and slow. They stumble that run fast" (II.iii.94). But teenage passion, the bustle of bourgeois family life, and the energy of hotheaded duelists are not to be regulated by such a schedule. Romeo and Juliet have no leisure in their headlong rush toward "engrossing death" (V.iii.115) for the longer and more reassuring view of temporality that comes with age and religious contemplation. For the lovers, loss of the beloved poisons life irreversibly in the here and now. Accordingly, Romeo seeks his release from time and the means to his reunion with Juliet in the shop of an apothecary who deals in the dried remnants and infertile appurtenances of horticulture—"Green earthen pots, bladders, and musty seeds, / Remnants of packthread, and old cakes of roses" (V.i.46–47). The friar speaks futilely of disposing Juliet "among a sisterhood of holy nuns," trying to pluck what hope he can from the "greater power than we can contradict" (V.iii.153–157) that thwarts human purposes. But he runs in fear from the tomb, leaving us with a sense that the darker and more powerful truth lies with the lovers and their final commitment to each other.

The motif of the green world in *Romeo and Juliet* is only one among many elements in a rich and complex structure. Obviously, for the sake of argument, I have exaggerated its prominence, for it is axiomatic that in tragedy the garden, the forest, or the orchard must remain subordinate to the throne room, the public square, the battlefield, or the tomb. My motive has been to illustrate a double, or ambivalent, attitude toward nature and natural order that appears to me, with appropriate differences of emphasis, to permeate most of Shakespeare's early works, whether comic, tragic, or, in the case of the histories, some combination of the two. From the beginning Shakespeare seems to have counterpointed optimistic and pessimistic views of human nature, as well as of the universal forces with which it must interact, by associating it in a wide variety of experiences and modes with the world of growing things. Since tragedy almost by definition dramatizes conflicts of good and evil, it is scarcely surprising that such conflicts should be reflected in settings and imagery that relate man symbolically to his environment. A useful means of suggesting the fundamental pattern of moral conflict extended into and connected with the physical universe is to portray nature both as a standard of order that man selfishly violates and as a mirror of his fallen condition, as a reflector of specific moral and emotional states. There was, of course, abundant literary and theological precedent for such a procedure in classical, medieval, and Renaissance tradition. We may observe Shakespeare already employing the technique in his first attempts to render tragic experience—in *Titus Andronicus* (1589–91), in *The Rape of Lucrece* (1593–94), and even in the semitragic *Venus and Adonis* (1592–93).

III

The first and bloodiest of the Roman tragedies depicts a savage struggle between civilization and barbarism, between an ideal of political and family order on the one side and a "wilderness of tigers" (*Titus Andronicus*, III.i.54) on the other. The verdant, idyllically described forest that serves as the ironic setting for the rape and mutilation of Lavinia, for the brutal murder of Bassianus, and for the trapping and false accusation of Titus's innocent sons is clearly meant to suggest a norm of moral goodness and natural repose that contrasts heraldically with the hellish cruelty, lust, and betrayal that Aaron, Tamora, Demetrius, and Chiron will introduce into it. Shakespeare goes out of his way to emphasize the benignity of the place:

> The birds chant melody on every bush,
> The snake lies rolled in the cheerful sun,
> The green leaves quiver with the cooling wind
> And make a checker'd shadow on the ground
> Under their sweet shade.
>
> (II.iii.12–16)

Mention of the serpent provides a hint of approaching disaster, but the attractive details, including an allusion to the union of Dido and Aeneas in the cave and a reference to "golden slumber" (II.iii.26), create, at least superficially, an impression of nature in harmony with a system of universal order and potential happiness.

Dramatically, of course, the speech is disturbing, for the barbaric Tamora is speaking to her black lover Aaron, and the love envisioned is adulterous. Moreover, disquiet is greatly aggravated if we recall that only two scenes earlier Aaron has proposed to Tamora's sons that the forest will be the perfect location for their monstrous crimes:

> The forest walks are wide and spacious,
> And many unfrequented plots there are
> Fitted by kind for rape and villainy.
> Single you thither then this dainty doe,
> And strike her home by force, if not by words.
> . . . .
> The woods are ruthless, dreadful, deaf, and dull.
> There speak, and strike, brave boys, and take your turns;
> There serve your lust, shadow'd from heaven's eye,
> And revel in Lavinia's treasury.
>
> (II.i.114–131)

Between these utterances by the master villains of the play, Titus looks forward cheerfully to a sportive day in the forest that will lead to bereaving him of three of his children:

> The hunt is up, the morn is bright and grey,
> The fields are fragrant and the woods are green.
>
> (II.ii.1–2)

The dramatist thus presents the woodland setting in a double light—as a place that, by virtue of its inherent sweetness and harmony, should resist violence, and yet that, because of its sequestration from civilized influences, actually shelters and encourages it.

Shortly after Tamora expatiates so lyrically on the beauties of the forest, she gives us a totally contrasting description of the place, now charging falsely that Bassianus and Lavinia have enticed her to a dangerous ground. Her purpose, of course, is to provide her sons with a pretext for their outrages against the married couple:

> A barren detested vale you see it is;
> The trees, though summer, yet forlorn and lean,
> Overcome with moss and baleful mistletoe;
> Here never shines the sun; here nothing breeds,
> Unless the nightly owl or fatal raven.
> And when they show'd me this abhorred pit,
> They told me, here, at dead time of the night,
> A thousand fiends, a thousand hissing snakes,
> Ten thousand swelling toads, as many urchins,
> Would make such fearful and confused cries
> As any mortal body hearing it
> Should straight fall mad, or else die suddenly.
> No sooner had they told this hellish tale,
> But straight they told me they would bind me here
> Unto the body of a dismal yew,

And leave me to this miserable death.

(II.iii.93–108)

Tamora, in advance of the horrific deeds that her sons are about to perpetrate, has already transformed the landscape from a pleasance to a jungle, from a place of romance and security into one of horror and bloodshed. After the crimes have been committed, the grief-stricken Titus sees nature in the same depressing light as his enemies. For him too, now, the woods are "ruthless, vast, and gloomy"—a place, like that in which Ovid's Philomel was ravished, "by nature made for murders and for rapes" (IV.i.55–60).

Shakespeare later reflects the extreme suffering and devastation of the victims by combining the orderly and disorderly, the human and the antihuman, aspects of nature in grotesque fashion.[7] Demetrius's metaphor for rape, "First thrash the corn, then after burn the straw" (II.iii.123), points up the contrast between the natural and human order of the play, as does Tamora's more conventional verb "deflow'r" (II.iii.191). Martius and Quintus, when they discover the hole containing Bassianus's corpse, notice the "rude-growing briers, / Upon whose leaves are drops of new-shed blood / As fresh as morning dew distill'd on flowers" (II.iii.199–201). The "fatal place" (II.iii.202) is marked by "nettles" and an "elder-tree / Which overshades the mouth" (II.iii.272–273) of the pit. Lavinia, deprived of her hands, is a tree "lopp'd and hew'd and made . . . bare / Of her two branches" (II.iv.17–18), while the tears on her cheeks are like "the honey-dew / Upon a gath'red lily almost withered" (III.i.112–113). Grief not only echoes but outdoes nature. Titus's "whole months of tears" make an "hour's storm," which "will drown the fragrant meads" (II.iv.54–55), seem insignificant by comparison; the "stain'd" cheeks of the mourners resemble "meadows yet not dry, / With miry slime left on them by a flood" (III.i.125–126). Titus offers to chop off his own hand to save his sons, since "such with'red herbs as these / Are meet for plucking up" (III.i.177–178).

Shakespeare also relates the politics of the play to natural processes and their disruption. Titus votes for Saturninus as emperor in the hope that his "virtues will . . . / Reflect on Rome as Titan's rays on earth, / And ripen justice in this commonweal" (I.i.229–231); but the ruler, "but newly planted in [his] throne" (I.i.448), immediately shows signs of tyranny. At the end of the play, when Lucius and the Goths gather their forces to unseat Saturninus, the tyrant likens himself to a victim of seasonal change: "These tidings nip me, and I hang my head / As flowers with frost or grass beat down with storms" (IV.iv.70–71). The invaders pursue the corrupt emperor "Like stinging bees in hottest summer's day / Led by their master to the flow'red fields" (V.i.14–15). After all the slaughter, it remains for Titus's brother to urge the Romans "to knit again / This scattered corn into one mutual sheaf" (V.iii.70–71) and restore the body politic to its natural wholeness and unity.

The sanguinary evils of *Titus Andronicus* are largely conceived as egregious violations of a normally healthy and harmonious universe, a universe whose essential fertility and goodness are symbolized by its trees, grass, flowers, and ripening grain. Lavinia's child nephew, one of the guileless survivors of the carnage, is a "tender sapling" whose grief almost "melt[s his] life away" (III.ii.50–51). Titus begs in vain for the life of his sons, promising hyperbolically to "befriend" the parched earth with the "rain" of his grateful tears, relieving "summer's drought" and "melt[ing]" winter's "snow" to "keep eternal springtime" (III.i.16–21) on the faces of the tribunes. But the tragedy also recognizes the stubborn persistence and inexplicability of evil as a force inherent in the fallen world.

Aaron, of course, is the embodiment of this fallenness, and one of his proverbs associates malignity not with any violation of nature but with nature itself:

> For all the water in the ocean
> Can never turn the swan's black legs to white,
> Although she lave them hourly in the flood.
>   (IV.ii.103–105)

Shakespeare identifies the Moor not only as "chief architect and plotter of [the play's] woes" (V.iii.122) but also as a diabolic influence from which the landscape can never be wholly free. Aaron makes "poor men's cattle break their necks, / Set[s] fire on barns and haystalks in the night," and carves "Let not your sorrow die" in the "bark of trees" (V.i.132–140). His bastard child suggests the perpetuity of evil in the ecology of the tragedy—a "brat" (V.i.28) nourished in the wild "on berries and on roots" (IV.ii.180).

Similarly divided ideas of nature reappear in the narrative poems, embedded in decorative imagery that frequently resembles that of *Titus*. In *The Rape of Lucrece* both rapist and victim are likened to trees. She is a "low shrub" before whose defenselessness the proud "cedar" (Tarquin) will not "stoop" (ll. 664–665); but after her tragedy she feels like a "lofty pine" stripped of its protective bark—a tree whose "leaves will wither and his sap decay" (ll. 1167–1169). Collatine, who has won fame "in the fields of fruitful Italy" (l. 107), creates by his untimely absence a "hasty spring" (l. 49) vulnerable to wintry blasts. Lucrece is a "sweet grape" for the taste of whom Tarquin is willing to destroy the "vine" (l. 215). The ravisher's fear is overwhelmed by his lust as "corn" is "o'ergrown by weeds" (ll. 281–282). Lucrece pleads in vain with her violator: "How will thy shame be seeded in thine age, / When thus thy vices bud before thy spring?" (ll. 603–604). Tarquin is not only a "worm intrud[ing] the maiden bud" (l. 848) but also a "lurking serpent" (l. 362) in the garden. She is the "withered flow'r," he the "rough winter that the flow'r hath kill'd" (ll. 1254–1255). In an extraordinary amalgam of the artificial with the natural, Shakespeare envisions Lucrece's "fair hand" resting on the "green coverlet" of her bed, its "perfect white / Show[ing] like an April daisy on the grass" (ll. 393–395). The grief of Lucrece's maid is as elaborately fanciful as Lavinia's or Titus's:

> But as the earth doth weep, the sun being set,
> Each flow'r moist'ned like a melting eye,
> Even so the maid with swelling drops gan wet
> Her circled eyne, enforc'd by sympathy
> Of those fair suns set in her mistress' sky,
>   Who in a salt-wav'd ocean quench their light,
>   Which makes the maid weep like the dewy night.
>   (Ll. 1226–1232)

In combination such details idealize the green world even as they acknowledge its imperfection. The principal action occurs wholly indoors; but the poem, through its tireless elaboration of conceits, invites the reader to accumulate a landscape of moral and psychological significance in his own imagination—to construct a kind of green backdrop by means of which he may sharpen his emotional focus or widen his interpretive horizon. By applying a system of allusion and cross-reference to the natural world, Shakespeare is able to invoke it both as an earthly revelation of higher good and as a mirror of tragic defection from that good. At one symbolic level Tarquin, by violating Lucrece, recapitulates the Fall. His irreversible act constitutes an attack on cosmic order itself, a conscious spurning "at right, at law, at reason"; he "seize[s] . . . souls" and makes "the vestal violate her oath" (ll. 880–883). Tarquin is the satanic agent who converts innocence to guilt, beauty to ugliness, summer to winter, growth to decay. By "deflow'r[ing]" Lucrece (l. 348), he deflowers Nature herself, bringing death into the world and all our woe. Yet his pathetic victim already inhabits a world where circumstances, human vulnerability, and especially time (upon whose tragic implications the poet dwells at length) cooperate with the ravisher. Time, the "tutor to both good and bad" (l. 995), not only hastens Tarquin toward outrage but "stay[s]" Collatine's "aid" (ll. 912–917). The green world that the poem projects also incorporates this melancholy truth, for Time's property is indifferently "to dry the old oak's sap and cherish springs" (l. 950). The emblematic garden of Lucrece's didactic rhetoric is one in which good and evil must coexist, a garden where "unwholesome weeds take root with precious flow'rs" and "the adder hisses where the sweet birds sing" (ll. 870–871).

Unlike *Lucrece, Venus and Adonis* is in major respects a comic poem. Not unexpectedly, Shakespeare sets its humorous eroticism in a lush context of greenery that promotes a sense of nature as fecund, burgeoning, even juicy. As in *Titus Andronicus*, the poet imposes landscape anthropomorphically upon character. If Lavinia's savaged person is a branchless tree, Venus's nubile body is a "park" through which Adonis, her favorite "deer," may range. The goddess invites him to "graze on [her] lips" and explore the "pleasant fountains" that lie lower; her sexual charms also include "sweet bottom-grass," a "high delightful plain," "round rising hillocks," and "brakes obscure and rough, / To shelter [him] from tempest and from rain" (ll. 231–238). Adonis is "the field's chief flower, sweet above compare," a figure whom Nature created to be "at strife" with herself and whose death, hyperbolically, would be coterminous with the world's "ending" (ll. 8–12). Venus wishes that her "cheeks were gardens full of flowers" (l. 65) and that her beloved's lips could forever retain their "verdure" (l. 507) so as to breathe forth plague-dispelling freshness. The reluctant boy insists poutingly that he is a "green" as opposed to a "mellow plum" and should, therefore, not be "early plucked" (ll. 527–528). From Venus's point of view, sexual indulgence is the logical extension of the libertinism and fertility already implicit in the green world; Adonis's prudish resistance is out of key with a setting "where never serpent hisses" (l. 17), with a place obviously designed for love and suitably furnished with a "primrose bank," "forceless flowers" (ll. 151–152), and "blue-veined violets" on which to "lean" (l. 125). The seductress invokes the familiar argument of Shakespeare himself in the sonnets to his own young Adonis:

> By law of nature thou art bound to breed,
> That thine may live when thou thyself art dead;
> And so, in spite of death, thou dost survive,
> In that thy likeness still is left alive.
>
> (Ll. 171–174)

And, as if to confirm her point, a "breeding jennet, lusty, young and proud" (l. 260), excites the boy's tethered courser, causing him to break rein.

The famous episode of the mating horses represents an obvious displacement into natural surroundings of Venus's frustrated desire. But the later and equally admired account of "poor Wat" (l. 697), the hare pursued by hounds, renders with equal verve and empathy the plight of Adonis, for whom Venus is a predator. This latter description foreshadows Adonis's death as a victim of the boar, the poem's emblem of murderous lust. *Venus and Adonis*, then, presents a dialectic between opposing attitudes toward sex, both of them reflected in activities—animal copulation and hunting—that commonly occur in the countryside. For Venus, the satisfaction of desire is not only nature's law but, through offspring, an anodyne to death. For Adonis, unwanted erotic aggression amounts at first to an embarrassment from which he can flee, but ultimately it implies mortality. The poem thus modulates from erotic comedy to a tragedy of unfulfilled passion with disturbing implications on the identification of love with death.

Increasingly, nature is perceived (even by Venus herself) to contain the conditions of sexual disappointment and hostile violence. At first the goddess fantasizes that if Adonis stumbles in his hasty withdrawal, it is because the "earth" is "in love" with him and will trip him up to steal a "kiss" (ll. 722–723). But later, when she hurries "to a myrtle grove" to listen for sounds of the hunting party, "the bushes . . . catch her by the neck, some kiss her face, / Some twine about her thigh to make her stay" (ll. 865–873). The green world is imagined as both an aid and an impediment to passion, a force to promote but also to encumber love. Supposedly jealous of Adonis's radiance and determined to make trouble for her sister deity, chaste Cynthia is accused of causing nature "To mingle beauty with infirmities / And pure perfection with impure defeature" (ll. 735–736). Thoughts of the "angry-chafing boar," as native to the forest as the foliage, cause Venus to foresee the "blood" of Adonis "upon the fresh flowers being shed," thus "mak[ing] them droop with grief and hang the head" (ll. 662–666). When the feared catastrophe occurs, the landscape (by convention of the pathetic fallacy) actually participates in the gory sacrifice: "No flow'r was nigh, no grass, herb, leaf or weed, / But stole his blood and seem'd with him to bleed" (ll. 1055–1056). For the bereaved goddess "black chaos comes again" (l. 1020). The Ovidian metamorphosis with which the poem concludes neatly encapsulates the unresolved antithesis between the green and the red, the cool and the hot, the peaceful and the violent conceptions of nature that Shakespeare has so elegantly polarized in the texture of his imagery.[8] The red-and-white flower that springs up to memorialize Adonis not only transfigures bloodshed, reincorporating it, so to speak, into the vegetable world, but also repeats the erotic flesh tones of Petrarchan convention, reminding us of Venus's initial dotage on the youth. The colors also evoke the war between passion and chastity that is thematically central to the poem as a whole. Finally, Venus plucks "the new-sprung flower to smell," and the stalk exudes "green dropping sap, which she compares to tears" (ll. 1171–1176). Love and death, grief and regeneration, pessimism and optimism, violence and repose, nature and antinature unite curiously in a single frail anemone.

IV

In the tragic masterpieces of his maturity Shakespeare dramatized conflicts of good and evil with greater psychological intensity than had previously been possible and in ways that raised profounder doubts about metaphysical order than the earlier works had done. One of the many symptoms of this advance in complexity seems to be a perceptible shift in the old balance between the more and less hopeful symbology of the green world that tends to characterize the plays and poems discussed above. Not that the dramatist ever abandoned the antithesis completely. The powerful dramatization of a fallen world necessarily implies some reference, however muted, to an unfallen state. The witches' blasted heath, with its "fog and filthy air" (*Macbeth*, I.i.12), would in some sense be meaningless without the countervailing image of Macbeth's castle, whose fertile atmosphere "sweetly recommends itself" to Duncan's "gentle senses" and reminds Banquo of "heaven's breath" (I.vi.2–5). But the chief effect of this contrast is piercing irony because we know, as the visitors do not, that the castle and the heath are symbolically the same—different venues, so to say, in the geography of hell. Macbeth turns all Scotland into a land barren of order and growth (he himself falls "into the sear, the yellow leaf" [V.iii.23]), and greenness can only return when foreigners invade, bringing Birnam wood to Dunsinane. Yet even this "regreening" of the nation involves much bloodshed and the deceptive use of boughs that have been severed from the trees that gave them life. Even the restoration of nature to a place that has become unnatural seems to imply some violation of nature's usual order. This darker and more skeptical conception of natural law as conveyed through symbols of the green world can already be discerned in *Julius Caesar* and *Hamlet*.

Shakespeare's second Roman tragedy, unlike his first, is remarkable for its calculated avoidance of vegetative ambience as regards both setting and imagery. The mainly political action of *Julius Caesar* begins in the turbulent streets of the capital and moves to the desert plains of Philippi, shaded only by "ravens, crows, and kites" (V.i.84). The natural world impinges on Rome in storms and prodigies—"scolding winds" that split the "knotty oaks" (I.iii.5–6), "blue lightning" that opens the "breast of heaven" (I.iii.50–51), a lioness whelping in the streets, the "bird of night" sitting "at noon-day upon the market-place, / Hooting and shrieking" (I.iii.26–28). The "earth" is "full of faults" (I.iii.45), and, as Casca chorically observes, nature itself is in revolt: "Things change from their ordinance, / Their natures, and preformed faculties, / To monstrous quality" (I.iii.66–68). The few references to the green world that do appear are introduced in contexts of political and moral disorder. The fickle crowds "strew flowers" (I.i.50) before Caesar as they had once honored Pompey. The superstitious conqueror imagines "trees" as the means to betray "unicorns" (II.i.204). Antony sees the whole world as providing the evil context for Caesar's murder, the "forest" in which the conspirators could hunt down so noble a "hart" (III.i.208). Contemptuously, he plans to expel Lepidus from the triumvirate—to turn him out to pasture, where he may "graze in commons" like the "empty ass" (IV.i.26–27) he has shown himself to be. Caesar bequeaths his "private arbors and new-planted orchards" (III.ii.246) to Rome as a public park, but the mention of even this oasis is tainted by the demagogy of Antony's manipulative funeral oration.

The unique green setting of the play is Brutus's "*orchard*" (II.i.1), where his "state of man . . . suffers . . . The nature of an insurrection" (II.i.67–69), and where the revolutionaries meet to formulate strategy; but Shakespeare rigorously suppresses any sense of foliage or benign natural environment.[9] The pivotal soliloquy in which Brutus decides on assassination is replete with serpent imagery that, although he applies it to Caesar, reflects ironically on the speaker, making him a serpent of sorts in his own garden. The orchard is as dark as the purposes it engenders and, in contrast to its counterpart in *Romeo and Juliet*, is unromantically illuminated by "exhalations whizzing in the air" (II.i.44) rather than by stars and moonlight. Masking the "monstrous visage" of conspiracy, the place suggests "Erebus" (II.i.81–84). Instead of fragrance, a "rheumy and unpurged air" full of "vile contagion" (II.i.265–266) suffuses the orchard. The garden suffers from a malaise as debilitating as that of its owner. In *Julius Caesar* nature seems almost wholly to echo the tragic disorders of men, whether individually or collectively; and connections between the green world and the order of grace, if they exist at all, are left to be inferred from their absence.

With respect to the symbolism of the plant world, Hamlet's Denmark is not radically dissimilar from Brutus's Rome. Growing things figure more saliently in the language of *Hamlet* than in that of *Julius Caesar* but most often in contexts that also suggest disorder, corruption, disease, and imminent death. Excessive lushness, however, rather than barrenness, is a leading motif, for as Claudius reminds Laertes, even "goodness, growing to a plurisy, / Dies in his own too much" (*Hamlet*, IV.vii.117–118). Also Shakespeare associates lechery, incest, adultery, and rottenness with luxuriant growth. Hamlet regards his entire world as an "unweeded garden" choked by "things rank and gross in nature" (I.ii.135–136); but what is true of Denmark is just as true of individuals. Shakespeare links many of the characters with the corruptions and excesses of nature, often with an implication of inherent weakness or malignancy. Laertes warns his sister about the "canker" of lust that "galls the infants of the spring . . . before their buttons can be disclos'd" (I.iii.39–40); she ripostes with a tart reference to the "primrose path of dalliance" (I.iii.50) to which his libertinism makes him liable. The Ghost, who has been "Cut off . . . in the blossoms of [his] sin" (I.v.77), "his crimes broad blown, as flush as May" (III.iii.81), urges Hamlet to shun dullness, a state induced by the "fat weed / That roots itself in ease on Lethe wharf" (I.v.33–34). Polonius's eyes, like exotic plants, repulsively exude "thick amber and plum-tree gum" (II.ii.199). Poison bids fair to being nature's chief product in *Hamlet*. The prince's father dies in an orchard by means of a "leprous distillment," the "juice of cursed hebona" (I.v.63–65). In the play-within-the-play Lucianus reenacts this murder *"upon a bank of flowers"* (III.ii.133), using a lethal "mixture rank, of midnight weeds collected" (III.ii.255), and Claudius employs against young Hamlet a similar "unction," or "contagion," so deadly that "all simples that have virtue / Under the moon" (IV.vii.141–147) are powerless against it. Claudius himself is a "mildew'd ear, / Blasting his wholesome brother" (III.iv.65–66), and Hamlet enjoins Gertrude not to "spread the compost on the weeds" to make her past sins "ranker" (III.iv.158–159). Even a total change in her habits, as Hamlet comes close to admitting, cannot *wholly* "change the stamp of nature" (III.iv.175). Evil is conceived as endemic to the processes of growth, an unhappy fact whose evidences are to be discerned in gardens as well as in palaces.

If natural images are allowed to represent ideality as opposed to the flawed aspects of reality, they do so only briefly and are often obliterated or undercut by uglier ones that immediately supplant them. Ophelia characterizes Hamlet as "Th' expectancy and rose of the fair state" only to bewail him as the "unmatch'd form and feature of blown youth / Blasted with ecstasy" (III.i.155–163). Hamlet suggests that "the rose" of his mother's "innocent love" has been replaced by a "blister" (III.iv.43–45). Ophelia's quasi-pastoral lyrics, grotesque mixtures of grief and bawdry, not only portray a mind diseased but also recall the past. They remind us sadly of what might have been, conveying a sense of innocence betrayed and of natural beauty spoiled.

More than any other character in the tragedy, Ophelia embodies the theme of flux and mutability, and indeed this is an important reason for the flower symbolism that insistently surrounds her. Laertes teaches that she must think of her love for the prince as "A violet in the youth of primy nature, / Forward, not permanent, sweet, not lasting, / The perfume and suppliance of a minute" (I.iii.7–9). When her brother first sees her deranged, he cries out "O rose of May!" (IV.v.159). The image brings the freshness of her past into painful contact with the present. Violets, the traditional emblems of faithfulness as well as of perishability, return in the mad scene: "I would give you some violets, but they wither'd all when my father died" (IV.v.185–187). And, of course, Shakespeare repeats the flower motif in the graveyard—not only in the "virgin crants" with which the corpse is adorned and in the "maiden strewments" (V.i.232–233) of the queen but also in the "violets" that Laertes fancies as springing from his sister's "fair and unpolluted flesh" (V.i.239–240).

By setting Ophelia's tragedy in the context of the green world, Shakespeare connects the idea of human frailty with the theme of time's ravages. The wildflowers and herbs that the demented girl distributes suggest a kind of atavism—a return to nature in its raw, formless, and uncultivated state and, therefore, a regression from a rational to a subrational plane of existence. This is pathetic enough, but the plants that she mentions tend also to emblematize specific sins and weaknesses or in some way evoke painful responses to these. As most editors point out, for Elizabethans the rosemary symbolized remembrance of the dead, pansies thoughts of love (or courtship), the fennel flattery, the columbines unchastity (or perhaps ingratitude), the rue repentance, and the daisies faithlessness (or dissembling). All link human failings or regret for such failings to the landscape and suggest a tenuous kind of identity with it. In some cases the flowers seem appropriate to the moral or emotional states of their recipients (Gertrude, for instance, "may wear [her] rue with a difference" [IV.v.184–185]), but Ophelia in some sense also engages in a chaotic dispersion of herself into fragments, acts out a floral ritual of self-disintegration. The wildflowers associate a human crack-up with a sense of dissolution and flux in nature itself.

One of the subtleties of Ophelia's drowning, so lyrically described by the queen, is that Shakespeare here confers a decorative beauty on a natural process that he elsewhere makes repellent. The deaths of Polonius and Yorick provoke thoughts of worms and the stench of decaying flesh. Ophelia returns to her primordial mud in poetic slow motion, borne up by clothes in water, garlanded by "crow-flowers, nettles, daisies, and long purples" (IV.vii.169), and accompanied by music. All the natural details (the drooping willow, with its "hoar leaves"; the flowers, with their mixed connotations of pleasure, pain, sexuality, and death; the "envious sliver" that cracks under the climber's weight; the "weeping brook") project the experience of Ophelia's passing as one of poignant reabsorption into the green world—as a cyclical return to that natural "element" to which she was already a "creature native and indued" (IV.vii.167–179). Despite the fanciful and romantic tradition of attributing human emotions to trees and brooks, the burden of the passage is to emphasize the inescapable reality of all tragedies—the inevitability of death. This is perhaps the most basic truth that the world of nature has to teach us in *Hamlet*. Laertes remarks of his sister that "she turns to favor and to prettiness" the tragic realities of life—"Thought and afflictions, passion, hell itself" (IV.v.189–190). The queen's bittersweet elegy on Ophelia performs a similar function for the play. But however inviting the green world may appear in *Hamlet*, it remains a world in which death is the fundamental and most operant power. Even when the tragedy suggests a more positive and comprehensive order in nature, it tends to do so by negative example.

The "special providence" that Hamlet, echoing Matthew 10:29, mentions as he moves toward his own death reveals itself "in the fall of a sparrow" (V.ii.217–218).

V

Shakespeare evokes the green world with some regularity in his tragedies and, at the beginning of his career, gives us reason to view its benevolent manifestation, familiar to us from the comedies, as providing, at least in one dimension, a standard by which to judge the unnatural. In the earliest plays and poems, the green world comprises a kind of subtext or underworld that allows us to regard the dialectic between good and evil, between hope and despair, as having a basis in the fabric of nature itself. Here, at any rate in theory, the landscape still reflects the order of grace and embodies the moral imperatives of natural law. But in the Jacobean tragedies and in those that immediately precede them, the green world shows signs of becoming desacralized. The healthy and orderly gardens of the older world are beginning to go to seed, to revert to weeds, or to specialize in the horticulture of exotic drugs and poisons. And the landscapes, when they appear at all, are more likely to be barren than green—forbidding and hostile places such as treeless and storm-torn heaths, chalky cliffs, deserts, and caves where only roots sustain life.[10]

8

Perdita's Distribution of Flowers and the Function of Lyricism in The Winter's Tale

I

Perdita. [*To Polixenes and Camillo*] Reverend sirs,
　　For you there's rosemary and rue; these keep
　　Seeming and savor all the winter long.
　　Grace and remembrance be to you both,
　　And welcome to our shearing!

　　. . . . .
　　the year growing ancient,
　　Not yet on summer's death, nor on the birth
　　Of trembling winter, the fairest flow'rs o' th' season
　　Are our carnations and streak'd gillyvors,
　　Which some call nature's bastards. Of that kind
　　Our rustic garden's barren, and I care not
　　To get slips of them.

　　. . . . .
　　Here's flow'rs for you:
　　Hot lavender, mints, savory, marjoram;
　　The marigold, that goes to bed wi' th' sun
　　And with him rises weeping. These are flow'rs
　　Of middle summer, and I think they are given
　　To men of middle age.

　　. . . . .
　　　　　　[*To Florizel*] Now, my fair'st friend,
　　I would I had some flow'rs o' th' spring that might
　　Become your time of day; [*To Shepherdesses*] and yours, and yours,
　　That wear upon your virgin branches yet
　　Your maidenheads growing. O Proserpina,
　　For the flow'rs now that, frighted, thou let'st fall
　　From Dis's wagon! Daffodils,

That come before the swallow dares, and take
The winds of March with beauty; violets dim,
But sweeter than the lids of Juno's eyes
Or Cytherea's breath; pale primroses,
That die unmarried, ere they can behold
Bright Phoebus in his strength—a malady
Most incident to maids; bold oxlips and
The crown imperial; lilies of all kinds,
The flow'r-de-luce being one. O, these I lack,
To make you garlands of, and my sweet friend,
To strew him o'er and o'er!

Florizel.   What, like a corse?

Perdita. No, like a bank for love to lie and play on,
Not like a corse; or if, not to be buried,
But quick and in mine arms. Come, take your flow'rs.
Methinks I play as I have seen them do
In Whitsun pastorals. Sure this robe of mine
Does change my disposition.

                                   (*The Winter's Tale*, IV.iv.73–135)

Ever since Hazlitt admired this famous sequence, comparing Shakespeare's floral imagination to Milton's as expressed in "Lycidas" ("we dare not give the preference"),[1] commentators and anthologists have singled it out as a jewel of poetic lyricism set in a play that, apart from Autolycus's delightful songs, is characterized by tangled syntax, elliptical, interruptive, or headlong utterance, and a degree of verbal compactness that not infrequently approaches opacity. Shakespeare embeds Perdita's distribution and catalogue of flowers in the sunniest and most pastoral episode of the play, as if to give dramatic focus to his major structural and thematic contrasts—winter and summer, age and youth, separation and reunion, sin and repentance, death and fertility, "things dying" and "things new-born" (III.iii.110–111). As the passage gradually dilates to encompass widening symbolic resonances, it also becomes rhythmically smoother and more incantatory; its emotional climax, reached with the evocation of spring flowers that must be fetched from the memory of a season already past and from the artifice of myth, employs comparatively few of the light and weak endings used more liberally elsewhere. Moreover, the rhetorical principle of *copia*—the rich accumulation of pictorial and sensory details (color, movement, texture, and scent) mediated subtly through verbal sound—invites us to enjoy the speech aesthetically for its own sake—as we might respond to an artfully arranged bouquet with its own internal patterns and form within the larger structure of a well-appointed room.

Although Perdita, costumed as a kind of Flora, acts in a ceremonial capacity, welcoming both friends and strangers as mistress of the sheepshearing festival, Shakespeare virtually suspends the forward movement of the plot at this point in order to refresh his audience—onstage as well as off—with a pause. The flower episode seems to function as a deliberate retard, or "hold" (to employ a theatrical director's term), that keeps the action of a play at some strategically appropriate point from unfolding too precipitously— rather in the way that Mercutio's Queen Mab speech (*Romeo and Juliet*, I.iv.53–95) or Jaques' discourse on the seven ages of man (*As You Like It*, II.vii.138–165) or the allegorical garden scene in *Richard II* (III.iv) or Katharine and Griffith's meditation on Wolsey's death and her subsequent "vision" (*Henry VIII*, IV.ii.31–84) operate in similar circumstances. The dramaturgical parenthesis with its obvious kinship to song and masque confers several benefits upon the spectators. It allows for reflection: the brief debate with Polixenes over the merits of a primitivist versus a hybridizing horticulture becomes a direct by-product of Perdita's lyric celebration of the delights of the garden. It encourages pleasure in art—in evocative imagery and poetic expressiveness, in the techniques of the "speaking picture," to borrow Sidney's pregnant phrase.[2] It permits vicarious sharing in an idealized love affair, for Perdita's rapture over Florizel informs the most ardent and harmonious part of her flower speech. Lastly, it both glamorizes and subtilizes the character of the speaker by associating her with a range of experiences and ideas, literary and imaginative as well as natural and earth-rooted. Somehow her listeners perceive her as at once goddess and peasant, idealized archetype and fully enfleshed personality, capable of alluding to Proserpina, Juno, and Cytherea yet charmingly unsophisticated on the subject of grafting. She impresses us as supremely fresh, uncommon, even refined in her representation of what is most attractive in humanity at its humblest and least pretentious. The union of royalty with noble instinct in the moral as well as the aristocratic sense is already implicit, although the stage audience remains ironically ignorant of Perdita's true rank.

The values conveyed here are among those traditionally ascribed to literary pastoral, but as Greg has sensitively pointed out, Shakespeare, despite his considerable debt to Greene's *Pandosto*, deliberately eschews reliance on the bloodless clichés and stereotypical formalities of pastoral convention: "the shepherd scenes . . . represent solely the idealization of [the poet's] own observation" and may be regarded as perfected versions of his earlier "sketches of natural man and woman, as he found them in the English fields and lanes."[3] The mention of "Whitsun pastorals," traditionally associated with May games, morris dancing, and Robin Hood plays, obviously strengthens the impression of native rather than of classical models of pastoralism and probably reflects Shakespeare's firsthand knowledge of the Warwickshire landscape.

What is clearest of all, however, is that the floral passage stands out from both its immediate context in an exceptionally long and varied scene and from its even broader context in *The Winter's Tale* as a totality. As such, it has something of the detachability and independence of an operatic aria. And, like many such arias, it serves to heighten pleasure and intensify emotion at an important point in the progress of the whole. Just previously Perdita has expressed nervousness to Florizel about their supposedly differing social positions, ironically transposed in his "swain's wearing" (IV.iv.9) and in her "unusual weeds" as "queen" of the feast (IV.iv.1–5); and the speech leads up to the "*dance of Shepherds and Shepherdesses*," Autolycus's merry vending of his dishonestly acquired "trifles," the "rough" satyr antimasque with its carnal overtones, and finally the menacing disclosure of Polixenes' identity, which casts its chilling shadow over the happiness of the lovers. Shakespeare sandwiches the seemingly innocent delight in flowers between material that presages clouds at the beginning of the scene and that actually brings a storm of anger and threatened retribution at its end. Nevertheless, the passage is designed to produce its special effects in a way that seems incidental, or at least tangential, to the development of the narrative line and to the unfolding of the dramatic action. We grasp the structural irony only as a function of hindsight.

Such lyrical set pieces are common enough in Shakespeare. One thinks, for example, of arias like the queen's description of Ophelia's drowning in *Hamlet* or of Enobarbus's magnificent account of Cleopatra on her barge—speeches essentially narrative and descriptive in content that can be recalled as separate entities—paintings in a gallery, so to speak, that seem to possess a life and coherence of their own. Indeed, at an earlier stage of the dramatist's career, the luxuriant, self-contained speech had become so pervasive or dominant as to characterize the style of an entire drama. *Love's Labor's Lost, A Midsummer Night's Dream, Romeo and Juliet,* and *Richard II* are all said to be "lyrical" plays, largely because they abound in florid orations or at least in rhetoric that self-consciously calls attention to its own musical and verbal extravagance—the "three-pil'd hyperboles," "taffeta phrases," and "silken terms precise" that Berowne of *Love's Labor's Lost* (V.ii.407–408) instances in his witty effusion on the relationship of courtly eloquence to sincerity.

In these plays the lyrical style often serves to separate a character or the subjectivity of his interior world from the threat or mundanity of an enforced context. The lyrical speech can offer a figure on the stage escape into a poetic universe of his own fashioning, a chance to redefine his own identity, to shape reality afresh in a way more congruent with private desire than with the intrusive or uncooperative surroundings to which destiny and circumstance have consigned him. The so-called arias of Shakespeare's early plays often have the effect of freeing their speakers from social, familial, and political constraints, allowing them, through temporary disengagement, to proclaim the untrammeled centrality of the self and imaginatively to reconstitute their relation to the pressures of temporal and spatial actuality. Inside the lyrical mode, which is often to say within a speaker's personal vision or reverie, time may be released from the strictures of chronological sequence or even abrogated altogether.[4] This is one reason why such speeches typically require a stasis in the progress of the story: the speaker removes himself or is removed from the usual circuits of discourse so as to explore or create a new or fancied space proper solely to his inner need, to impose coherence and expressive form upon it, and to endow the entire experience with the satisfactions of fixity and closure forbidden him by the intractable and ceaseless flux of quotidian reality. The lyrical mode is frequently optative, as in Juliet's desire for the consummation of her marriage in "Gallop apace you fiery-footed steeds" (*Romeo and Juliet*, III.ii.1–31), or in Perdita's wish for flowers no longer in season.

The relevance of this paradigm to the tragedies and histories is more apparent than it is to the comedies. Romeo and Juliet, whether together or apart, express the private intensity of their romance through aureate speeches confessedly indebted to the traditions of Petrarchan sonneteering—speeches that establish the lovers as inhabiting a world elsewhere, a self-conceived, absolutist sphere beyond space and time in which family and civic considerations, even physical death, can have no final importance. Richard II sits upon the ground "to tell sad stories of the death of kings" (III.ii.156), poeticizing his royal isolation by identifying himself with the venerable art of *de casibus* tragedy and weaving a tapestry of magniloquent sensibility out of the paradoxes of his unique double identity as sacramental monarch and fallible mortal. In Richard's construction of this specialized poetic universe—a universe in which he alone can play a theatrically compelling role and that his coarser political rival cannot hope to share—lies both his defeat and his triumph, his sentimental escapism and his tragic dignity.

The comedies, by definition concerned more than the histories and tragedies with social integration, make use of the lyrical style in a less obviously isolative way. Here the set speeches can sometimes be didactic (like Portia's famous words on mercy [*The Merchant of Venice*, IV.i.182–203]) or comically pyrotechnical (like Biondello's prose poem on the chaos of Petruchio's wedding garments [*The Taming of the Shrew*, III.ii.43–70]) or astringent-sweet and pathetic-ironic (like Viola's personification of her frustration in love as "Patience on a monument, / Smiling at grief" [*Twelfth Night*, II.iv.114–115]). But, as in the case of the other genres, the comedies also employ deliberately heightened and melodious rhetoric to set characters and special kinds of experience apart from their contexts.

The King of Navarre and his fellow academicians in *Love's Labor's Lost* make fashionably clever and conceited expression a kind of *raison d'être*; and their showy flights of verse become the most obvious symptom of their naïve Platonizing and of their risible failure to acknowledge biology and the other demands that real life makes upon young men. Interestingly, too, lyrical rhetoric becomes the medium through which Berowne and his friends learn to recognize their foolishness and begin to rethink their inadequate definitions of the self. The most exquisitely lyrical meditation of *The Merchant of Venice*, commencing with "How sweet the moonlight sleeps upon this bank" (V.i.54), situates Lorenzo and Jessica in their private romantic green world under the stars; and although the poetry adumbrates universal consonances that will eventually include *all* the amorous couples of the play, Lorenzo's dulcet intimations of cosmic harmony would somehow be unthinkable as a "public" speech. As with the *aubade* scene of *Romeo and Juliet* (III.v), the ethos is too tender, intimate, and personal for the more neutral language of social intercourse. And of course the speech sunders Jessica from Shylock's vengeful mind-set as completely as a daughter could ever be removed from her father. Even Oberon's "I know a bank where the wild thyme blows" (*A Midsummer Night's Dream*, II.i.249), an aria that invites comparison with Perdita's speech because of its floral content, functions separately to some extent; for the fairy king is evoking the supernatural realm of Titania and her gossamer court—the moonshine domain of the forest that becomes a complex symbol for the creative imagination, irrationality, the mystery of love, subconscious desire, the tricks of illusion, and indeed all the baffling subjectivities that challenge the reasonable, orderly, and daylight world of Theseus.

Although Perdita's beautiful speech may seem to function contrastively like some of the examples mentioned above, it differs significantly from them in being more public than most: it is part of a social ritual that involves not only her lover Florizel but also the unrecognized guests Polixenes and Camillo as well as the entire community of rustics. The inclusiveness of the episode (with its mixture of aristocracy and peasantry and with its combination of relaxed jollity and potential for harm in the person of the disguised king who has come to destroy his son's happiness) should alert us to the truth that although Shakespeare sets Perdita's Bohemia with its unspoiled freshness in striking contrast to the obsessive jealousy, madness, and cruelty of Leontes' court, he also wishes to prevent our accepting the pastoral environment uncritically or sentimentally as though we had suddenly reentered Arcadia or had miraculously recovered Eden or the Age of Gold. I wish to argue, in fact, that Perdita's flower aria, despite its apparent tonal and stylistic independence, is of a piece with the drama as a whole—that it functions subtly as a kind of microcosm, reflecting in its symbolism realities that are past, present, and in prospect as well as touching upon most of the major thematic nodes of the play. If such a function can be demonstrated, as I think it can, it would suggest that Shakespeare used his supreme lyrical gifts somewhat differently in *The Winter's Tale* than in plays written during the 1590s. Perhaps (if we take the use here to be typical of his late style) it would even imply that he attempted to integrate the lyrical speeches of the romances as a group more tightly into the warp and woof of these mixed, probing, and emblematically dense structures while nevertheless preserving a luminous and limpid clarity of effect at the moment of their utterance.

II

The seasonal motif is probably the most obvious aspect of Perdita's poetic bouquet. First she presents rosemary and rue, winter herbs that retain their "seeming and savor" beyond the growing season, to her elderly visitors, one of whom wears a "white beard" (IV.iv.404). Then, fearful that she may have tactlessly offended by calling attention to their age, she mentions less ordinary flowers ("carnations and streaked gillyvors") that appear in late summer or early autumn—blooms symbolically more flattering to the advanced in years but that she nevertheless cannot offer, refusing, as she does, to cultivate impure or bastardly hybrids—the products of nature corrupted (or, depending on one's point of view, perfected) by art. Instead of these she bestows "flow'rs / Of middle summer" upon the strangers, those that combine beauty with domestic utility (lavender, mint, savory, marjoram) but that are also perfectly in rhythm with nature (including the heliotropic marigold that closes its petals at sunset and begins to open them dewily at dawn). Turning finally to the young (Florizel and the virgin shepherdesses), Perdita nostalgically elaborates her list of spring flowers, those no longer available in June or late summer—blossoms that she must call up imaginatively as purely verbal gifts through mythical allusion and other devices of poetic art. As the pedantic Holofernes might have said, she invokes the "golden cadence of poesy, . . . smelling out the odoriferous flowers of fancy" (*Love's Labor's Lost*, IV.ii.121–124).

Although scholars disagree about the actual season in which the sheepshearing holiday occurs (June would be the normal time to harvest wool, but there is debate as to whether the references to the imminence of winter apply to the literal present or are simply a means of specifying the proper season for carnations and gillyflowers),[5] it is plain that Perdita's imagery, cumulatively received, evokes all four seasons of the year in such a way as to underscore their continuity and interdependence. At the same time the language implies that the different stages of human life, which by a Renaissance commonplace corresponded to the changes of season,[6] participate in a similar cycle or continuum. Today's young are tomorrow's old, as the figure of Time reminds us in his choric leap over the sixteen years that divide the two generational emphases, and therefore the two halves, of the play; and the natural recurrence of growth and decay that Perdita subtly acknowledges in her speech makes all periods, as well as the emotions appropriate to them, evanescent. In addition, since youth and age operate as metaphors for spiritual and moral conditions as much as for physical states, the destructive and regenerative phases of life need not coincide precisely with winter and summer. The delicate innocence of Hermione and the springlike boyhood of Mamillius can be dramatically present in the winter of Leontes' palace, just as the cold brutality of Polixenes toward his son can mar the "green-sward" (IV.iv.157) of "fair Bohemia" (IV.i.21). Moreover Perdita serves in some sort as a replacement for the dead Mamillius, so that youth and innocence may be seen as symbolically renewable or recoverable. And Hermione is to return to life after a protracted absence strangely more beautiful, despite the wrinkles of age, than when she had left it so poignantly. The result of course, together with the reunion of parents and children and the reconciliation of boyhood friends, is a kind of new birth for everyone, whether young or old.

If the seasonal imagery of Perdita's speech betokens a certain thoughtful blurring of the contrasts between age and youth and between wrongdoing and innocence, it complicates the usual binary opposition between nature and art and between court and country in an analogous way. The dramatic irony that the heroine's disapproval of grafting produces when she, a supposed rustic, accepts the courtly attentions of a prince has often been remarked; but Shakespeare produces a subtler irony by making Perdita represent nature in its purest and least-adulterated state while participating in a ritual that involves artificialities of costume, masque, and poetic refinement appropriate to a more sophisticated setting. Polixenes notes that she "smacks of something greater than herself" and is "too noble for this place" (IV.iv.158–159). She may feel uncomfortable as hostess in her "borrowed flaunts" (IV.iv.23) and may stubbornly resist the doctrine that "art . . . mend[s] nature" (IV.iv.95–96), but she does not hesitate to embroider her floral evocation with a reference to Pluto and Proserpina, plucked by Shakespeare probably from Golding's Ovid (*Metamorphoses*, V, 491–500). It is interesting to notice also that some of Perdita's flowers are physical—stage properties that can be handled—while others are made present to our fancy exclusively through the charms of lyric description. The uncertain hovering between a palpable and a merely verbal presentation of the floral offering necessarily involves an audience in the mysterious tension between illusion and reality or between the objective world and their subjective apprehension of it. This is a theme central to the early acts in which Leontes insanely misperceives his wife and to the final act in which an apparent statue miraculously moves and speaks.

That Perdita should recite the lyric passage on flowers is fitting in the most exact way. She has become the virtual apotheosis of what Time refers to as "th' freshest things now reigning" (IV.i.13), and Antigonus, as the storm rises and just before he falls victim to the bear, prepares us for her flower episode by referring to his royal infant as "Blossom" (III.iii.45), a sobriquet that hints at her survival, growth, and providential happiness. Shakespeare picks up this thread later when Autolycus mentions "the blossoms of [the older and younger shepherds'] fortune" (V.ii.126–127) after they have been snatched from a horrible death, restored to the good graces of King Polixenes, and raised to gentlemanly rank. In act IV Perdita presides over a verdant landscape that had years before been thought of by Antigonus as "the deserts of Bohemia," a place of storms and "famous for . . . creatures / Of prey" (III.iii.2–12). The fertile atmosphere may also recall the "garden" (I.ii.178) to which Hermione and Polixenes withdrew after first observing the sudden agitation of Leontes, as well as the "fertile . . . isle" of Delphos with its "delicate" climate and "air most sweet" (III.i.1–2), where the oracle of Apollo, god of art, sunshine, and enlightenment, had delivered the truth of Hermione's innocence. There is an obvious correlation between the floral sequence and Florizel's name, which Shakespeare seems to have appropriated from *Amadis de Grecia*, a Spanish sequel to *Amadis de Gaule*;[7] and the sense of fertility that the name projects reaches dramatic fruition when Leontes welcomes him and Perdita to Sicily "as . . . the spring to the earth" (V.i.152).

The specific details of Perdita's speech, however, extend well beyond a diffuse impression of vegetative profusion, fructification, and foison. Whether instinctively or by conscious design, Shakespeare loads it with an imagery and vocabulary that radiate connectively to the most diverse parts of the drama, thereby making it a thematic matrix or distilled synthesis of the whole. Not surprisingly—at least for those who recall Ophelia's painful scene with herbs—the poet treats individual flowers iconographically, for Elizabethans, as is well known, liked to see moral, emotional, and religious significances in the most minute and particular facets of nature.

Rosemary and rue, the "winter" plants with which Perdita begins her performance, stand respectively for remembrance after death (or friendship) and repentance. The first invites us to cast our minds back to relationships and events of the past—specifically perhaps to the loss of Mamillius and Hermione and beyond them to the close companionship of the two kings before their falling out and separation. Rue clearly evokes the whole issue of contrition, forgiveness, and spiritual regeneration; but it is also called "herb of grace," a name derived from *grace* in the theological sense but that also, as Mahood has pointed out,[8] suggests a number of alternative meanings—graciousness in manners, bodily grace, social or political favor (as in being in someone's grace), aristocratic breeding, gracefulness in art, and even royalty or high nobility (as used in a title or formal mode of address). The word *grace* together with its derivatives appears at least a dozen times in the play (most of the above significations are included). Therefore, in addition to the central concern of how divine grace may manifest itself through nature while, in another sense, being opposed to nature in its baser or fallen aspect, the word also connects with other themes. Among these are nature versus nurture, or true gentleness in relation to genetic origin, class, and rearing (Perdita is at once nobly born and nobly raised by her surrogate shepherd father), and physical beauty in relation to moral and spiritual radiance. The accompanying welcome "to our shearing" in the presence of playful but virgin shepherdesses—and of Polixenes himself—of course invites us to recall the latter's description of his own boyhood innocence with Leontes: the two lads "were as twinned lambs that did frisk i' th' sun" and "knew not / The doctrine of illdoing, nor dreamed / That any did" (I.ii.67–71).

Perdita's naïve disdain for the flowers produced by grafting—"nature's bastards" as she calls them—initiates the debate on whether one may legitimately tamper with the processes of growth, on the relationship of the human to the divine order of things; ironically also the language reminds us of the ugly scene in which Leontes had rejected this very speaker as a "female bastard" (II.iii.175). Grafting can be as relevant to the human as to the vegetable kingdom, as when a man is suspected of siring a child on another man's wife, or when the scion of a royal house aspires to marry a shepherdess; and we may remember also that Leontes had sought to make Camillo, "a servant grafted in [his] serious trust" (I.ii.245), the murderer of his dearest friend. The physically absent carnations and streaked gillyflowers, mixtures of human and superhuman creativity, are crammed with suggestiveness too. The first derive their name from the word for crowning and therefore imply royalty, perhaps coronation (Florizel and Perdita will one day wear crowns, and she is the "queen of curds and cream" [IV.iv.161] even as she speaks); one recalls Lennox's metaphor for the state as "the sovereign flower" (*Macbeth*, V.ii.30). But, as Traversi has noticed, the word may also involve a kind of double entendre on the stem of *carn*ality,[9] with backward glances at Leontes' obsession with cuckoldry and Autolycus's vital world of "the doxy over the dale," "the red blood" that "reigns in the winter's pale," and "tumbling in the hay" (IV.iii.2–12). After all, Mistress Quickly, responding to Falstaff's reputed characterization of loose women as "devils incarnate," had unconsciously associated the flower with the flesh, in her malapropistic observation, "'A could never abide carnation; 'twas a color he never lik'd" (*Henry V*, II.iii.30–33). The "hot lavender" may equally convey sexual overtones (how can one forget Leontes' outburst, "Too hot, too hot! / To mingle friendship far is mingling bloods" [I.ii.109]), although the literal meaning is technical and has to do with distinctions in the natural world between "hot" and "cold" plants, those that bloom earlier or later because of their relatively quick or slow receptivity to the sun. The image of the solisequious marigold with its opening and closing corolla, its "weeping" commencement of the day and its noontide splendor, subtly implies the interrelatedness, or balance, of sadness and joy that pervades *The Winter's Tale* as regards both its tragicomic action and its mingled tone.

When she comes to her imagined spring flowers, Perdita carries the principle of floral anthropomorphism even further. She begins by likening the maidenheads of the shepherdesses to buds that remain as yet ungathered "upon [their] virgin branches," an image that leads by natural association to the story of Proserpina's rape by Pluto, a violent and sudden action not unlike Leontes' frightening assault upon Hermione and, later, Polixenes' intrusive attempt to break up the young love affair. The falling of the flowers "from Dis's wagon" embodies the notion of disaster and chaos unpredictably ruining happiness and order, a pattern that the action of the play repeats several times in the quick reversals of fortune that beset so many of the characters. But the Pluto-Proserpina myth, besides accounting for the separation of the year into cold and warm seasons, also reinforces the idea of their fundamental indivisibility. The king of the underworld and the queen of spring are married after all, and although their realms of death and rebirth are spatially distinct, the poignant force of the story lies in the perception that each side of the contrast defines itself in relation to the other. Perdita's bright pastoralism could have no true significance without the wintry preface of her father's descent into darkness, coldness, and death.

Now the symbolic vibrations begin to proliferate as rapidly as Perdita can name the flowers. The daffodils, most forward of the spring blooms, precede even the swallows and brave the March winds as Antigonus and the mariners had braved the fatal storm. Again the clash of life with the natural forces of destruction can be inferred, but the emphasis is on survival and the power of beauty rather than death, just as Autolycus's rollicking song in the previous scene, "When daffodils begin to peer" (IV.iii.1), conveys more delight in the rising sap of the season than fear of a vagabond's roguery. The delicate blossoms "take," or enchant, the wind, rendering it harmless. The violets, traditional Shakespearean emblems of fragility and evanescence, are the briefest and most perishable flowers in the list. They suggest the precarious hold that tenderness and delicacy have upon life. Again we think of Mamillius's early demise, the unforeseen death of gentle Antigonus, and the miracle of survival when a newborn child is exposed to the elements. But the allusion to Juno's eyelids is interesting as well: the shaded violets are "sweeter" to observe than the best feature on the face of the fabled queen of the gods, the Olympian deity who, as wife to Jupiter, presides over wedded love. There are of course a number of marriages in the play—one deeply troubled by Leontes' jealousy and ultimately restored to health, another broken by Antigonus's mission to Bohemia and the cruel death that flows from it, and, finally, Paulina's remarriage to Camillo at the end, in neat parallel with the royal coupling of Florizel and Perdita—both of these latter being rewards, of a kind, for loyalty and endurance. The allusion to Juno, patroness of happy and unhappy, old and young marriages, would seem to point in different ways to all the relationships just named.

Additionally, however, the erotic component in love, whether of the married kind or not, is suggested by the comparison of the violets to "Cytherea's breath." Venus, the goddess of sexual passion, enjoys a wide range of devotees in *The Winter's Tale*, illusory as well as real: Polixenes and Hermione are wrongly accused of lust; Autolycus consorts with "doxies," "aunts," and "drabs" (IV.iii.2, 11, 26); the shepherd who finds Perdita (the apparent evidence of "some stair-work, some trunk-work, some behind-door-work") complains that the younger rustics go in for the "getting wenches with child" (III.iii.60–61, 72–73), among their other disorders; and the speaker herself is shortly to envision her flowers as love garlands for Florizel, the fitting appurtenances of "a bank for love to lie and play on." The erotic element in the floral symbolism obviously comprehends the disruptiveness of sin at one extreme and the idealized passion of approved romance at the other with a certain amount of morally neutral realism placed somewhere between.

The "pale primroses, / That die unmarried" introduce another note of pathos and frustration into the social bouquet that Perdita is imagining. The stage is filled with virginal shepherdesses, some of whom are undoubtedly destined to be cut off by disease or some other disaster before their romantic dreams can be fulfilled. Shakespeare's audience would have been only too aware of the high mortality rate of adolescents— including, of course, the untimely deaths of royal children such as Edward VI and Francis II (first husband of Mary Queen of Scots) in the mid-sixteenth century or Prince Henry a year or so after *The Winter's Tale* was composed. We think again of Mamillius. But Perdita's flowers are conceived in the main as feminine—extensions in some sense of herself. And the contrast here is chiefly internal; for as commentators have pointed out, the poet is playing wittily with the opposition between the marigold, known also as bride of the sun (*sponsus solis*), and the greenish-yellow flower, colored like the complexion of girls who suffered from greensickness ("a malady / Most incident to maids") that expires before it can be united with Phoebus, its intended spouse. Phoebus, an alternative name for Apollo, also reminds us of the oracle whose light finally penetrates the darkness of Leontes' suspicions.

The list concludes with "bold oxslips" (stronger and more assertive than cowslips), the "crown imperial" (the tall yellow fritillary recently imported into England from the Ottoman Empire), and "lilies of all kinds" including the "flow'r-de-luce" (or iris). Here the dramatist combines associations of strength, regal stature, erotic romance (Jonson in *The Masque of Beauty* [1608] makes Venus carry lilies, calling them "speciall *Hiero-glyphicks* of *louelinesse*"),[10] and perhaps kingship, the French *fleur de lys* being a feature of royal heraldry. These have the effect of contrasting in various ways with the more sheltered and impermanent aspects of love as suggested by the fragile violets and sickly primroses. And Shakespeare combines the hopeful and pessimistic attitudes toward love in Florizel's jesting response to his lady's wish for garlands of flowers with which to "strew him o'er and o'er": "What, like a corse?" Her instantaneous reply is that she would bury him "quick and in [her] arms" rather than in his grave, but the exchange makes us aware that flowers are equally a tribute for funerals as for weddings. Again the interdependence of spring and winter, of Proserpina and Dis, is implied. Death is not only the opponent of Love but, as Romeo knew, in some deeper sense, his paramour.

The flower aria ends on a jocular note with the speaker's self-conscious awareness of her function as an actress, a player of roles. Again we are forced to confront the way in which the freshest and most natural emotions get mediated through symbolic costume and stylized gesture, through the aural and visual devices of theatricality. At one level of the fiction, Perdita is a princess; at another she is a shepherdess; at still another she is hostess of a ceremonial ritual or masque, "most goddess-like prank'd up" (IV.iv.10); and at the most basic level of all, of course, she is a boy actor in female attire, probably rouged, wigged, and falsely bosomed. This layering of identity consists brilliantly with the mixed mode of the long flower speech, helping to suggest in another way its subtle blend of the natural with the artificial.

III

Rosalie Colie in her brilliant book, *The Resources of Kind*, observes that to the Renaissance mind a genre, or literary "kind," was a means of taking a "fix" on the world, a formal way of seeing experience through a recognized frame or from a particular angle of vision.[11] Each mode, be it lyric, pastoral, satire, tragedy, love comedy, romance, epic, or whatever, had its own set of conventions and predictable features appropriate to the set of attitudes or the perspective being rendered. She goes on to show how various mixtures and composites of these conventions, those associated with quite different genres, frequently result in the most interesting, complex, and original works. Perdita's flower speech might profitably be viewed in this way. On its surface, it satisfies several expectations of pastoral—the quiet but dignified rusticity, the delight in nature, the romantic idealism, the lyric musicality, the touches of classical mythology, the self-consciousness about art as a medium, for example. But without the least sense of strain or difficulty, it also gathers to itself themes, ideas, and points of view that characterize the tragicomic mode of the play at other important points in its kaleidoscopic and diverse range of actions, effects, and emotions. It manages, for instance, to suggest the typical opposition between the innocence of the country and the corruptions of the court through the contrast between natural and "bastard" flowers, but not content with this simplistic and conventional attitude, it also implies the alliance—even the fusion—of civilized elegance with what Hamlet, in his speech to the players, calls "the modesty of nature" (*Hamlet*, III.ii.19). Perdita manages to synthesize in the most pleasing and least-awkward way the apparently contrary values of the palace and the shepherd's cottage. Her lyrical speech contains elements that elicit the memory of past events and subtly anticipate future ones; it mingles a sense of the tragic with the comic, allowing us subliminally to harmonize and emotionally transmute a wide disparity of human experiences and conditions including violence, gentleness, sexual energy, chastity, spontaneity, naïveté, sophistication, irony, charm, jocularity, youth, age, vitality, and death.

The subtly modulated style of the speech with its combinative rhythms, tending toward lyric regularity but flexible and irregular enough to suggest natural impulse and unrehearsed delivery, bridges the gap between Autolycus's carefree songs and the contorted verse of Leontes at his most paranoid. It is worth noting too that the verse rhythms of the play move in the direction of increased lyricism just as the flower passage itself does. The songs are concentrated in two successive scenes of the fourth act, and most of them occur very near Perdita's iambic pentameter speech. It has long been recognized of course that music plays an especially prominent role in the romances as a group, partly, as Nosworthy suggests, because of Robert Johnson whom the King's

Company were regularly employing to supply incidental music for the stage.[12] In *The Winter's Tale* such music functions importantly at the climactic moment when the statue comes alive—an obvious symbol of the re-creative and regenerative forces that are at work in the drama as a whole. Perdita's beautiful speech on flowers, which at its most ravishing seems to aspire to the condition of song, obviously plays its part in the larger musical-philosophical design of the work. Perhaps, too, Perdita's eloquence at this point illustrates the recrudescence of the mother's rhetorical skills in the daughter. When he is a guest in Sicily, Polixenes allows Hermione to persuade him to extend his visit after the inducements of Leontes have failed. And Hermione's moving, dignified, and restrained defense of her own integrity at the trial prepares us for the similar impression of sincerity that illuminates Perdita's more decorative aria.

Enough has been said, I trust, to allow us to dismiss forever Lytton Strachey's assertion, made originally in 1904, that in *The Winter's Tale* and the other plays with which it is usually grouped Shakespeare was "bored with real life, bored with drama, bored, in fact, with everything except poetry and poetical dreams."[13] At least at the deeper levels of perception, there is no divorce, as I have tried to show, between "drama" or "life" and the poetry of Perdita's much-excerpted speech. On the contrary, the aria constitutes a remarkable example of how "poetical dreams" in the hands of a master artist can encapsulate the very stuff of a complex play that deals as powerfully with the actual as with the imaginary; and the passage also demonstrates that during a charming pause in the ongoing rush of stage action, a dramatist may delicately touch chords that help his audience, through memory and association, to synthesize the actions and emotions that have led them to a point of temporary rest, and that can point forward in a similarly thematic manner to events and resolutions yet to be presented.

Copiousness of language as an ornament in poetry had been endorsed by rhetoricians as far back as Quintilian and was obviously much cultivated by the Elizabethans; but behind the pursuit of richness in imagery and linguistic detail lay the desire for inclusiveness of experience. The ideal in other words was to use ornament not merely for its own sake but as an adjunct to meaning. George Puttenham held that although speech in the formal sense "is artificiall and made by man," the ability to speak "is giuen by nature" for the "perswasion of others" as well as for self-understanding. Another sixteenth-century theorist of rhetoric, Henry Peacham, speaks of poetry as "a pleasant proportion, & as it were . . . a sweet & musicall harmonie," whose true function is not only to delight but to work "by the secret and mightie power of perswasion."[14] Perdita's speech can hardly be called persuasive in the sense that the orations of Brutus and Antony over the body of Caesar are intended to persuade. But it is nevertheless urgent in its own way, both morally and emotionally, and it is imbued with ideas as much as with delicious sounds and pleasing imagery. Moreover, it reflects character. As Margreta de Grazia has shown, the fullest and most satisfying kind of communication, according to Renaissance theory, involved the principle that truly good speakers must be good persons: the finest kind of verbal expressiveness should disclose and irradiate the essential charity of the speaker, for, as charity reins in sinful pride and egotism, it may also subdue the imperfections and artificialities of the verbal medium in which one Christian soul addresses another.[15] Shakespeare arranges for us to intuit at least that in the flower speech Perdita meets this test.

The attractive yet essentially mysterious blend of sincerity and verbal artifice that appears to be the hallmark of Perdita's eloquence in the pastoral episode would seem to reflect ambiguous attitudes toward language itself that were current in Shakespeare's age. The dramatist could play movingly with the skeptical notion, voiced by Montaigne and others, that the link between a word and the reality to which it referred was tenuous at best. Juliet's "What's in a name? That which we call a rose / By any other word would smell as sweet" (*Romeo and Juliet*, II.ii.43–44) makes drama out of the self-conscious gap between poetry and meaning. But Othello defends himself before the Venetian senate in "a round unvarnish'd tale" (*Othello*, I.iii.92) that positively exfoliates in luxuriant verbiage and exotic imagery without conveying the least hint of rhetorical calculation or of the speaker's having studied the arts of persuasion. Othello's words, whatever their debt to the subtleties of poetic art, flow naturally and spontaneously from the heart. As Richard Lanham has suggested, eloquence is fundamentally two-faced, looking in one direction toward the frank pleasures of rhetorical invention (a species of play) and in the other toward the duty of communicating higher truth and, in the process, of authenticating the serious self. Lanham cites Castiglione's *Courtier* in Hoby's famous translation as an example of the "middle style," that is, a work that mediates subtly and successfully between the two impulses. The courtly dialogue at Urbino, in its idyllic semirural setting, combines wit, *sprezzatura*, aristocratic elegance, even a certain theatricalization of the self, with passion, sincerity, and, in Cardinal Bembo's great paean to love, a dynamic Platonic idealism. The style employed here allows speakers to oscillate, as Lanham phrases it, "from word to concept and back," and as the successful courtier builds into his created public image a sense of otherness without eradicating the true center from which the image is generated, so "the mature stylist . . . internalize[s] his own sense of decorum," maintaining a "poise between extremes."[16] Something like this balance between the artificial and the genuine, between fulfilling the expectations of a role and voicing the holiness of the heart's affections, can be enjoyed in Perdita's floral speech.

9

The Idea of Time in
Shakespeare's Second Historical Tetralogy

> For the Methode of a Poet historical is not such, as of an
> Historiographer. For an Historiographer discourseth of
> affayres orderly as they were donne, accounting as well the
> times as the actions, but a Poet thrusteth into the middest,
> euen where it most concerneth him, and there recoursing to
> the thinges forepaste, and diuining of thinges to come, maketh
> a pleasing Analysis of all.
> —Edmund Spenser's letter to Sir Walter
> Raleigh, prefixed to *The Faerie Queene*

I

That eight of the ten Shakespearean histories are arranged into tetralogies—two sequences of four plays each—suggests an important point about the form of the history play as opposed to the form of the other major genres, comedy and tragedy—namely, that the history play (almost by the nature of its subject) is an *open*, as opposed to a *closed*, form.[1] History is a continuum, and any historical drama must, in an important sense, commence *in medias res*. Of course, each of the four plays in the two tetralogies has its own organic structure and may be performed as a self-contained unit. But all these plays contain prominent references to what went before as well as predictions or foreshadowings of what is to come, so that an important part of our experience of a history play consists of being caught up dramatically in the stream of events as these impinge upon us immediately, while being constantly made aware that there are longer vistas of cause and effect that cannot be ignored.

Comedy is a self-contained and generally closed form because it creates its own fictional world tied to a completed narrative and a set of characters who exist only to fulfill the particular requirements of the fiction. When Orlando and Rosalind in *As You Like It* or Bassanio and Portia in *The Merchant of Venice* join hands as married couples in the fifth act, the drama is over, and the world they have brought to life before us ceases to exist except as memory. These plays do not encourage us to imagine the young lovers twenty years later as the parents of children, growing thicker in the waist, losing their hair, or having problems with gout or lumbago. In another way, the same point may be made about tragedy. Elizabethan tragedies always end with death—the most absolute kind of closure we know—and the devastation is usually such that we are forced to look backward over what was or what might have been rather than at what may follow. After Hamlet's death no one cares very much about a Denmark under Fortinbras's rule, and at the end of *King Lear*, the future will scarcely bear thinking about at all. Edgar's final words sum up the typical mood at the end of tragedy:

> The weight of this sad time we must obey,
> Speak what we feel, not what we ought to say.
> The oldest hath borne most; we that are young
> Shall never see so much, nor live so long.
> *(King Lear*, V.iii.328–331)

This is obviously not the way that *Richard II* (even though the word "tragedy" appears in its title) or *2 Henry IV*, for instance, conclude. Bolingbroke in the first play is just beginning a reign that will be as important for England as the one that has just ended with Richard's assassination. We hear of the new king's concern for his "unthrifty son" (V.iii.1), even though Prince Hal has not yet appeared as a stage character; so we know that Henry IV is already saddled with a family problem that remains very much unresolved. Moreover, Henry's political difficulties, far from being over, are just commencing. He hopes to make a voyage to the Holy Land to wash the bloody guilt of Richard's murder from his hands, but we already know from Aumerle's abortive revolt, if not from the Bishop of Carlisle's ominous prophecy in act IV, that more or less continuous rebellion will keep him at home and never permit him to go on crusade. Hence the poignant irony of his dying two plays later in the Jerusalem chamber of his London palace. Also, the dying king advises his son to "busy giddy minds / With foreign quarrels" (*2 Henry IV*, IV.v.213–214) and, after the rejection of Falstaff, Prince Hal's brother, John of Lancaster, lays the foundation for the next play by anticipating the great triumph of Agincourt:

> I will lay odds that, ere this year expire,
> We bear our civil swords and native fire
> As far as France. I heard a bird so sing,
> Whose music, to my thinking, pleas'd the King.
> *(2 Henry IV*, V.v.106–109)

Shakespeare's histories have a more ambiguous sense of ending than the comedies and tragedies, not merely because in eight cases out of ten they are parts of a larger sequence, but also because they deal, for the most part, with actual events that cannot be neatly separated from their origins and consequences—with events, by the way, that were near enough in the cultural memory of the Elizabethans to seem contiguous to the present. Americans regard their own Civil War not only as an episode from the past but also as exerting a formative kind of pressure on their present culture. British subjects feel the same way about the long and multi-faceted reign of Queen Victoria. In an analogous way, Shakespeare and his audience were interested in the political struggles of the fourteenth and fifteenth centuries because these turbulent times allowed them to make sense of their own national heritage. The older age was seen as helping to shape their own age—even, in a way, as reflecting contemporary issues—and as having the potential, theoretically at least, to yield insight into what the future might be like.[2] The form of the history play as Shakespeare develops and refines it becomes, then, the dramatic means by which we as an audience experience time. The duration of the play in the theatre—what Shakespeare referred to in *Romeo and Juliet* as "the two hours traffic of our stage" (Prologue, l. 12)—is an artistic convention that permits Shakespeare and (through his artistry) permits us to explore the endlessly fascinating phenomenon of time and temporality in a complex way.

Renaissance historiography regarded the purpose of history as being principally didactic. Shakespeare might have said (with Santayana and, later, Churchill) that those who cannot remember their past are condemned to repeat it. But Shakespeare and his age knew that the past was both different from, and similar to, the present, and also that the future would in some mysterious way be a product of both present and past. They also knew, as we do, that today's past was yesterday's present and that today is tomorrow's past. Also, of course, in a more puzzlingly philosophical or epistemological sense, they were aware, as we are, that one could only know either past or future through the mediation of the present. There is a kind of truth in saying that past and future exist only in the mind as it confronts these through the medium of imagination. In one sense all historians *create* the past—reconstruct it out of materials not wholly available to the age being represented. Everyone's re-creation of the past and the meaning stamped upon it, moreover, will differ according to the historian's particular angle of vision, or his cultural, religious, and moral biases. Shakespeare's histories as a group raise these issues powerfully to our consciousness—but dramatically rather than discursively, concretely rather than abstractly—by clothing the intellectual paradoxes with human flesh and giving us not only a vivid sense of the past but also the essence or process of historical flow in both its universal and particular aspects. My purpose in this chapter, keeping these generalizations in mind, is to illustrate a few of the ways in which the concept of time, which must underlie all historical inquiry, lends a special kind of richness and significance to *Richard II*, the two *Henry IV* plays, and *Henry V* considered as an unfolding progression.

II

Elizabethan England inherited two models of the shape of human history—one classical, the other medieval. The notion of historical movement that Shakespeare derived, indirectly, from Thucydides and, more particularly, from Polybius was cyclical. In this view, civilization had its happy and its unhappy periods, its fortunate and unfortunate phases, but recurrence was its defining feature. The ups and downs of one period could be expected to replicate themselves in succeeding times, and (at least in Polybius's analysis) in more or less the same—or analogous—sequence. The past thus became the mirror of present and future ages, but since all change obeyed an ineluctable rule of predictable but unending alteration, the sense of long-range direction, progress, or purpose in history could be only relative and contingent. Eternal flux was the irreducible law of nature, and a kind of saturnine determinism its final implication. Of necessity, the practical historian must focus his attention upon some particular segment of a movement that had no ultimate beginning or end but that nevertheless might disturb or reassure through the recurring impressions of *déjà vu* that it afforded.

Contrastingly, the medieval concept of history regarded all human events of whatever period as part of salvation history under the aegis of Christian revelation. Saint Augustine, for instance, viewed time as a uniquely human condition and its wearisome pressure as a consequence of the Fall. Time had an identifiable beginning (the Creation as described in Genesis) and an identifiable end (the Last Judgment as foretold in the Book of Revelation). It also enclosed two intermediate points of vast significance—the Fall of Man (through Adam's Original Sin) and the salvation of man (through the sacrifice of Jesus Christ, the second Adam). All human activity from genesis to apocalypse, from the Creation until the end of the world, was thus seen theologically as an aspect of divine providence. Any historical period or pattern of change must then be interpreted as part of an overarching and eternal pattern in which time itself becomes a mere parenthesis (the phrase is Sir Thomas Browne's) between the nothingness out of which God made the world and the physical nothingness to which He will ultimately reconvert it. History in the medieval view becomes teleological, part of the pilgrimage of the soul through earthly changes and vicissitudes to its final destination, the City of God. Even if Shakespeare did not read the Church Fathers, he could have absorbed this latter view of time by attending the biblical plays of the late Middle Ages—the Corpus Christi pageant cycle that survived in certain provincial English towns into the period of the dramatist's boyhood. These plays, performed in sequence on wagons, began with a dramatization of the Creation and ended with the Final Judgment, orienting the most famous stories of the Old and New Testaments between these absolute termini to the central fact of Christ's death and Resurrection.

Both of these historical perspectives appear in Shakespeare's tetralogy, superimposed—as it were—to create an interesting ambiguity or indeterminacy of response to the characters and events dramatized. Richard II's deposition and murder tended to be interpreted by Shakespeare's chronicle sources (particularly by Edward Hall and, even here, partly by implication) as analogous to the Fall, as a kind of Original Sin in its political dimension. The unlawful removal of an anointed king by the illegitimate usurper Bolingbroke fundamentally disturbed the created universe as ordained by God, the inevitable consequence being perpetual unrest in the body politic, continuing rebellion, and a sociopolitical chaos that did not run its full course until Richard III, a monster-king deformed in body as in soul, brought England to the verge of ruin. This was a nadir from which only Queen Elizabeth's grandfather, Henry VII, the first Tudor monarch, could deliver the nation.[3] Shakespeare gives us a clue to this kind of historical thinking by having Richard II's queen refer to her husband's impending disaster as "a second fall" (*Richard II*, III.iv.76). Moreover, Richard II so weds his conception of self to the doctrine of the divine right of kings, regarding himself as an extension of God on earth, that he fatally confuses his timeless and eternal body with his time-bound and finite body. Thus, he can unblushingly compare himself to Christ and his persecutors and betrayers to Pontius Pilate and Judas Iscariot. He sentences Bolingbroke and Mowbray to banishment with a kind of finality that suggests the assumption of divine rather than human judgment. Bolingbroke comments bitterly on the difference between a king's sense of time and a mere subject's:

> How long a time lies in one little word!
> Four lagging winters and four wanton springs
> End in a word; such is the breath of kings.
>   (I.iii.213–215)

Richard's words of banishment ironically take on something of the force of the Word in Saint John's sense of *logos*.

But the youthful king, of course, proves all too fallible and human as a ruler, and Shakespeare shows that he is very much the victim of time as well as, in another sense, its theologically privileged voice. Richard violates the very sanctions that entitle him to his own special authority. By confiscating his cousin's estates to finance his war in Ireland, he interrupts the orderly sequence of events over which he theoretically presides and of whose eternal law he considers himself to be the temporal enshrinement. York warns him of the disastrous inconsistency:

> Take Hereford's rights away, and take from Time
> His charters and his customary rights;
> Let not tomorrow then ensue today;
> Be not thyself; for how art thou a king
> But by fair sequence and succession?
>   (II.i.195–199)

The later plays contain many nostalgic allusions to Richard, and Shakespeare preserves the idea, inherited from the chronicles, that the multifarious sufferings of England flow in some primordial way from the crime of deposing a legitimate monarch, the "deputy elected by the Lord" (*Richard II*, III.ii.57). But he also undercuts this long-range Christian and mythic concept of historical causation by showing us Richard's ironically partial and self-deceived view of his own nature and by bringing him at length to a tragic recognition of his own time-boundness and finitude: "I wasted time, and now doth time waste me" (V.v.49). And the unfolding events of the whole tetralogy repeatedly confirm our awareness of cyclical change, of bafflingly rapid fluctuation in political affairs, that runs counter to any sense of purposive or linear advance and that leaves us with a profound skepticism about historical providence or teleology.

Bolingbroke as king, sleeplessly speculating on how inscrutable the future is to those who would read her secrets, voices a more realistic and less comforting attitude toward historical process that cannot be set aside:

> O God, that one might read the book of fate,
> And see the revolution of the times
> Make mountains level, and the continent,
> Weary of solid firmness, melt itself
> Into the sea. . . .
> . . . .
>   O, if this were seen,
> The happiest youth, viewing his progress through,
> What perils past, what crosses to ensue,

Would shut the book, and sit him down and die.
(2 Henry IV, III.i.45–56)

Henry continues, pessimistically reviewing the paradoxical shifts in human alliances that alter the course of nations:

'Tis not ten years gone
Since Richard and Northumberland, great friends,
Did feast together, and in two years after
Were they at wars. It is but eight years since
This Percy was the man nearest my soul,
Who like a brother toil'd in my affairs
And laid his love and life under my foot.
(III.i.57–63)

Thus does Bolingbroke notice—and Shakespeare through his words—that (to borrow a tragic phrase from *Romeo and Juliet*) "all things change them to the contrary" (IV.v.90). Shakespearean chronicle plays may give some sense of a divine purpose in history, but they also create a countervailing weariness about the hope of plucking comfort from the giddy revolutions of Fortune's wheel. Bolingbroke's reaction to the "necessities" of mutability—even though (because of the principle of recurrence) they may enable us to look into the seeds of time—must be a gloomy stoicism:

Are these things then necessities?
Then let us meet them like necessities.
(2 Henry IV, III.i.92–93)

Since the opposed views of time suggested here nudge and modify each other in Shakespeare's dramatic practice, it is interesting to note that the histories as a group embrace both comedy and tragedy without succumbing totally to the generic dictates of either. Perhaps the dual perspective on history presupposes this combination: the medieval Christian view, though not lacking in tragic emphases (the murder of Abel, the sacrifice of Isaac, and the Crucifixion, for instance), is essentially comic in direction, while the classical view, though allowing for moments or periods that might justify optimism, is essentially pessimistic in its positing of ceaseless change and in the obscurity it implies as to final purpose.

The *Henry IV* plays balance comedy against tragedy brilliantly in the contrasted worlds of tavern and rebel camp. Both worlds are defined in part by their radically different sense of time. Indeed, opposing attitudes toward clock and calendar become a major device of characterization in these dramas. When we first meet Falstaff, the very incarnation of the comic spirit not only in the history plays but in all of Shakespeare, the fat knight is asking Hal, "What time of day is it, lad?" (*1 Henry IV*, I.ii.1). The prince's elaborate reply to this routine question is, of course, no answer at all, but a facetiously extended analysis of why the question itself has no relevance to Falstaff's style of life:

Thou art so fat-witted with drinking of old sack and unbuttoning thee after supper, and sleeping upon benches after noon, that thou hast forgotten to demand that truly which thou wouldst truly know. What a devil hast thou to do with the time of the day? Unless hours were cups of sack, and minutes capons, and clocks the tongues of bawds, and dials the signs of leaping-houses, and the blessed sun himself a fair hot wench in flame-color'd taffeta, I see no reason why thou shouldst be so superfluous to demand the time of the day.

(I.ii.2–12)

In the ethos of the tavern, which, incidentally, Falstaff carries with him both to Gadshill and to Shrewsbury, urgency has no meaning. Time is suspended for the sake of pleasurable escape from the grimmer realities of life. Refusing to acknowledge the discomforts of age in the robbery scene ("They hate us youth" [II.ii.85], the old coward bellows), Falstaff willfully inhabits a fantasy world of playful adolescence, of eternal gaming and holiday, that does not fully dissipate until Hal's crushing rejection of him at the end of *Henry IV, Part II*. Even as late as the scenes in Gloucestershire, Falstaff, "play[ing] the fool . . . with the time" (*2 Henry IV*, II.ii.134) in the prince's phrase, finds his actual past too painful to contemplate seriously and insists on a comic world of present amusement and future hope. To Shallow's senile reminiscences of their youthful highjinks fifty-five years ago when, as students, they "lay all night in the Windmill in Saint George's Field," Falstaff can only rejoin, "No more of that, good Master Shallow, no more of that" (*2 Henry IV*, III.ii.193–196); and he begs Doll Tearsheet, who reminds him of his age, not to "speak like a death's-head," not to "bid [him] remember [his] end" (II.iv.232–233).

If the aging Falstaff symbolizes the comic refusal to accept mortality by insisting on a world of eternal youth, Hotspur, his ironically youthful foil in the first Henry IV play, is wedded to the tragic necessity—indeed almost the desire—of death for honor's sake. As his name implies, everything Hotspur says or does is associated with risk and with speed: "O, let the hours be short / Till fields and blows and groans applaud our sport!" (*1 Henry IV*, I.iii.301–302). With a romantic's appetite for high adventure and importunity, he recognizes the brevity of life and measures human dignity not in years but in the quality and intensity of the life lived:

> O gentlemen, the time of life is short!
> To spend that shortness basely were too long
> If life did ride upon a dial's point,
> Still ending at the arrival of an hour.
> And if we live, we live to tread on kings;
> If die, brave death, when princes die with us!
> (*1 Henry IV*, V.ii.81–86)

Earlier, disdaining the politic caution of Worcester and his cooler-headed colleagues, Hotspur even magnifies the odds against him for the sake of greater glory:

> Come, let us take a muster speedily.
> Doomsday is near; die all, die merrily.
> (IV.i.133–134)

Like Tennyson's "Light Brigade," Hotspur rides cheerfully into the jaws of death, savoring each moment the more because it is likely to be among his last. Nowhere does Shakespeare make the contrary views of time—the comic versus the tragic—more emblematic than in the scene at Shrewsbury where Prince Hal stands between two apparent corpses—the athletic body of Hotspur, whom he has just robbed of his youth, and the decrepit body of Falstaff, who feigns death in order to evade its terrors and who then pops up like a jack-in-the-box the moment it is safe to do so. Tragedy and Comedy, the death wish and the life-force, symbolically occupy the right and left sides of the same stage.[4]

Prince Hal, who assimilates some of Falstaff's wit and love of fun without his cowardice and some of Hotspur's bravery and idealism without his rashness, embodies a more complex attitude toward time than either of his opponents in verbal or military combat. Hal may seem to ignore the importunities of the court and the battlefield temporarily, "awhile uphold[ing] / The unyoked humor of . . . idleness" (*1 Henry IV*, I.ii.189–190), but his game-playing, unlike Falstaff's, is self-consciously calculated and accommodated to a longer temporal perspective. In its consciousness of foreseeable ends, Hal's sense of time may partake of both the comic and tragic attitudes, but in essence, it is political. The playacting episode in the Boar's Head tavern ends with Falstaff (in the role of Hal) pleading with the prince (in the role of his father) not to banish his corpulent companion: "banish plump Jack, and banish all the world." Characteristically, the prince answers with a double voice: "I do, I will" (*1 Henry IV*, II.iv.474–476). Falstaff draws no line between the charade and the reality it parodies, but the prince, by his change of tense, shows us that he carefully distinguishes between the present fun and the future reform. Hal's playfulness is not escapist, not rooted in the confusion of recreation with work. The boy knows, like his rapidly aging father, that a prince has only one life in which to make his mark and, unlike Hotspur, that one cannot afford to be too intense or obsessively single-minded in his loyalties. As a consequence, we are slightly repelled by the coldly utilitarian construction that he seems to put upon his association with his tavern cronies.

In his death speech Hotspur reminds us poignantly that life is "time's fool, / And time, that takes survey of all the world, / Must have a stop" (*1 Henry IV*, V.iv.81–83). Hotspur stops the clock tragically for himself by getting himself killed in a mistaken cause. Falstaff tries to stop the clock in another sense by willfully refusing to acknowledge its existence. Hal can absorb something of value from both associations without opposing himself to the inevitable flow of time. He grows from boy to man, from tavern roisterer to the princely savior of his father's life—finally to the kingly hero of Agincourt—by moving *with*, rather than *against*, the tide of history and, in some sense, harmonizing the political and the moral, the realistic and the Christian insights into temporality. Through a synthesis of attitudes toward the relaxations and pressures of history, he "make[s] offense a skill, / Redeeming time when men think least [he] will" (*1 Henry IV*, I.ii.210–211).

III

Not content with playing off the interlocking worlds of comedy, tragedy, and politics against each other in respect of their varying responses to time, Shakespeare also makes us aware of other temporal contrasts and concerns. One of his most effective techniques is the counterpointing of an external, objective sense of time with a more internal, subjective sense of it, so that, as an audience, we may experience history both from the perspective of a dispassionate looker-on and also through the eyes of feeling individuals. The external sense of time is, of course, linked to the action and could hardly be avoided by any dramatist. Thus, the plays are full of simple information about scheduling, such as Bolingbroke's announcement after the deposition of Richard, "On Wednesday next we solemnly proclaim / Our coronation. Lords, be ready all" (*Richard II*, IV.i.320–321), or Mortimer's statement about the rebel plans: "Tomorrow, cousin Percy, you and I / And my good Lord of Worcester will set forth / To meet your father and the Scottish power . . . at Shrewsbury" (*1 Henry IV*, III.i.80–83). But the ordinary sequence of events is constantly being intersected by a more private sense of time that discloses personality or lights up the moral or spiritual interior of a speaker. Richard II's heartless remark at the news of Gaunt's death shows us the flippant and youthful king at his most shallow:

> The ripest fruit first falls, and so doth he;
> His time is spent, our pilgrimage must be.
> So much for that.
> (*Richard II*, II.i.153–155)

Then later on we are exposed to a deeper and more sympathetic example of Richard's interior sense of the clock, when, for the first and only time he is alone in the entire drama, he plays painfully at manufacturing a whole private microcosm based on the psychology of isolation. He works out an intricate poetical conceit by which his thoughts become minutes, his eyes the outward watch, his heart a bell that tolls the hours, and his finger, wiping away tears of grief, a dial's point:

> So sighs and tears and groans
> Show minutes, times, and hours. But my time
> Runs posting on in Bolingbroke's proud joy,
> While I stand here, his Jack of the clock.
> (V.v.57–60)

Richard constructs an inner world of time out of thoughts and emotions in a therapeutic attempt to adjust to an exterior onslaught of time that has passed him by. Thus does Shakespeare dramatize through a moving soliloquy how sorrow and joy make for different experiences of time and how dynastic change alters the tempo of life in diverse ways, depending on whether one is the loser or the winner.

Some of the playwright's most trenchant ironies arise from niceties of historical timing. In the very scene in which Richard II disinherits his cousin, we learn that Bolingbroke has already raised an army and is even then making for England "with all due expedience" (*Richard II*, II.i.287), apparently ignorant of the king's action against him.[5] Then, after Bolingbroke has already consolidated his power, Richard himself returns from Ireland "one day too late" (III.ii.67) to prevent the defection of his own adherents, and Salisbury wishes futilely that the inexorable march of the calendar could be reversed:

> O, call back yesterday, bid time return,
> And thou shalt have twelve thousand fighting men!

Today, today, unhappy day, too late,
O'erthrows thy joys, friends, fortune, and thy state;
For all the Welshmen, hearing thou wert dead,
Are gone to Bolingbroke, dispers'd and fled.
(III.ii.69–74)

In this dramatic juxtaposition Shakespeare hints that Bolingbroke ambitiously rushes the time for his own political advantage, while Richard's more leisurely and passive approach to political crisis is self-defeating. The king loses even before he can begin to fight. Bolingbroke makes time his servant. Richard becomes time's prey.

The collision of two differing misperceptions of time in *2 Henry IV* makes for one of the most memorably ironic episodes of the entire tetralogy. Prince Hal enters the bed-chamber of his father and, thinking the king dead, reverently takes his crown from its pillow in the belief that his most solemn moment of responsibility has at last arrived. Then the king awakes and, doubtless remembering his own youthful seizure of the diadem from Richard, misinterprets his son's behavior as an act of usurpation:

Dost thou so hunger for mine empty chair
That thou wilt needs invest thee with my honors
Before thy hour be ripe? O foolish youth,
Thou seek'st the greatness that will overwhelm thee.
Stay but a little, for my cloud of dignity
Is held from falling with so weak a wind
That it will quickly drop. My day is dim.
Thou hast stol'n that which after some few hours
Were thine without offense, and at my death
Thou hast seal'd up my expectation.
Thy life did manifest thou lov'dst me not,
And thou wilt have me die assur'd of it.
Thou hid'st a thousand daggers in thy thoughts,
Which thou hast whetted on thy stony heart,
To stab at half an hour of my life.
What, canst thou not forbear me half an hour?
Then get thee gone and dig my grave thyself.
(*2 Henry IV*, IV.v.94–110)

Henry IV protracts this misplaced rebuke to his son almost unendurably, bitterly alleging that "a time is come to mock at form" (IV.v.118) at the very moment when Hal's consciousness of kingly form and identity has been raised to its highest pitch of intensity.

One of the ways in which Shakespeare conveys the sense of history developing and exfoliating before our eyes is to intermingle immediate with more remote, short-term with longer-term, measurements of time. The histories are replete with a feeling for temporality in its quotidian and urgent aspects. Historical drama depends for its back-ground effects on verisimilar touches of location and period that lend a sense of "then-ness" to the play; but, in addition, its dramatic movement requires relationships of rapid cause and effect, of quick stimulus and response. The play, to come alive onstage, must make us care about the links between what happened ten minutes ago and what is happening now or will happen very soon—or, in the time scheme of the drama itself, between yesterday, today, and tomorrow. This is the sensation of temporality that Shakespeare dramatizes when he shows us Hotspur rushing fatally into battle without pausing to read important letters ("I cannot read them now!" [*1 Henry IV*, V.ii.80]), or when messages arrive at the Boar's Head summoning Falstaff and Hal to the colors ("I'll to the court in the morning. We must all to the wars. . . . I'll procure this fat rogue a charge of foot" [*1 Henry IV*, II.iv.538–540]).

But longer perspectives interrupt this sense of daily bustle, connecting present urgencies with a more distant awareness of both past and future. The rebels are forever revising the past as a way of displacing their own guilt. When Henry IV, the usurper whom they have helped bring to power, disappoints their expectations, they reclothe Richard's memory in the robes of sentimentality and besmirch their own former leader. From the new revisionist angle of perception, Richard becomes "that sweet lovely rose," and the king who supplanted him "this thorn, this canker, Bolingbroke" (*1 Henry IV*, I.iii.175–176). The meritorious exile whose injustice they had once claimed to be righting has suddenly been transformed through self-deceptive rhetoric into "a poor unminded outlaw sneaking home" (IV.iii.58). The gap between the original "then" and the "then" as perceived in this curiously skewed "now" becomes a major source of dramatic irony.

The prophecies with which the histories are laden also produce a sense of temporal distance in the forward direction—and with no less irony. The Bishop of Carlisle predicts that the deposition of an anointed king will transform England into a second Golgotha, bringing in its wake "disorder, horror, fear, and mutiny" (*Richard II*, IV.i.143) to successive generations; and he is instantly arrested for speaking a truth that everyone in the audience knew had already come to pass. Richard himself correctly predicts that Northumberland will be just as disloyal to his new master as to his old, and when this happens in the plays that follow, Shakespeare pointedly reminds his audience of what was said but ignored in the first instance:

> *King Henry.* But which of you was by—
> [*To Warwick.*] You, cousin Nevil, as I may remember—
> When Richard, with his eye brimful of tears,
> Then check'd and rated by Northumberland,
> Did speak these words, now prov'd a prophecy?
> "Northumberland, thou ladder by the which
> My cousin Bolingbroke ascends my throne"—
> Though then, God knows, I had no such intent,
> But that necessity so bow'd the state
> That I and greatness were compell'd to kiss—
> "The time shall come," thus did he follow it,
> "The time will come, that foul sin, gathering head,
> Shall break into corruption"—so went on,
> Foretelling this same time's condition
> And the division of our amity.
> *Warwick.* There is a history in all men's lives,
>   Figuring the nature of the times deceas'd,
>   The which observ'd, a man may prophesy,

> With a near aim, of the main chance of things
> As yet not come to life.
>
> (*2 Henry IV*, III.i.65–84)

The long-range perspectives, whether of past or future, tend to endow immediate actions with something like the status of myth, thus conferring upon them a cultural dignity and significance they might otherwise lack. This dilation or expansion of a particular political context thus deepens the dramatic resonance effectively. Richard of Bordeaux, for instance, sees his own tragedy as part of a venerable literary tradition: the "lamentable tale of me" (*Richard II*, V.i.44) that he enjoins his wife to narrate to future auditors in France becomes one more addition to that swelling anthology of "sad stories of the death of kings" (III.ii.156) to which he had earlier referred. But Richard becomes the type of the murdered and desecrated monarch, not merely another example, through the literary and biblical traditions with which he so self-consciously associates himself. And Henry V before Agincourt inspires his troops with the promise that their bravery against almost impossible odds will enshrine them forever in the national memory:

> He that shall see this day, and live old age,
> Will yearly on the vigil feast his neighbors,
> And say, "Tomorrow is Saint Crispian."
> Then will he strip his sleeve and show his scars,
> And say, "These wounds I had on Crispin's day."
> Old men forget; yet all shall be forgot,
> But he'll remember with advantages
> What feats he did that day. Then shall our names,
> Familiar in his mouth as household words,
> Harry the King, Bedford and Exeter,
> Warwick and Talbot, Salisbury and Gloucester,
> Be in their flowing cups freshly rememb'red.
> This story shall the good man teach his son;
> And Crispin Crispian shall ne'er go by,
> From this day to the ending of the world,
> But we in it shall be remembered—
> We few, we happy few, we band of brothers.
>
> (*Henry V*, IV.iii.44–60)

Nor is the tetralogy without its comic memories. Shallow lives wholly in the distant past—the frail relic of a bygone age the sexual excitements of which he vastly exaggerates in the impotence of his present condition: "Jesu, Jesu, the mad days that I have spent!" (*2 Henry IV*, III.ii.33). The even wispier Silence joins the concept of time past to a unique compound of pathos and hilarity. When Silence, somewhat surprisingly, breaks into a drinking song and Falstaff is astonished to discover that he possesses enough vocal energy for the feat, the old man's response is delicious: "Who I? I have been merry twice and once ere now" (V.iii.39–40).

IV

Thus does Shakespeare weave the mingled yarn of pastness, presentness, and futurity into the richest of dramatic tapestries. Prince Hal can drink in Eastcheap with Poins while reminding us of our common parent (he refers in passing to "the old days of goodman Adam" [*1 Henry IV*, II.iv.93]), and Hotspur can locate his own demise in the wider context of time's ultimate cessation at the last trump. But if, in some sense, Shakespeare takes all of time for his province, what finally may we say that his concept of it was?

The answer must be, I think, that the complexity of the individual plays—not to mention the additional complexity of their interrelatedness—makes it hazardous to affix labels. Many attitudes toward time are embodied in the plays I have been discussing, and there are still others to be found elsewhere in Shakespeare. But by way of conclusion it might be well to notice that the second tetralogy ends paradoxically with the same mixture of comic and tragic implications about time that we have been remarking throughout the series. The emergence of Prince Hal as "the mirror of all Christian kings" (*Henry V*, II; Prologue, l. 6) and the miraculous victor of Agincourt suggests the happy resolution of comedy. In marrying Katharine and joining England to France, Henry V concludes the final play in a way that reminds us of a romance structure with its "happily-ever-after" sense of finality. Certainly the closure of this history play implies a sunnier future for the nation than we have ever had reason to expect at earlier points in the historical sequence. England under Henry seems to have realized her greatest and most heroic potential, and Agincourt seems to have culminated her finest hour.

But the epilogue sounds a disquieting chord, reminding the audience that Henry's reign, however "greatly lived," was but a "small time" (l. 5). The longer shadow that time inevitably casts darkened the glory of "this star of England" (l. 6), and the poet sadly reminds us that Henry's son, who inherited the crown as a babe in arms, "lost France" through his weakness and, in the civil chaos that ensued, once more "made his England bleed" (l. 12). The historical wheel, in other words, continues to revolve, and in this case, it comes full circle, for Shakespeare returns our memories to the internecine strife that he had dramatized in his earliest chronicle plays, the three parts of *Henry VI*. And as if this were not enough to dampen the comic optimism, Shakespeare gives us a funny but also pathetic account of Falstaff's death through the uncomprehending lips of Mistress Quickly. If the whirligig of time has brought Henry V success as a king, it has also brought in its revenges, for it diminishes him as a man through the rejection and loss of his most affectionate and emotionally vital companion.

Part III

The Family

V PON a Cock, heere *Ganimede* doth fit,
   Who erft rode mounted on *IOVES* Eagles back,
One hand holdes *Circes* wand, and ioind with it,
A cup top-fil'd with poifon, deadly black:
   The other Meddals, of bafe mettals wrought,
   With fundry moneyes, counterfeit and nought.

Thefe be thofe crimes, abhorr'd of God and man,
Which Iuftice fhould correct, with lawes fevere,
In * *Ganimed*, the foule Sodomitan:
Within the Cock, vile inceft doth appeare:
   Witchcraft, and murder, by that cup and wand,
   And by the reft, falfe coine you vnderftand.

* O fuge te tene-
ræ puerorum cre-
dere turbæ,
Nam caufam in-
iufti
femper amoris
habent.
Tibullus.

Ifta a te puniantur (ô Rex) ne tu pro illis puniaris.   Ciprian.
de vtilitate Pœnitentiæ.

Virtutem

3. Emblem of Ganymede riding a cock, from Henry Peacham's *Minerva Britanna, Or a Garden of Heroical Deuises* (London, 1612), p. 48

10

"A Little More than Kin, and Less than Kind": Incest, Intimacy, Narcissism, and Identity in Elizabethan and Stuart Drama

I

After Shakespeare makes Hamlet bemoan the "most wicked speed" with which his mother and uncle have posted to "incestuous sheets" (*Hamlet*, I.ii.156–157), the hero sustains the shock of learning from the Ghost that "the royal bed of Denmark," now "A couch for luxury and damned incest" (I.v.83–84), shelters not only a fratricide but also a probable adulteress. In this sequence the dramatist was raising a sensational subject guaranteed simultaneously to horrify and attract sophisticated thinkers and ignorant groundlings alike. That Renaissance culture was fascinated by forbidden forms of sexuality—especially desire within the confines of the family—is attested by the popularity of the subject in the poetry, prose fiction, and drama of the period. Spenser, for instance, touched upon it in *The Faerie Queene* (III.vii.47, 48; III.xi.3, 4), allegorizing the most extreme form of unchastity imaginable in the twin giants Ollyphant and Argante, monsters incestuously conceived by a Titaness in union with her own son, who reduplicated the incest of their conception by uniting with each other while still in the womb. More centrally, Milton adapted Saint James's homily on the unholy triad of lust, sin, and death (James 1:15) in a similarly double incest: in *Paradise Lost* (II, 761–767) Satan fathers Death upon Sin (his own daughter); then Death rapes the figure who has become both his mother and his sister.

Arthurian romance also made much of incest. In Malory's redaction of the legend, for instance, King Arthur begets his bastard son Mordred upon his sister Morgause; then Mordred compounds the incestuous circumstances of his engendering by seeking to commit adultery with Guenevere, his stepmother—a notorious example of the "bold bawdrye" of which Ascham so disapproved in *The Scholemaster* (1570).[1] Since Arthur expires from a wound inflicted by Mordred, incest might well be thought to condition the events leading to his death. Thomas Hughes's Senecan tragedy, *The Misfortunes of Arthur* (1588), incorporated the tradition of fatal incest and transmitted it to the stage. Continental writers of fiction who treated incest include such well-known names as Marguerite of Navarre, Basile, Bandello, Cinthio, and Montemayor, many of whose tales readily found their way into English.[2] Greene's *Pandosto* (Shakespeare's source

141

for *The Winter's Tale*) and the story of Apollonius of Tyre (which lies behind *Pericles*) are both typical of romance in their inclusion of the incest motif.

Reviewing my somewhat desultory reading of Renaissance plays, I count no fewer than thirty-eight dramatists who made various uses of the incest theme—mostly in plots but occasionally also in imagery—in some sixty comedies, tragedies, tragicomedies, moralities, histories, romances, and pastorals. The range of genres is no less impressive than the widespread authorship. Shakespeare himself produced six plays in which incest figures directly or by implication—*Richard III* (a history), *Hamlet* and *Lear* (tragedies), *The Comedy of Errors* (a Plautine farce), *Measure for Measure* (a dark comedy), and *Pericles* (a romance);[3] and *All's Well That Ends Well* and *Henry VIII*, for reasons that will become apparent later, might be added to the Shakespearean list, although neither play actually mentions incest or specifically underlines any sexual impropriety in connection with it. But the roster extends also to dramas by Phillip, Gascoigne, Preston, Lyly, Lodge, Greene, Peele, Hughes, Chettle, Haughton, Jonson, Marston, Chapman, Dekker, Mason, Barnes, Webster, Beaumont and Fletcher, Middleton, Tourneur, Ford, Massinger, Shirley, Wilson, and Brome. Seven of the *Tenne Tragedies* of Seneca, collected by Thomas Newton in 1581 and translated by himself, Jasper Heywood, and others, involve incest directly or as background; and even courtly and academic amateurs such as Margaret Cavendish, Walter Montague, Samuel Harding, Joseph Rutter, Lodowick Carlell, Thomas Randolph, and Sir John Suckling wrote plays that turn on incest.[4] It is therefore possible to deny unequivocally a recent statement by Denis Gauer, a writer on Ford, that "incest has seldom been treated by literature or drama,"[5] and to suggest that Marlowe alone among the playwrights of the first rank avoided the topic as a subject for dramatization—perhaps because homosexuality, an alternative form of sexual nonconformity, engaged his attention more urgently.

Renaissance concern with the theatrical possibilities of incest is hardly surprising. Freud in *Civilization and Its Discontents* held that the almost universal prohibition in Western culture against coition with close relatives amounted to "perhaps the most drastic mutilation which man's erotic life has in all time experienced."[6] According to Freud and his school, social order has always required us to resist our primary instinctual passion for the parent of the opposite sex, repressing or diverting it to more acceptable objects; nevertheless, the depth and pervasiveness of the resulting neuroses continue to prove, as Freud demonstrates, how formidable and difficult the process of transference or sublimation inevitably becomes. Anthropology, the handmaiden of psychology, has likewise tended to insist on the centrality of the incest taboo for the construction and development of civilization.[7] One can say, then, that Elizabethan drama, like the art of other periods, simply represents a particularly imaginative attempt to take account of socio-psychological tensions inherent in the human situation—the more so, perhaps, because drama as a genre especially thrives on such conflicts. I would suggest, however, that special environmental factors more proximate than the Oedipal archetype account for the particular proliferation of incest stories and figures of speech on the Elizabethan stage. The most important of these intellectual and sociological pressures may be attributed to the humanistic literary tradition, the emotional climate within the family, and recent dynastic history (with its related theological debates concerning marriage, divorce, and remarriage).

II

Steeped as they were in classical mythology and history, the Elizabethans were constantly being reminded in their reading of incestuous situations and relationships. Plato, in *The Republic*, had notably relaxed traditional restrictions against incest for the purpose of breeding intellectual strength through eugenics, even going so far as to propose that "the law [of the ideal city] will allow brothers and sisters to cohabit if the lot so falls out and the Delphic oracle approves." Tacitus and Suetonius had gossiped about the lurid incests of the Roman emperors—of Claudius's marriage to his niece Agrippina, of Nero's dalliance with his mother (that same Agrippina who, as a younger woman, had attracted his stepfather), of Caligula's copulation with two different sisters, and of Domitian's seduction of his niece. Cicero in his *Pro Caelio* had hinted at the sexual liaison between the notorious Clodia (Catullus's "Lesbia") and her brother Publius Clodius, while Quintus Cicero, Asconius, and Plutarch (in works that Jonson would use as the basis for a passage in his second Roman tragedy) recounted how Catiline had debauched both his sister and his daughter. Classical drama, both Greek and Roman, was replete with incest, Sophocles, Euripides, Aristophanes, Seneca, Plautus, Terence, and Menander all being cases in point. Seneca was especially fertile ground, for the English translations mentioned above include dramatizations of the stories of Thyestes, Hippolytus, Oedipus, Agamemnon, and Octavia, all of which turn to some extent on incestuous affairs. Thyestes deflowered both his sister-in-law Aerope and his daughter Pelopeia; Hippolytus was seduced by his mother Phaedra; Oedipus slept unwittingly with his mother Jocasta (Gascoigne and Kinwelmersh adapted the Euripidean version of the same myth in their drama, *Jocasta*); Agamemnon's wife Clytemnestra took Aegisthus (the offspring of Thyestes' incestuous union with Pelopeia) as her lover; and Octavia, daughter of the emperor Claudius, married Nero, her uncle.

Juvenal made seduction inside the family circle one of his targets in *Satire I*, while in *Satire II* he alluded pointedly to the emperor Domitian's incest with his niece Julia, to be imitated by Marston, who invoked the same scandal to spice up *The Scourge of Villanie* (1598). Herodotus related the barbaric and incestuous monstrosities of Cambyses, King of Persia, in an account that indirectly became the source for Thomas Preston's early Elizabethan shocker. And the promiscuous life of Cleopatra, who successively married two of her brothers in accordance with the incestuous tradition of the house of Ptolemy, obviously riveted the Renaissance imagination; Dio Cassius (in a passage that Shakespeare may have known) mentioned how Julius Caesar, when the Queen of Egypt was his mistress, settled both her and her brother-husband in his house at Rome "so that he . . . derived an ill repute on account of both of them." The mythographers Parthenius and Hyginus both recounted the familiar tale of how Harpalyce was ravished by her father Clymenus, who was later horribly punished (like Thyestes) by having his son, the product of the incest, served up to him in a meal. And Fulgentius moralized the lusts of Semiramis, legendary Queen of Assyria, who "flamed with desire for her own son" Ninus, consuming "her dignity as a mother" to become "his bride," the horrors of which story the Italian playwright Muzio Manfredi dramatized on the stage in 1593.[8]

But the poet whom everyone read was of course Ovid, who, in his *Heroides* (XI), drew upon the myth of the children of Aeolus. In this legend five pairs of brothers and sisters, apparently not realizing the forbidden nature of their attraction, coupled with each other after the example of their youngest siblings Macareus and Canace. As a consequence, Canace was forced to commit suicide while the parallel incests, perhaps because the participants enjoyed divine status, went unpunished.[9] The *Metamorphoses* (both in the original and in Golding's famous translation) provided an even more accessible collection of incest myths. Here one could read of Nyctimene's defiling of her father's bed (II, 742–745), of Menephron's rape of his mother (VII, 492–494), of Byblis's ungovernable lust for her twin brother Caune (she pursued him relentlessly until frustration turned her into a weeping fountain [IX, 542–786]), of Myrrha's passion for her father King Cinyras, from whose union Adonis sprang forth (X, 327–588), and of Phaedra's perverse attraction to her stepson Hippolytus and its fatal consequences (XV, 550–613).[10]

At one point in Ovid's extraordinarily popular poem Byblis bewails the fate of mortals, who, unlike the gods, are denied the pleasure of incestuous cohabitation. She envies Saturn and Ops, Oceanus and Tethys, Jupiter and Juno, and the children of Aeolus, all of whom (in Golding's words) "matched with theyr [brothers and] susters" without reproach and therefore "are farre in better case than wee" (IX, 590–591). A little later Ovid makes Myrrha extend her envy to "dame nature" because that lady embraces within the pale of her sexual tolerance all earthly creatures *except* human beings: how can incest infringe the "bondes of godlynesse" when even beasts enjoy a privilege proscribed to mankind?

> The Hecfer [i.e., heifer] thinkes no shame
> Too beare her father on her backe: The Horse beestrydes the same
> Of whom he is the syre: The Gote dooth bucke the Kid that hee
> Himself begate: and birdes doo tread the self same birdes wee see
> Of whom they hatched were before. In happye cace they are
> That may doo so without offence. But mans malicious care
> Hath made a brydle for it self, and spyghtfull lawes restreyne
> The things that nature setteth free.
>
> (X, 360–367)[11]

In these passages Ovid visualizes the plight of human sexuality as essentially tragic: humankind is compelled by its very nature to forgo desires that both deities and animals may indulge without restraint but that men and women, uniquely, can pursue only at the cost of their certain destruction.

Incestuous lovers on the Jacobean and Caroline stage sometimes complain in just such Ovidian terms, seeking to justify forbidden longings against the tyranny of the moral law. Thus Arbasces in Beaumont and Fletcher's *A King and No King* can condemn himself for bestial appetite in lusting for his supposed sister Panthea yet wish that he could live uninhibited by the scruples inherent to his humanity:

> Accursed man,
> Thou bought'st thy reason at too dear a rate,
> For thou hast all thy actions bounded in
> With curious rules when every beast is free.
> What is there that acknowledges a kindred
> But wretched man? Whoever saw the bull

Fearfully leave the heifer that he lik'd
Because they had one dam?
(IV.iv.131–138)[12]

Giovanni in Ford's *'Tis Pity She's a Whore* tries to rationalize his incestuous desire for Annabella in the opposite way by identifying her, in a perverted kind of Platonism, with deity:

Must I not praise
That beauty which, if framed anew, the gods
Would make a god of if they had it there,
And kneel to it, as I do kneel to them?
(I.i.20–23)[13]

(This line of reasoning is not far removed from that of King Rasni in Greene and Lodge's *A Looking Glass for London and England* [1590], who tries to justify his marriage to a sister Remilia by citing the incest of Jupiter and Juno as a precedent [I.i.87–91].) Ford's confused young man, however, also tries to rationalize his obsession on grounds of the natural affinity between *human* siblings:

Say that we had one father, say one womb
(Curse to my joys!) gave both us life and birth;
Are we not therefore each to other bound
So much the more by nature? by the links
Of blood, of reason? nay, if you will have 't,
Even of religion, to be ever one,
One soul, one flesh, one love, one heart, one *all*?
(I.i.28–34)

And again: "Nearness in birth or blood doth but persuade / A nearer nearness of affection" (I.ii.239–240).

Giovanni's argument from nature is deliberate and quasi-logical, unlike the attitude of Aeolus's sons and daughters who, failing to understand "that incest among humans was displeasing to the gods," as Robert Graves phrases it, "innocently paired off . . . as husbands and wives." But the naïve lovers of Montemayor's incest story in *Diana* take a line similar to that of Ford's ardent youth by suggesting that their supposed kinship actually accounts for the erotic attraction they feel toward each other:

But tel me now (I pray thee) what certaintie hast thou, that we are brother and sister? No other (saide she) then of the great love I beare thee. . . . And if we were not brother and sister (saide I) wouldest thou then love me so much as thou dost? . . . I understand thee not said she, but (me thinkes) (being brother and sister) it binds us to love one another naturally.[14]

Classical literature and myth, together with their later redactions, then, provided ample precedent for the ambivalent attitude toward incest in the drama of Shakespeare's age— precedents that not only reinforced the Judeo-Christian horror of sexual relationships within the family but also offered sympathy for persons who violated, or wished to violate, the taboo.

In a sizable number of Renaissance plays, usually comic or tragicomic, the plot turns on the amorous attraction of supposed brothers and sisters who cannot marry until the fact that they are congenitally unrelated emerges surprisingly at the denouement; or, alternatively, on the obverse of this pattern—that is, on love affairs between apparently unrelated persons whose incestuous marriages are prevented almost at the steps of the altar by a revelation of their true parentage. In the latter situation, theatrical sleight of hand typically permits the threatened incests to be converted into nuptial realignments that satisfy the requirements of social respectability and romantic fulfillment at the same time.[15] The dramas of averted incest include titles as diverse as Lyly's *Mother Bombie*, Beaumont and Fletcher's *A King and No King*, Middleton's *No Wit, No Help Like a Woman's*, Shirley's *The Coronation* and *The Court Secret*, Randolph's *The Jealous Lovers*, and Carlell's *The Deserving Favorite*. Plays that involve the incest-mistaken identity nexus more tangentially or obliquely are Jonson's *The Case Is Altered*, Fletcher's *Women Pleased*, Massinger's *The Guardian*, and Shirley's *The Opportunity*. An interesting reversal of the pattern of incest avoidance appears in Shirley's *The Gentleman of Venice*, a comedy in which the hidden kinship of two lovers (they are first cousins only) actually makes an otherwise unacceptable marriage possible; for when the noble-spirited and gently spoken hero of this play (a gardener named Giovanni) turns out to be the Duke's son (by reason of babies secretly exchanged in their cradles), he now qualifies for the hand of a royal lady. Giovanni's instinctive drift toward a blood relation, despite her initial spurning of him as a mere commoner, only proves that heredity is a better guide to the discovery of a fitting spouse than humility, however crucial the latter may in fact have been. What we may call a permissible incest—that is, marriage that threatens but never actually violates the carefully drawn boundaries of illicit consanguinity—becomes meritorious in Shirley's play and validates the time-honored aristocratic and romantic principle that blood will tell.

III

The wide appeal of plots that connect the threat or magnetic pull of incest with confusions of identity would seem to reflect a deep insecurity in upper-class families of the period about genetic origin and lineage. Sons and daughters of more prominent families were often farmed out to wet nurses in their infancy and thereby deprived as children of parental nurture and affection. The literary cliché, anciently derived from romance tradition, of the midwife or wet nurse who substitutes her own child or that of a confidante for that of her master (usually out of political or economic motives) must have raised in the minds of some playgoers the specter of illegitimacy, if it did not stimulate fantasies of being elevated suddenly to wealth and noble rank.

Lawrence Stone in his revealing study of the emotional and sexual climate of the family in Renaissance England describes a number of conditions that support the hypothesis that links the desire for closer intimacy with uneasiness about identity. Although respect for patriarchal authority was strongly enforced, little in Elizabethan upper-class houses sustained close affectional ties within the nucleus. Personal relationships between husbands and wives, between parents and children, and between siblings of the same sex tended to be cool if not strife-ridden and acrimonious. The number of bastard children who figure in Elizabethan and Stuart plays is partly a reflection of the numerous adulteries that constantly disrupted family harmony, particularly at the upper and lower ends of the social spectrum. Church canons forbidding the divorce of unhappily wedded partners undoubtedly encouraged sexual infidelity, and indeed the discovery of incest or arguments about too close a genealogical affinity could be among the few valid excuses for dissolving a marriage. Blood or family ties, then, were likely to be regarded as having immense political and social importance, even as their emotional implications might either threaten or subversively excite. As Stone puts it, "marriage meant not so much intimate association with an individual as entry into a new world of the spouse's relatives, uncles, nephews and distant cousins. . . . Kinship was an institution whose purpose was the mutual economic, social and psychological advancement of the group."[16] The emotional or psychological gratification of individuals enjoyed very low priority and was not consid- ered to be a rational objective of marriage, which, in any case, was likely to be decided by one's parents or guardian on grounds wholly unrelated to empathic or romantic considerations.

Primogeniture tended to stir up animosities between the heir to an estate and his younger brothers, whose prospects for a secure future would be uncertain at best, unless, of course, the heir should meet with some untimely (and perhaps secretly desired) misfortune. Rivalry among marriageable daughters over which of them should be auc- tioned off first to a rich or influential spouse, and with how generous a dowry, could be as intense as that between brothers. Shakespeare gives us some sense of the all-too- common malaise between siblings in *The Taming of the Shrew*, *As You Like It*, and *King Lear*, whereas Webster's two great tragedies raise hostility between brothers and between brothers and sisters to the level of criminal pathology.

George Wilkins's *The Miseries of Enforced Marriage* (1607), a play based to some extent on historical persons, presents a veritable anthology of strained family situations— a young man compelled by his autocratic guardian to desert his true love and marry a girl for whom he has no feeling, a sister whose chief motive for marriage is the desire to relieve the poverty of her brothers, a son who is glad to learn of his father's death, and the intense jealousy of deprived younger brothers, directed against an elder spend- thrift one. Heywood and Rowley's domestic drama, *Fortune by Land and Sea* (c. 1607– 09), also reflects a significant demystification of the family. Here Philip Harding is reduced to menial status in his own household by a tyrannical father (who intends to disinherit him) for presuming, for romantic reasons, to marry a girl of no means, while two hateful younger sons, spoiled, irresponsible, and grasping, despise their older brother and are finally punished for their arrogance by being made to depend upon him totally, once he has come into the family estate. In a more satiric vein, city comedies by Jonson (such as *Volpone* and *Epicoene*) and by Middleton (such as *The Family of Love*, *A Trick to Catch the Old One*, and *A Chaste Maid in Cheapside*) also depict family life as characterized by suspicion, jealousy, greed, fragmentation, and sexual infidelity. Given the predictable tensions between siblings of the same sex and between offspring and parents who often forced them into marital alliances for nakedly unromantic purposes, it is hardly unlikely that many children grew up with the simultaneous fear of, and unsatisfied need for, greater intimacy with their closest kin.

Since so many of the incestuous or would-be incestuous relationships in Elizabethan drama concern involvements between brothers and sisters, it is interesting to notice in Stone's analysis the relative absence of reasons to assume coolness or affectional distance between sons and daughters of the same household. It is probably more than mere coincidence, for instance, that the affection of the two brother-and-sister pairs in *Fortune by Land and Sea* (Susan Forrest and young Forrest, Anne Harding and her brother, a merchant) is as warm as any in the play—a play, as has been pointed out, that makes a maltreated elder son the brunt of ill feeling from both his father and his younger brothers. Indeed, as Stone suggests, "the brother-sister relationship" in the sixteenth and seventeenth centuries, simply because it would be comparatively untainted by marital and economic pressures, may often have been "the closest in the family."[17] If this was true, the social context may throw light upon the darkly troubled love-hatred of characters like Vittoria and Flamineo in *The White Devil* or of Duke Ferdinand and the title figure of *The Duchess of Malfi* with its strong infusion of fraternal sadomasochism and undertow of carnal attraction. Frank Whigham even goes so far as to interpret Ferdinand's incestuous impulse toward his sister, because it is coupled with his contempt for the baseness of her alliance to a mere servant, as a radical sexualization of the threatened aristocrat's fear of the contamination of his class; in this reading, a smotheringly close attraction to a sister becomes a symbol of the need to insist upon endogamy within a rigidly defined elite—"a *social posture* of hysterical compensation—a desperate expression of the desire to evade degrading association with inferiors."[18]

As for the numerous dramatic plots that feature lovers who do not know that they are brother and sister, it is tempting to regard these as symbolic expressions of an unconscious desire for closer emotional affinity within families that tend to deny or deprecate such intimacies. Such plays usually awaken their lovers to a fresh or heightened sense of identity through a happy ending that discloses their true parentage, while releasing them to marry in a way that unites the satisfactions of intimacy with economic, political, and class approval—that is, with the values of a limited exogamy on which family stability and social enhancement are taken to depend. Such plays, in other words, may be interpreted as gratifying their audiences through a kind of psycho-sociological wish-fulfillment by means of the manipulations of a theatrical technique that capitalizes on both predictability and surprise.

Dramatists sometimes complicate our responses to the more tragic examples of incestuous involvement on the stage by silhouetting the forbidden attraction against a backdrop of worldliness, vulgarity, cynicism, or brutality. In *Women Beware Women*, for instance, Middleton forces us to assess Isabella's involvement in a sexual liaison with Hippolito (her uncle), by contrasting it with the most repellent of alternatives—forced marriage to the rich but imbecilic Ward, whom the reluctant bride "loathe[s] . . . more than beauty can hate death / Or age, her spiteful neighbour" (II.i.84–85).[19] Isabella must be trotted out for inspection by her repulsive and witless bridegroom like a brood mare at Smithfield Market to have her "good parts" (III.iii.5)—her hair, her eyes, her nose, her teeth, her breasts, her voice, her bum, her posture—put on public display for the consideration of the prospective wife-shopper. This degrading commercial ritual makes the competing union between uncle and niece almost desirable by comparison, and, in fact, Middleton uses the contrast to dramatize a pattern of emotional displacement that tends to equate incest with the only psychosexual fulfillment available to lovers in the play.

Guardiano, uncle to the Ward and cynical promoter of the unsuitable marriage, describes Isabella's close companionship with Hippolito before he pushes his idiot nephew in her direction:

> *Guardiano.*   take one mark more:
> Thou shalt ne'er find her hand out of her uncle's,
> Or else his out of hers, if she be near him.
> The love of kindred never yet stuck closer
> Than theirs to one another; he that weds her
> Marries her uncle's heart too.
> *Ward.*   Say you so, sir,
> Then I'll be asked i' th' church to both of them.
>
> (III.iii.14–20)

And, in fact, Isabella's father—a man who thinks of his daughter as a mere breeding machine—has commented already on the special intimacy between his brother and her:

> Look out her uncle, and y' are sure of her.
> Those two are ne'er asunder; they've been heard
> In argument [i.e., conversation] at midnight, moonshine nights
> Are noondays with them: they walk out their sleeps,
> Or rather at those hours appear like those
> That walk in 'em, for so they did to me.
> Look you, I told you truth; they're like a chain:
> Draw but one link, all follows.
>
> (I.ii.62–69)

To which Guardiano responds with ironic blindness: "Oh affinity . . . / 'Tis work clean wrought, for there's no lust, but love in 't, / And that abundantly" (I.ii.69–72).

In her distress at being paired off lovelessly with a mental defective, Isabella, naturally enough, turns to Hippolito, her "best friend" (I.ii.186), who loves her "dearlier than an uncle can," "as a man loves his wife" (I.ii.211–217). Hippolito, for all the "black lust" (IV.ii.66) of his incestuous behavior and, later, his murderous mission against Leantio (the anti-hero of the coördinate plot), at least possesses intelligence; and when the retarded Ward wants a demonstration of Isabella's dancing (Middleton gives the dancing distinctly sexual overtones), it is symbolically her uncle rather than the oafish fiancé who takes her as partner on the floor. Afterward, when the Ward himself attempts to dance with his would-be wife, the stage direction tells us that *"he ridiculously imitates Hippolito"* (III.iii.227). The sexual displacement is dramatized in terms of a social ritual at once comic and sinister.

But Middleton complicates responses still further, as Dodson has argued,[20] by suggesting that Livia, the sophisticated, amoral worldling of the tragedy, diverts her potentially incestuous affinity for her brother by subconsciously displacing it upon her niece. Early in the play she speaks to Hippolito in language of suspiciously unique ardor:

> *Livia.* My best and dearest brother, I could dwell here;
> There is not such another seat on earth

> Where all good parts better express themselves.
> *Hippolito*. You'll make me blush anon.
> *Livia*. . . . .
> thou art all a feast,
> And she that has thee a most happy guest.
> Prithee cheer up thy niece with special counsel.
> (I.ii.144–151)

The quasi-erotic attraction of sister to brother expresses itself as a smoothing of the way for his seduction of his more youthful and naïve female relation, a girl whom they both call niece.

Glossing over Hippolito's moral scruples as of no true importance compared to the gratification of his physical desire, Livia relieves his "fearful" and guilty "grief" (II.i.20) by arranging to cover the incest with the lie (to Isabella) that the younger woman is not in fact related to him at all:

> 'tis but a hazarding
> Of grace and virtue, and I can bring forth
> As pleasant fruits as sensuality wishes
> In all her teeming longings. This I can do.
>
> . . . .
> You are not the first, brother, has attempted
> Things more forbidden than this seems to be.
> (II.i.29–47)

Then, having dealt with her half-acknowledged desire for her brother by rechanneling it into a sexual union of uncle and niece, Livia supplies her own carnal needs by taking on as a surrogate the virile young bourgeois Leantio, whose adulterous wife Bianca has just displaced him by allowing herself, through naïve entrapment, to become the mistress of a duke. *Women Beware Women*, as its title subtly implies, articulates a tangle of sexual and emotional substitutions in which incest becomes a significant factor in the symbolism. The tragedy explores kinship in its biological, moral, social, and psychosexual dimensions, making brilliant dramatic capital out of their elaborate, subtle, and ironic cross-relations.

The figure of the coarse and brutal husband with whom a more refined woman is forced to cohabit appears in two of Ford's major plays. In both cases incest becomes part of the contrastive structure. In *'Tis Pity She's a Whore* the neurotic, sensitive, and intellectually gifted student Giovanni is set off, in his hothouse obsession for his sister Annabella, against a trio of suitors, each of them less attractive than he—Grimaldi (the cowardly cutthroat who ambushes rivals in the dark), Bergetto (a parcel of stupidity cut from the same cloth as Middleton's Ward), and Soranzo (the hypocritical philanderer whom Annabella actually marries to conceal the shame of her brother's having made her pregnant). Ford portrays Soranzo as a more acceptable spouse for Annabella than his two rivals, but after he discovers that his wife is with child, he becomes a jealous monster of the most rebarbative sort, physically abusing her onstage as a "notable harlot," raging at her "hot itch and plurisy of lust" (IV.iii.4–8), and threatening (in an ironic prolepsis of Giovanni's incestuous sacrifice) to "rip up [her] heart" so that he may discover the identity of "the prodigious lecher" who has supplanted him and "Tear" him "joint by joint" (IV.iii.53–55) with his teeth. Ultimately, of course, Giovanni exceeds even Soranzo's monstrosity when, having turned madman, he ritually murders his sister to preserve the perverted exclusiveness of their special and (to him) inviolable love; but until the tragic climax, Ford treats the incestuous relationship with considerable sympathy—not as a bestial abomination but as a tragic but humanly comprehensible error, in comparison with which arranged and affectionless marriages are crude, destructive, and even barbaric.

The Broken Heart, at one point, also dramatizes the same contrast between a sensitive brother-sister intimacy and the "torture" and "barbarous thraldom" (I.i.49–54)[21] of the lady's marriage to an insanely jealous, superannuated dotard. Bassanes, the suspicious old man who keeps his beautiful wife under lock and key, has virtually "buried" Penthea in her own "bride-bed" (II.ii.38). Ironically, it is the brother Ithocles who has unnaturally condemned his sister to this living hell, but in a private reunion with her that underscores the mysterious emotional affinity of long-separated twins, the brother repents his former cruelty and shares with Penthea the secret of his own love for the Princess Calantha, which he dares not communicate even to his closest friend or to the lady herself.

Ford's dialogue verges on the erotic, mingling Ithocles' "languishing affections" (III.ii.53), that is, his remorse for his wrecking of Penthea's emotional happiness, his joy at being reunited with her, and his need to relieve a bottled up desire for Calantha by confessing it to the sole confidante who may serve immediately as a surrogate object of devotion and, later on, as an intercessor or proxy wooer:

> *Ithocles.* Sit nearer, sister, to me; nearer yet.
>   We had one father, in one womb took life,
>   Were brought up twins together, yet have lived
>   At distance like two strangers. I could wish
>   That the first pillow whereon I was cradled
>   Had proved to me a grave.
> *Penthea.*   You had been happy.
>   Then had you never known that sin of life
>   Which blots all following glories with a vengeance,
>   For forfeiting the last will of the dead,
>   From whom you had your being.
> *Ithocles.*   Sad Penthea,
>   Thou canst not be too cruel. My rash spleen
>   Hath with a violent hand plucked from thy bosom
>   A lover-blest heart, to grind it into dust;
>   For which mine's now a-breaking.
>
> . . . .
>
> *Penthea.*   Pray kill me.
>   Rid me from living with a jealous husband.
>   Then we will join in friendship, be again
>   Brother and sister.
>
>   (III.ii.33–67)

It is scarcely astonishing that the brutish Bassanes, excluded from this exquisite, quasi-amorous closeness, breaks in upon it with a drawn dagger, wildly accusing his wife of "bed-sports" and the "swine-security of bestial incest" (III.ii.135–150). Bassanes' rage is almost comic in its violence—a stage illustration of what Burton describes in *The Anatomy of Melancholy* under the category of postnuptial love melancholia. Prominent among the symptoms of such husbandly jealousy is the "suspecting not strangers only, but brothers and sisters, father and mother, nearest and dearest friends."[22] Soranzo in *'Tis Pity* and Bassanes in *The Broken Heart* both approach the status of Burtonian caricature in their most irrational moments; hence, in context, they make intimacies between brother and sister, whether overtly incestuous or not, seem comparatively refined and idealistic. In any case Ford's Annabella and Penthea, as well as Middleton's Isabella—each one a victim of enforced marriage—are all complex women and suffer the indignity of being paired with gross, stupid, or unfeeling men who treat them as mere goods and chattels. Such women remind us of Penelope Devereux, the "Stella" of Sidney's sonnets, who was married off in youth to the intellectually limited Baron Rich (an unattractive peer whose vast wealth made a pun of his name). This unhappy match proved so unpalatable that the couple soon separated; and it is an index of the degree to which respectable society must have sympathized with her plight that Lady Rich was permitted to live in open adultery with Charles Blount, Lord Mountjoy, whose several children she bore. It is also relevant to note that throughout her marital difficulties she remained especially close to her brother, the Earl of Essex, at whose house in the Strand she was often resident. Lady Rich's admirer, Sir Philip Sidney, as his dedication of the *Arcadia* shows, was himself particularly fond of his sister Mary; the gossipmongering John Aubrey in his *Brief Lives* even passes on the report of certain "old Gentlemen" that "there was so great love between" them that "they lay together, and it was thought the first Philip Earle of Pembroke was begot by him, but he inherited not the witt of either brother or sister."[23]

IV

If the domestic and marital climate of Renaissance England made for ambivalent attitudes toward incest, both stimulating and repressing it by turns, the political and theological debates of the period only confused matters further. Indeed we may speculate whether psychic conflicts that surfaced or half surfaced within the home would not inevitably be mirrored, in some manifestation or other, at the more public levels of Church and State. With the Reformation came considerable relaxation of the medieval canons prohibiting marriage between distant cousins and between persons related ecclesiastically such as godparents and godchildren. In 1563 Matthew Parker, Elizabeth's Archbishop of Canterbury, issued a table reducing to thirty the relationships (counting the male and female equivalents together) that fell within the proscribed degrees of kindred and affinity. By 1603 these had become canonical in ecclesiastical law, and modern reprints of the Anglican Prayer Book of 1662, still in official use in England, often append a table of twenty-five prohibited relationships along with the Thirty-nine Articles. It was not until 1907 that Parliament repealed the old law prohibiting marriage between brothers and sisters-in-law, and indeed the history of proscribed degrees in matrimony is forbiddingly labyrinthine. Not surprisingly, there was much disagreement and uncertainty in the sixteenth century on the subject as well as conflict on certain points between ecclesiastical and civil law.[24]

In any event, conservative views continued to engage more liberal ones throughout the Tudor and early Stuart reigns. Marriages within the same family for purposes of dynastic expansion and aggrandizement were frequently sought and solemnized, usually requiring a papal or archiepiscopal dispensation. Richard III in Shakespeare's play attempts unsuccessfully to marry his niece, Elizabeth of York, with a view to legitimating his tenure of the crown and co-opting possible opposition.[25] The marriage that takes place instead between Elizabeth and Henry Tudor is portrayed as uniting at long last the white rose with the red. The symbolic, propagandistic, and political desirability of such a union is obvious in the play, but Shakespeare makes little of the actual degrees of kindred and affinity between the new king and queen (they descended in different branches from a common ancestor—Catherine Swynford, third wife of John of Gaunt) and ignores the historical fact that special permission from the pope was required to legalize their nuptials.[26]

In *Hamlet* the hasty marriage between his uncle and his mother obviously disgusts the young Prince of Denmark, shaking his faith in human nature to its core; yet what Hamlet and his father's Ghost choose to regard as the blackest of sexual transgressions seems to occasion no great objection in Denmark generally. Hamlet's sardonic comment on his unwelcome sonship to the usurper of his father's throne, "A little more than kin, and less than kind" (I.ii.65), encapsulates a complex irony, for although the speaker puns bitterly on "kind," implying that the new marriage shows his uncle to have acted both cruelly and against nature, he unintentionally points up the isolated state of his own indignation. And one effect of the remark, as Sir Thomas Hamner noted in the eighteenth century, is simply to call attention, through the use of a proverb, to a relationship "so confused and blended that it was hard to define."[27] Horatio, Hamlet's ally, expresses no open disapproval, and even the couple themselves feel minimal guilt. Of course the king and queen must put as good a face as possible on their marriage in public, but privately also, they are remarkably untroubled by bad conscience. Claudius in his agonized prayer soliloquy is almost wholly concerned with the murder of his brother, not his incest, and Hamlet has to work very hard to bring his mother to a sense of sexual sin; even then, we cannot be sure that her conversion is permanent.[28] One reason for the apparently wide acceptance of the new marriage may be territorial, for Claudius refers to Gertrude in his opening speech as "th' imperial jointress to this warlike state" (I.ii.9). That is to say, the title may imply not only that the queen holds authority co-extensively with her husband but that she has also brought a valuable jointure to the Danish throne—probably lands or a strategically important estate that would make the kingdom politically, economically, or militarily stronger.

But, of course, royal or noble marriages might be contracted for precisely the opposite reason—that is, because the parties were *not* blood relations. One of the most convincing explanations that anthropology has yet advanced for an insistence on exogamy is not the fear of genetic malformations (as some still suppose) but rather the strongly felt imperative to strengthen the tribe through family ties to a political and economic power base beyond itself. The pattern survives in Shakespeare. When Henry V marries Katharine of Valois at the end of the second tetralogy, he symbolically strengthens England by absorbing what has now become a foreign culture and hostile territory into the national blood stream. Katharine asks, "Is it possible dat I sould love de ennemie of France?" And Henry responds, "I love France so well that I will not part with a village of it. I will have it all mine. And, Kate, when France is mine and I am yours, then yours is France and you are mine" (*Henry V*, V.ii.170–177). The annexation of France by a Plantagenet king who quarters his arms with the *fleur de lys*, yet speaks but a few syllables of broken French, neatly culminates in a dynastic marriage to a partner who is paradoxically both native and foreign—in a kind of geopolitical incest in which England weds her closest European sibling and historic enemy at a single stroke.

Incest, then, whether literal or symbolic, might be regarded as relatively beneficial or repugnant depending on particular circumstances. At all events, among the upper classes, intrafamilial intercourse and marriage often seem to have been officially deplored but covertly tolerated or at least lightly punished.[29] At the peasant level, crowded rural dwellings probably made it difficult to prevent, despite the strenuous prohibitions of the Church; but the argument against incest was economic as well as moral: if sexual attachment to close relations was dangerous to the soul, it was also injurious to the social fabric by concentrating too much wealth within a single family instead of spreading and diffusing it via the institution of exogamous wedlock. Dramatists and literary artists, if they were historically cognizant in a deliberate way, tended, of course, to look to the aristocracy for precedents and examples.

Elizabethans familiar with their recent past could hardly be unaware of how centrally the question of incest had dominated the reign of Henry VIII. Elizabeth's father, like Shakespeare's Claudius, had married his brother's widow when he came to the throne, and the usual papal dispensation had been obtained to allow the impediment of affinity to be set aside. But the threat of incest here was less shocking than in *Hamlet* because Katharine of Aragon (unlike Gertrude) had never consummated her marriage to Prince Arthur (Henry's older brother) and consequently (again unlike Gertrude) was childless.[30] Levirate marriage (the union of a brother's widow with her brother-in-law for the purpose of having children and thus preventing the extinction of a family) had ancient biblical sanction. Historians have often assumed that Henry's later "scruples" about the incestuous nature of his first marriage derived cynically from political necessity—his need to produce a male heir—and that this, in turn, impelled him to reject Katharine for Anne Boleyn, a spouse who seemed to promise greater fertility. The psychoanalytic historian, J. C. Flügel, has argued, however, that a simultaneous fear of, and attraction to, incestuous situations, whether symbolic or actual, tended to dominate Henry's sexual and marital life from start to finish.

Flügel points out that Henry's parents (Henry VII and Elizabeth of York) were technically incestuous, as noted already, and circumvented the impediment of kindred and affinity only through a papal exemption; that Henry VIII created a second symbolic incest after his marriage to Katharine by entering upon an affair with Mary Boleyn, the elder sister of the woman who was to become his second queen; that when the king executed Anne for treasonable adultery, the charges included the allegation that she had slept with her brother, Lord Rochford; that Henry's third marriage to Jane Seymour (the mother of Edward VI) involved still another breach of the affinity principle—affinity in the third degree—thus requiring a dispensation from Archbishop Cranmer; that Henry had approached Jane through Sir Edward Seymour, her brother, who acted as a co-participant in the courting process; that after Jane's death, Henry considered but rejected a marriage to Mary of Guise, who was already affianced to James V of Scotland, Henry's nephew; that Catherine Howard, Henry's fifth queen, was a first cousin of Anne Boleyn and therefore, technically, a relative; that Henry, in order to marry his sixth wife, had forced Catherine Parr to break off an engagement to his own brother-in-law, Sir Thomas Seymour, and so forth. In Flügel's analysis, Henry VIII's deep sexual conflicts—his unconscious wish to be opposed by, and to overcome, a sexual rival, his impulse toward, and horror of, incest, his irrational desire for a lover at once sexually experienced and chaste—were all interconnected and sprang, very likely, from the same source—a deeply embedded Oedipal pattern of jealousy for the father and sexual attraction to the mother.[31]

Renaissance dramatists could hardly have known the more intimate details of a king's love experiences, let alone have rationalized them according to the Freudian categories of Flügel, although a play such as *The Duchess of Malfi*, with its dark mixture of sexual attraction and sadistic jealousy in Ferdinand, suggests a pattern not wholly foreign to what Flügel describes in Henry VIII. But playwrights would certainly know that Henry's several marriages had been notorious for the sexual and moral controversies they had unleashed and for the political and dynastic consequences, both good and bad, that had flowed from them. Perhaps they reasoned that but for Henry's scruples about incest, Gloriana would never have ruled England at all. Or, if they were inclined to defend the incestuous necessities of nuptial politics within the royal family, they might nevertheless thrill to sensational crimes of incest emanating from a depraved country like Italy. Barnabe Barnes, for instance, in *The Devil's Charter* (1607), had dramatized the most lurid scandals of the Borgias, including Pope Alexander VI's copulation with Lucrezia (his own daughter) and her lustful affair with her brother Cesare (a cardinal turned soldier). Among Alexander's motives, of course, as the sources make clear, was family pride (one thinks again of Webster's Ferdinand) and the consolidation of power (as in the case of Richard III's marital strategies). The infamous history of Count Cenci, who had seduced his daughter Beatrice and then had been murdered at her behest, also fed the appetite for sensational horror, as did the story of Niccolo III, Marquess of Ferrara, who executed his wife and son on the same day for engaging in a secret love affair. This story, as already explained (see n.2[*b*] below), probably influenced *The Revenger's Tragedy*. Alessandro de Medici, another notorious lecher, attempted to seduce the aunt (or, in some versions, the sister) of his cousin Lorenzino, who then had him stabbed to death in the bedchamber where the assignation was to have taken place; a version of these well-known incidents was put on the stage by Shirley in *The Traitor* (1631), although Shirley circumvented the incest by removing the blood relationship between the lady and the seducer.[32] Although Dante's *Divine Comedy* would have to wait until the eighteenth century for an English translation, many Renaissance readers and poets would know of the famous incestuous affair (evoked with consummate pathos in canto V of *The Inferno*) between Francesca da Rimini and Paolo, the handsome brother of her physically deformed husband Gianciotto, son of Malatesta da Verrucchio. Here again forced marriage had cut athwart sexual romance with tragic consequences, for the ugly brother, surprising the illicit lovers at a moment of indiscretion, stabbed them both to death in 1285.

Closer to home was the scandal of Anne Lake, Lady Roos, who, quarreling with her husband, slandered the Countess of Exeter by charging her with "adulterie, incest, murther, poison and such like peccadillos"; at the trial in 1619 Lady Roos was exposed as a liar, and later, according to a report by John Chamberlain, accused (in the confession of an accomplice to her libel) of having herself had incestuous relations with her brother, Sir Arthur Lake.[33] In the background, too, was the unhappy awareness of the Spanish king Philip II and the memory of his dynastic marriage to Mary I, notorious persecutor of English Protestantism. After "Bloody Mary's" death, Philip remarried a third and fourth time, his final alliance being contracted with his own niece—Anne of Austria, daughter of the emperor Maximilian II. In 1587, just before the Armada sailed and when anti-Spanish sentiment in Britain was particularly intense, the puritan Job Throckmorton delivered an incendiary speech in Parliament denouncing His Most Catholic Majesty and infuriating Elizabeth because of the presumptuous attempt to interfere in royal foreign policy. Throckmorton fulminated against Philip's religion as "idolatrous," against his life as "licentious," and against his marriage as, "we all know, incestuous," the monarch being "great-uncle to his own children"; the speaker went on to characterize the entire house of Hapsburg as "an incestuous race of bastards."[34]

Considered alongside these events, Henry VIII's "great matter," his attempt to secure from Rome an annulment of his marriage to Katharine of Aragon, may appear somewhat less great; it nonetheless stimulated considerable theological discussion not only in England but on the continent. Learned churchmen were enlisted by all parties to the debate, and scholarship was ransacked for precedents.[35] The issue was thorny because scriptural exegetes could point to open contradictions and discrepancies in the Bible. The proof text on which Henry founded his case was Leviticus, which in two different places explicitly forbids marriage to a sister-in-law: "if a man shall take his brother's wife, it is an unclean thing: he hath uncovered his brother's nakedness; they shall be childless" (Leviticus 20:21; see also 18:16). The reasoning here apparently is that, since man and wife are one flesh, copulation with one's sister-in-law is tantamount to copulating with one's brother. But Katharine's supporters and defenders cited Deuteronomy 25:5, a passage that specifically enjoins a husband's brother to marry his widow, *if* there have been no children (as was of course the case with Prince Arthur and Katharine).[36] It goes without saying that the Church, on both Levitican and Pauline authority (see Leviticus 18:6–30 and 1 Corinthians 5:1–5), had anciently condemned more direct forms of incest—those involving consanguinity rather than mere affinity. This they associated with witches and demons as so self-evidently repugnant to the word of God that no intellectual or theological argument need be advanced against it. Incest prohibition, in effect, became the unequivocal answer to which it was unthinkable even to frame the question. In the Second Book of Samuel (13), for instance, Amnon's rape of his half sister (Tamar, daughter of King David) and the revenge taken by Absalom (a third of David's children) offered a classic example of what tragic results might flow from incestuous passion. Peele, indeed, had given this "kindlesse love" (l. 295) and "heinous lust" (l. 376) dramatic expression in *David and Bethsabe* (1587).[37] King Herod's marriage (after a divorce) to Herodias, the wife of his half brother Philip, presented another tragic instance of incest (see Matthew 14:3–12; Mark 6:17–29; Luke 3:19–20); for John the Baptist's rebuke of the immoral union had been a putative cause of his decapitation, as the official book of *Homilies* suggests.[38]

Still, for the curious or thoughtful, biblical riddles and problems remained. The children of Adam and Eve obviously had no choice but to commit incest in order to propagate the human race, and, in a sense, Eve was the daughter (or sister) of Adam, having come from his rib. In Genesis 19, the daughters of Lot had tricked their father through drunkenness into engendering Moab and Benammi, the progenitors of two important tribes (the Moabites and Ammonites).[39] And Sarah was the half sister of her husband, the revered Abraham. Closer to Henry VIII's situation was the case of Judah's three sons (Er, Onan, and Shelah) in Genesis 38, each of whom in succession married, or was to marry, Tamar in what would seem to be at least a partial vindication of the Deuteronomic text; but the matter was further complicated by the fact that Tamar went on to conceive twins by Judah himself, her father-in-law. Also, according to some interpreters of the early Church, the half brothers Heli and Jacob married the same woman in turn—a woman who became the mother of Saint Joseph (see Matthew 1:16; Luke 3:23).[40] In the Book of Ruth the title figure, a widow, took to husband Boaz, a kinsman of her deceased spouse Mahlon (Ruth 4:10–13). And, in addition, there was the puzzle in Luke's gospel of Christ's being questioned by the Sadducees as to which of seven brothers who married the same woman in succession would be acknowledged in heaven as her true husband (Luke 20:27–36).

By and large, the exegetical arguments for the validity of Henry's marriage to Katharine were weightier than those against (Shakespeare in *Henry VIII* scrupulously avoids taking clear sides in the debate, making the king refer cloudily to "many maz'd considerings" [II.iv.183]), but as Roland Frye shows, the cultural revulsion against all incests in principle persisted nevertheless, and the monarch's guilty feelings and dynastic needs had the effect of agitating the ecclesiastical waters turbidly. Suffice it to say, then, that the dramatists and writers of the period were composing in an intellectual, cultural, and political milieu that not only raised the subject of incest to unusual prominence but also nurtured contrary and discrepant attitudes towards it. Whether the imagined experience of incestuous attraction excited or repelled them—and often it seems to have done both—literary practitioners found the topic a useful vehicle for exploring themes and ideas central to the moral and psychological concerns of their art.

V

One of Marguerite of Navarre's tales from the *Heptameron*, englished as early as 1597, illustrates the special potency of incest as a fictional motif—a potency that would extend perhaps even more saliently to the drama. And, given the moralistic tendency of most sixteenth-century fiction, we are astonished to read at the conclusion, apropos of the incestuous lovers: "Never was there such love between husband and wife, never were a husband and wife so close. For she was his daughter, his sister, his wife. And he was her father, brother and husband. They endured for ever in this great love. . ." (p. 321).[41] Marguerite's Novella 30 tells of a youthful widow whose devotion to her dead husband and concern for her small son cause her to become a religious recluse. She vows never to remarry and cannot even attend a wedding or hear a church organ without suffering pangs of conscience. Her motive for this rigidity of life is to avoid any situation that might lead to sexual temptation and hence to sin. When her son reaches adolescence, he becomes sexually interested in his mother's maidservant, who then complains to her mistress about the boy's improper advances. The mother, who distrusts the report of her son's carnal behavior, decides to test it by having the maidservant arrange a tryst with the lad and then substituting herself in the bed. Intending to punish the boy if he should show any sign of lust, the mother, to her surprise, becomes sexually aroused herself. As the narrator phrases it,

> so fragile was her nature, that her anger turned to pleasure, a pleasure so abomina-
> ble, that she forgot she was a mother. Even as the dammed-up torrent flows more
> impetuously than the freely flowing stream, so it was with this poor lady whose
> pride and honour had lain in the restraints she had imposed upon her own body.

No sooner had she set foot on the first rung down the ladder of her chastity, than she found herself suddenly swept away to the bottom.

(p. 318)

Without her son's ever realizing that he has slept with his own mother, she conceives a child by him, for which sin her conscience torments her to the end of her days. The didactic emphasis of this ironic incest falls on the mother's spiritual pride and, by implication, on the unnatural ferocity with which she has repressed healthy and normal instincts: to quote Marguerite, "instead of humbling herself and recognizing how impossible it is for our flesh to do otherwise than sin unless we have God's help, she tried . . . through her own prudence, to avoid future evil" (p. 318).

Fearing further intimacy with her son, the mother sends him away next morning for military training without even saying goodbye, then conceals her pregnancy by visiting a "bastard brother" (p. 319) who lives far away—the only person in whom she feels she can confide. When the child (a daughter) is born, the midwife is told that the mother is the bastard brother's wife, so that a second symbolic incest is employed to clothe the first in the garb of respectability. The guilty mother hides the shameful evidence of coitus with her son by masquerading as the wife of a man who is actually her half brother. After giving birth, the mother returns home to live more austerely than ever, disciplining herself by fasts and other devotional rigors, while the baby girl is farmed out to a wet nurse by her supposed father, the bastard brother. At the age of puberty, the girl is sent to be reared at court so that her true identity may continue to be hidden, and so that, having no estate of her own, she may be suitably married off to a gentleman of aristocratic station. Meanwhile the son, now grown to manhood, wishes to visit his mother, from whom he has long been absent. She, however, still fearing the temptation to incest, imposes the condition that he first be married. The son therefore travels to court where he meets, and unwittingly weds, the girl who is also his sister and daughter. He now intends to bring home the happy bride to meet the woman who has just become her mother-in-law as well as her mother and symbolic grandmother. By satisfying his mother's demand that he marry—a demand intended to forestall incest—the son has in fact embraced the very disaster his mother had sought so sedulously to avoid.

The marriage of the son-father to his daughter-sister, both parties being ignorant of their consanguinity, completes a mounting progression of three incests in the tale—an escalation of familial entanglements with comic possibilities; but Marguerite's story divides itself neatly between comedy and tragedy by the double nature of its ending. The mother, when she perceives what horror she has wrought, almost dies in guilty despair but is finally driven to make her confession to a papal legate, who, after consulting "several doctors of theology" (p. 321), enjoins her to reveal nothing to her children but to do secret penance for the rest of her life. The father-brother-husband and his daughter-sister-wife are "very much in love" (p. 321) and live out their days in connubial felicity, while the mother-grandmother-mother-in-law suffers agonies of remorse, withdrawing to weep at the slightest expression of affection between the married pair. Awareness becomes the index of sin. The children are innocent because they committed incest without knowing it, whereas the mother knew what she did in sleeping with her son and so must endure perpetual grief for the extraordinary consequences. The story accommodates a dual perspective on incestuous love affairs, identifying them with suffering and a kind of spiritual death at the conscious level, yet also depicting them as potentially happy and fulfilling at the deeper stratum of the subconscious.

Marguerite's tale contains in embryo a surprising number of the motifs and ideas that Renaissance dramatists, even if they did not know her narrative, would develop variously in both comic and tragic directions. We may therefore use it as a kind of window through which to view at a distance, as it were, some of the more prominent landmarks of the diverse plays that make up the theatrical skyline of forbidden love.

The bed trick, of course, was hardly to be limited to plots involving physical incest, as Shakespeare's *All's Well That Ends Well* and *Measure for Measure* and Middleton's *The Changeling* remind us; but all three of these plays toy with the ironic intersection of moral and sexual identity in the dark, a theme of which the erotic substitution in Marguerite's tale might seem to be a fitting emblem. Nor should we forget that disturbing, unnatural, or monstrous conjunction as a concept enters these plays in metaphorical and symbolic ways. Thus when the Countess in *All's Well* portrays herself as a surrogate "mother" (I.iii.135) to Helena, her adopted "daughter" (I.iii.150) tries to evade the association, recognizing that her love for Bertram would then amount to incest of a kind: "the Count Rossillion cannot be my brother" (I.iii.152). Against this background the physical union of Bertram and Helena, during which the Count fails to recognize his cohabitant, seems somehow tainted—a troubling compound of the illicit with the chaste and permissible. Also when Claudio in the second Shakespearean comedy begs his sister to save his life at the price of her chastity, Isabella indignantly suggests that the substitution of a sister's maidenhead for a brother's head would be "a kind of incest" (III.i.138). In Middleton's tragedy, too, the horrible coitus between Beatrice and De Flores becomes figuratively consanguineous, since his physical ugliness is conceived as a projection, or extension, of her moral squalor; when she refers to herself in the final scene as the infected "blood" that has been purged from her father for his "better health" (V.iii.150–151),[42] the metaphor also appears to include her carnal partner who holds her wounded body in his arms.

Intimacies between brother and sister, whether physical or other, occur twice in Marguerite's tale—first, between the guardian and the parent and, second, between the children. It would be pointless to list the numerous Elizabethan and Stuart plays in which incest between siblings, whether contemplated or indulged, serves as a means of arousing prurience or horror or becomes the focus of dramatic suspense; Webster's *Duchess of Malfi*, Beaumont and Fletcher's *A King and No King*, Ford's *'Tis Pity She's a Whore*, and Brome's *The Lovesick Court* spring to mind. But it is worth emphasizing that Marguerite treats brother-sister relationships with special attention and sympathy, whether they are sexual or not (the royal authoress herself was renowned for being close to her brother, Francis I), even as the great majority of the playwrights do. The appearance of the bastard brother is also notable, reminding us of sexual noncompliance in a related key. The incestuous liaison in *The Revenger's Tragedy* is motivated partly by the resentment of an illegitimate son for his father. Innovatively, however, Tourneur (?) makes this incest between a bastard son and an adulterous stepmother not merely another illustration of courtly depravity but also an agency of vengeance. The lascivious Duke not only dies kissing the poisoned skull of a woman he had tried in vain to seduce but must bear the additional humiliation, as he dies, of watching himself incestuously cuckolded by the illegitimate issue of his own lechery.

The figure of the midwife is linked in Marguerite, as in many of the comedies and tragicomedies, with the falsification of parentage; and additionally, in the French tale, we have the use of the wet nurse and the separation of children from their parent and from each other so that they become unrecognizable when they meet as adults. In the *Heptameron* also, Marguerite makes it clear that choice of a marriage partner is anything but free. The incestuous union between the brother and sister comes about only because the mother of the tale insists on her son's taking a mate before he returns home, and because the sister's mentor (the Queen of Navarre), knowing that her charge's suitor is rich, handsome, and of noble birth, in effect instructs her to marry him. As we have seen already, enforced marriage on the stage is typically a form of emotional imprisonment from which incest offers a kind of desperate or illusory escape, whereas in Marguerite, the elders ironically drive the lovers—and drive them happily—into each other's arms.

Still another characteristic of Marguerite's tale that gets reflected obliquely in certain stage dramatizations of incest is the mixture of respect for, and skepticism of, ecclesiastical authority. The female protagonist of Marguerite's narrative unwittingly courts carnal knowledge of her son by imposing upon herself and, by implication, upon him an exaggerated and unnatural asceticism stemming from misdirected piety; a commentator in the frame story remarks that the heroine of the tale was probably "one of those foolish, vainglorious women who had had her head filled with nonsense by the Franciscans" (p. 322). Nonetheless, it is the papal legate, on the expert advice of theological scholars, who renders the nicely balanced judgment at the end—namely that she has sinned mortally, while her children are adjudged to have done nothing wrong. In this bifocal attitude toward the clergy (the Franciscan order, the legate of the pope, the doctors of theology) Marguerite adumbrates that commingling of sympathy for incestuous lovers with a genuine revulsion against incest itself that makes plays like Ford's *'Tis Pity* so subtly complex and problematic.

By her stress on the overlapping of roles (a young man who is father, brother, and husband to the same girl, a woman who is at once that same girl's grandmother, mother, and mother-in-law), Marguerite touches upon problems of psychic identity infinitely deeper and more disturbing than those implied by the changeling device and the misidentifications that issue from it. It is true that the son of the story never recognizes his blood kinship to either of his sexual partners; but apart from our titillation at his ignorance of the truth, the story fascinates us because of its frightening erasure of the definitional boundary lines that traditionally separate members of the same family and thereby confer a kind of security upon them. Plots that dissolve or merge these comforting distinctions of role threaten us with confusion and uncertainty, terrify us with the possibility of absorption into a trackless wilderness of liminality. For a few (Ford's student Giovanni may be a case in point) such an experience might qualify as a harrowingly pleasurable adventure, a Faustian assault upon the unknown; but for most, it equates with death, a crossing of that bourn from which no traveler returns.

One can recognize this matrix of fear, challenge, and the mergence of roles in a play like *Pericles,* where Antiochus attempts to maintain his incestuous relationship to his daughter by posing a riddle for prospective suitors to guess—at the risk of their lives, of course, should they fail:

> I am no viper, yet I feed
> On mother's flesh, which did me breed.

> I sought a husband, in which labor
> I found that kindness in a father.
> He's father, son, and husband mild;
> I mother, wife, and yet his child.
> How they may be, and yet in two,
> As you will live, resolve it you.
>
> (I.i.65–72)

The solution, of course, is that the daughter feeds on her mother's flesh because she sleeps with her father, who was once married to, and was so one flesh with, her mother. Antiochus is now both father and husband to his daughter-wife, and, in addition—by the same crazy logic that made the woman of Marguerite's story at once a mother and grandmother to the same girl—Antiochus is his own son-in-law because he functions as his daughter's spouse. Conversely, the daughter plays the role of her own mother-in-law by virtue of serving as her father's wife.

At the rhetorical level such superimpositions of role function like elaborate puns, *double entendres*, or exercises in metaphysical wit, but considered psychologically, they point toward chaos and death. They also suggest an overloading of the emotional circuits, the burdening of a single relationship with different but highly charged kinds of intensity—in the case of Antiochus, with the paternal and the husbandly, in the case of Marguerite's young man, with the paternal, the brotherly, and the husbandly (although he remains unaware of the first two). This surplus of propinquity, of course, constitutes one of the standard objections to incest. Montaigne, in his essay, "Of Moderation," cites Saint Thomas Aquinas as an authority for asserting that genital love within the "forbidden degrees" will necessarily be "immoderate": in the words of Florio's translation, "if the wedlocke, or husband-like affection be sound and perfect, as it ought to be, and also surcharged with that a man oweth to alliance and kindred, there is no doubt, but that surcease may easily transport a husband beyond the bounds of reason."[43] Criminal madness, extending even to murder, is precisely the result of the incestuous attraction that we observe in Webster's Ferdinand and Ford's Giovanni.

The symbolism of role confusion and the frustrations and agonies it can generate reaches a dizzying, even potentially absurd, complexity in Brome's *The Lovesick Court*, where the threat of incest gets entangled with the conflict, familiar from romance tradition, between the competing claims of love and friendship. Through a notably vermiculate plot, the dramatist manages to explore a number of issues implicit in the problem of incest, only a few of which would occur to a reader who considered Marguerite's narrative in isolation. But Brome's play is worth discussing in some detail if only because it shows, as the tale from the *Heptameron* does more simply, how incest can become the emblem for a whole congeries of role and identity puzzles basic to close emotional relationship. Early on, Brome telegraphs a clue that his play is to introduce the theme of incest by making the Delphic oracle announce in riddling fashion that a solution to the central amorous-dynastic conundrum "requires an *Oedipus* to construe it" (I.ii);[44] but the shadow of illicit sexuality emerges gradually, and we come to recognize its significance only at the denouement.

The Lovesick Court presents supposed twin brothers, Philocles and Philargus, who contend for the hand of the Princess Eudina (and hence for the crown of Thessaly), rather as Palamon and Arcite contend for Emilia in *The Two Noble Kinsmen*. The two young noblemen, believing that they are brothers, love each other as much as they love Eudina (at one point they invoke the myth of Castor and Pollux), while she, in turn, loves both of them with a devotion that will admit of no priority:

> O, ye Gods!
> Why made ye them two persons, and assign'd
> To both but one inseparable mind?
> Or, Why was I mark'd out to be that one,
> That loves and must embrace, or two, or none;
> O my perplexity.
>
> (I.ii; pp. 105–106)

Although the three figures are shown to waver under pressure, divided loyalty traps each in an emotional impasse. From the lady's point of view, the twin suitors represent the bifurcation of a single identity—one soul, as it were, occupying distinct bodies; and she must either complete herself psychologically by uniting with both or forgo romantic fulfillment altogether. (Shakespeare approaches the same idea in *Twelfth Night*—though with the important difference of separating the siblings by gender—when he makes Sebastian, a kind of duplicate of Cesario-Viola, so easily replace his twin in the affections of Olivia, who may now wed a male version of the same identity she has cherished from the beginning.)

Like Eudina, Philocles and Philargus also confront crises of self-completion; they must wrestle with the paradox of sacrificing their identities in the very process of realizing them, caught up, as they are, in the toils of emotional attachment and distancing. As Philocles puts it,

> I must proceed to gain *Eudinas* love
> From my *Philargus* or I loose my self.
> And gaining it, I must forgo *Philargus*,
> And equally be lost.
>
> (II.i; p. 110)

Maneuvered through deception into a duel over the lady, each combatant seeks to die unselfishly at the hands of the other; later, when Philocles abandons Eudina in favor of his rival, having lost in a drawing of lots, he prays that "she may lively find / She has my love in [Philargus's]" and "that in [him] / She has us both" (V.i; p. 156).

As early as the end of act II, it becomes clear that Brome has fashioned an equilateral triangle, each point of which is so tensely, reciprocally, and hopelessly drawn to the other two that the full satisfaction of everyone's desire would require the mergence of all three persons into a single being—the assimilation of their separate personalities into a kind of androgynous trinity in which individuality would be blurred or even obliterated. Such a state, of course, would be equivalent to death, so it is not surprising that in the course of the action each of the lovers wishes to die, while Philargus actually appears at one point to do so. Eudina exclaims that "love's number's one" (II.i; p. 115), and the brothers are "each / *Wedded* [emphasis added] to others friendship," each "more studious for the other then himself" (II.i; p. 118). Philargus verbalizes the fatal interdependency of the triad: if Eudina should be driven to suicide by the nature of her impossible choice, both he and his twin would also "fall by necessary consequence" (III.iii; p. 129). A little later she remarks that "one friendship, yet, must marry us all three" (III.iii; p. 130).

As in Marguerite's tale, family and romantic relationships tend to fuse. But in Brome, three distinct kinds of emotional involvement are in operation—erotic love, twinship (the closest kind of blood brotherhood), and passionate friendship, each emotion overlapping the others so that a painful and chaotic stasis results. Eudina wishes to "die . . . Rather than live in this confusion," but proposes weakly and fatalistically that all three participants "continue thus with Maiden love, / With modest freedom, unsuspected joyes, / *As we had all been formed in one womb* [emphasis added], / Till Heaven determine of us" (II.i; p. 118). Brome's figure of prenatal togetherness in a context of unfulfilled sexual desire is revealing; for in this drama incest not only enters the plot at two crucial points but also symbolizes, almost generically, the "lovesickness" of the title—that is, it stands for the problem of undifferentiated feeling and for the psychological overheating that results from the confounding and intermingling of intensities (heterosexual romance, biological fraternity, and male bonding) that society wisely controls by individuating and keeping apart. Of course the metaphorical retreat into the womb also implies immaturity, as though the adolescent lovers of this murky three-way relationship had yet to achieve adult personhood; indeed the boys' uncle, exasperated by the refusal of his nephews to compete strenuously enough for the princess, regards their sticky idealism as infantile: "I could even swadle 'em both for a brace of Babyes" (V.i; p. 153). Such symbolism also relieves the dramatist, it will be noted, of having to individualize his youthful characters in any but the most rudimentary and functional way, for the shifts and changes of the plot obviously require that the young men be interchangeable.

Brome breaks up his impossible triangle in the conventionally predictable way—that is, as in *Twelfth Night*, by introducing a fourth term so that it may be converted into a parallelogram. But the route to a happy resolution is unusually—one might almost say parodically—labyrinthine, since it involves not only the apparent death and resurrection of one of the principals but the prurience of two potentially incestuous love affairs as well.[45] Placilla, who is assumed until the end of the play to be a sister of the twin youths, tries to suppress an erotic attraction to Philocles, her feelings being rendered more painful by the fact that her "brother," the object of her guilty desire, charges her (with a kiss!)—as his other self—to woo Eudina in his behalf; thus, like Viola wooing Olivia for Orsino in Shakespeare's comedy, Placilla is compelled ironically not only to hide her love but also, frustratingly, to work against it.

The second potential incest involves Philocles and Eudina, who are about to marry at the play's end after poison seems to have eliminated the rival candidacy of Philargus; for just as the king is about to join the couple in matrimony, the long-hidden secret that they are really brother and sister and that the two boys are *not* after all twin brothers comes suddenly to light to surprise, titillate, and further perplex the audience. (Brome, like Marguerite, employs the time-honored device of a midwife, Garrula, although in this case the character possesses the secret knowledge of the children's true origin and so becomes a knowing, rather than an unwitting, party to the deception.) When it finally transpires that Philargus is no corpse (as was thought) but only drugged, his revival makes possible a double union. Placilla can now marry Philocles (the man she had guiltily regarded as her brother), and Eudina, who actually *is* the sister of Philocles, can marry Philargus, the symbolic, if nonbiological, twin of the man she had been on the point of espousing.

As in Marguerite, incest thus functions as at once problem and solution, although somewhat more cloudily than in the *Heptameron*. Actual brothers and sisters cannot finally be united, however much their sensual desire may generate theatrical suspense. As one speaker warns when the king is unwittingly about to marry his daughter to his son, "You will sooner joyn / The Wolfe and Lamb, Falcon and Dove together" (V.iii; p. 166). But Brome can nullify Placilla's guilt and satisfy her longing at the same time by making her beloved turn out to have different blood in his veins; and he can also overcome Eudina's inability to choose between two equally dear aspirants for her hand by revealing, at the last minute, that one is ineligible (by reason of being a blood brother); thus his "twin" may step handily into the role of husband (by reason of *not* being a kinsman) with no sacrifice of romantic excitement.

The technical flaw in this overly schematic solution is the final arbitrariness of the Placilla-Philocles union, which is patched up hurriedly in the last few moments of the drama. Brome's emphasis falls on the marriage of Eudina and Philargus and on the succession to the throne of Philocles (now revealed to be the dying king's heir) as a compensation of sorts for being denied his princess. Placilla's romantic wishes are at last gratified, as required by the artificial neatness of the ending, but we are given no indication that Philocles regards his supposed former sister as a happy substitute for Eudina or as an appropriate future queen. He appears merely to accept her with a shrug and a mythological allusion, casting her "as *Juno* to [his] *Jupiter*, / Sister and wife" (V.iii; p. 169).

The significant feature of this somewhat diffuse but psychologically suggestive play is its delight in showing not only how completely irrational emotional attachment can be but also how closely and dangerously illicit forms of sexual desire can tread upon the heels of the licit. Here, too, Brome shares common ground with Marguerite. Consanguinity, assumed in the relationship between Placilla and Philocles until the last moment, serves as the frailest of barriers, even though the actual kinship between him and Eudina, revealed with mysterious suddenness, snatches lovers back from the edge of a tragic abyss because the play must end comically. Accidents of birth become fortunate or unfortunate technicalities as fate decrees; but the implied lesson, as in the *Heptameron*, is that passion is all but irresistible and that, unchecked by such knowledge, it would easily override restraints or taboos that claim their authority only from religion and the culture. The play suggests also, through the mechanisms of plot rather than through any richness of characterization, that at some deep stratum of the psyche all attractions between people, whether they be brothers, sisters, lovers, or friends, are somehow unitary in nature; and that within this frighteningly undifferentiated nexus of magnetisms—sexual and nonsexual, romantic and fraternal, incestuous and nonincestuous—lies the possibility of annihilation as well as an opportunity to discover the uniqueness of the self. Brome, of course, is not up to *dramatizing* such self-discovery; it remains implicit merely as a proposition of the plotting. And the pattern of substitutions is equally intriguing, as we observe Placilla having to woo Eudina for Philocles, see Philocles end up with Placilla for his wife instead of Eudina, watch Eudina marry Philargus in lieu of Philocles, hear Philocles hand over Eudina to his "brother" as an extension of himself, and so on. Such actions suggest a disturbing fluidity, or instability, at the heart of personality and portend a world in which the vital demarcations in social, sexual, and family relations are at best only provisional. The theme of incest obviously plays its part in the evocation of this concept in both the *Heptameron* and Brome's tragicomedy.

Finally, Marguerite's tale suggests, although only distantly, the notion of incest as a buried metaphor for narcissism. The lady substitutes herself in her maid's bed out of the felt need to impose her own specialized attitudes upon an adolescent boy—to expose, punish, and repress natural biological impulses in the developing lad that would separate him morally, psychologically, and physically from herself, that would force her to acknowledge his independence. Subconsciously, at least, she wishes to regard her son as a duplicate of herself, a kind of mirror image, or reflexive extension, of her own commitment to chastity. The egotism that underlies this foolish attempt is already explicit in the tale; the narrator refers to her "root of pride" (p. 319), and a listener in the frame observes aphoristically that "he is a wise man . . . who recognizes no enemy but himself, and who distrusts his own will and counsel, however good and holy they may appear to be" (p. 321). Moreover, the fact of the son's unconscious gravitation to his own sister for a bride, when he might have chosen from all the eligible ladies of Navarre, again invites the concept of a self-enclosed or dangerously circular eroticism.

Pausanias in his *Description of Greece* (IX, 31) connects the myth of Narcissus to brother-sister love. This late classical work mentions an alternative version of the famous story, one in which "Narcissus fell in love with his [twin] sister, and when the girl died, would go to the spring, knowing that it was his reflection that he saw, but in spite of this knowledge finding some relief for his love in imagining that he saw, not his own reflection, but the likeness of his sister."[46] A similar suggestion shows up in Montemayor's *Diana* where the love affair between Abyndaraez and Xarifa, who suppose they are brother and sister, ripens near a "cristalline fountaine" in which the young man sees the image of his beloved "so lively represented, as if it had beene she her selfe": "I still beheld her . . . goodly counterfaite truely translated into verie hart. Then said I softly to my selfe. O, if I were now drowned in this fountaine, where with pride I behold my sweete Lady, how more fortunate should I die then *Narcissus*?"[47] As I have suggested elsewhere,[48] Webster gives us a twisted and frightening version of the symbolic union of self with twin sister in the tense scene of *The Duchess of Malfi* in which the heroine, combing out her hair as she looks into her mirror, suddenly catches the reflection of her brother's incestuously menacing presence. Here disease superimposes itself upon health, the image of brother upon sister, in a symbolic fusion of incest and narcissism, for of course it is an aspect of self that Ferdinand both loves and wishes to destroy in his twin.

Twinship, indeed (as we have already observed in Brome's *Lovesick Court*), is a not infrequent component of incest plots. In addition to Webster's *Duchess* (which involves physical twinship between the title character and Ferdinand, as well as symbolic twinship between the cruel brothers), we might instance Fletcher's *Monsieur Thomas* (a comedy) and Ford's *The Broken Heart* (a tragedy). The idea of incest as narcissistic twinship was of course already implicit in Plato's *Symposium*. In this dialogue Aristophanes accounts for both homo- and heterosexual attraction by his humorous myth of how Zeus, displeased with the overweening pride and complacency of mortals, split them down the middle, causing each half (with its independent set of genitalia) to seek reunion with its complement. Hence incest impinges upon the fascinating idea of the Doppelgänger, of the brother or sister as pursuing shadow or alter ego (often a symbolization of guilt) or, alternatively, as a projection of the ideal self (a way of imagining self-completion or union with one's own perfected essence). Although the symbolism of incest tends, of course, to be negative in Renaissance consciousness (as the link with narcissism would imply), the idea of union between the two aspects of an identity that is at once the same as, and yet other than, the self is not without its attractions. The narcissistic model of incest most often connotes an egocentric self limited to whatever authority the unique experience of that self can assert; hence it represents a psychosexual turning back upon the known, the safe, and the emotionally underdeveloped. But contrariwise, it may also point toward wholeness, spiritual enlargement, and even androgyny (as in Aristophanes' union of male and female halves that, in junction, reconstitute their original totality as a single being dynamically richer and more kinetic than the sum of its separated parts).

Milton suggests something like this in his conception of Adam and Eve, who were originally one until God, through the agency of Adam's rib, separated the female from the male body by endowing the woman with physical, psychological, and spiritual independence; the poet thereby envisioned our first parents as the prototypical incestuous couple. Adam and Eve are one flesh in the sense that they are husband and wife, but they are one flesh also—brother and sister or perhaps father and daughter—by virtue of their originally common blood stream. In *Paradise Lost* the prelapsarian sexuality of earth's first lovers, far from suggesting a solipsism, projects a relational structure in which, according to a recent commentator, "each partner enriches the life of the other because imagination and feeling, reason and desire, the life of spirit and the life of the senses, are not categorically isolated according to gender. . . . identity is not other than community . . . [and] the distributions of domestic power are conditioned by the greater power of unselfish love."[49] In other words, when Adam calls Eve "best image of my self and dearer half" (V, 95), he expresses a sexual ideal, at least symbolically incestuous, that represents the precise opposite of the detestable incest of Sin and Death in the same poem. To quote once more from the essay cited above, Milton explores "the movement from self-absorbed primary narcissism to a recognition of the self as an image of an other": to "become an image of an other is to give that other visible, palpable, significant presence in the world, to provide symbolic form to the other's self. Eve thus stands in the same identifying relation to Adam as the Son stands in relation to the Father."[50] Although it is probably impossible to cite a close analogue to Milton's myth of "incestuous" and mutual self-completion as an ideal in the largely secular drama of the Renaissance, the author of *Paradise Lost* may serve to remind us that automatic or merely reflex condemnations of incest on the stage are likely to oversimplify and therefore short-circuit issues that cry out for more sophisticated analysis.

We may now consider two well-known dramas on the theme of incest that approach the problem of narcissism from different directions—Beaumont and Fletcher's *A King and No King* and Ford's *'Tis Pity She's a Whore*. In the tragicomedy, the militaristic King Arbasces is characterized as a compound of opposites, "vainglorious and humble," "angry and patient," "merry and dull," "joyful and sorrowful" (I.i.84–85). Nevertheless, arrogance and self-absorption dominate his character in the early acts, and when he praises the sister from whom he has been separated since childhood, he conceives her as a female version of his ideal self: "Nature did her wrong / To print continual conquest on her cheeks / And make no man worthy for her to take / But me that am too near her . . ." (I.i.167–170). Later when he is smitten irresistibly by love for her, and she for him, he tries irrationally to deny her independent existence, to expunge the forbidden lust he feels by annulling her symbolically into a nonpresence, by reconstituting her as a kind of psychological ghost of his interior being: "She is no kin to me nor shall she be; / If she were any, I create her none, / And which of you can question this?" (III.i.165–167). Thus, from his own troubled perspective, Panthea incarnates the image of the warfare between reason and passion, between the angel and the beast, that rages in Arbasces' breast. Simultaneously she represents to him "blessedness / Eternal" (III.i.138–139) and "damnation" (III.i.189); she is "fair and wise / And virtuous" (III.i.190–191)—a female mirror of his brightest ideals—but also "a disease," "an ungodly sickness" (III.i.193–195), who gives back a shadow of the loathsome temptation and guilty desire that gather so threateningly in the darker recesses of his incipient depravity.

The only way to penetrate this psychic and moral impasse is of course to reveal that Arbasces is, in actuality, neither the king nor the brother that he thought himself to be. A familiar device of plotting does service in a somewhat unexpected way, for a sudden and dramatic metamorphosis of genetic identity allows Beaumont and Fletcher to close the apparently unbridgeable divide between moral idealism and carnal desire. A new genealogical self makes possible a new psychological self, so that passion and reason can be reconciled in a healthy Christian marriage. Arbasces' discovery that Panthea is not after all his sister allows him to break out of the narcissistic and solipsistic box in which he had been confined and to acknowledge his beloved's otherness. Marriage can now fulfill its proper psychological function as the institution that traditionally sanctifies and confirms the individuality of lovers while at the same time making them one flesh.

Ford's Giovanni, perhaps even more than Arbasces, is the narcissist *par excellence*, for in his autointoxication with his sister Annabella, he sees a kind of perfection that would remove her from external reality and set her up as a private, arbitrary icon of his own subjective fashioning. Not content to share his sister with the world, he demands, as a perceptive critic puts it, "a unity more complete, more self-sufficient than human life permits."[51] In the face of all social and religious pressures to the contrary—indeed partly *because* of these pressures—Giovanni is swept along in his self-isolating passion to contract a secret incestuous union with Annabella that he equates with the sacred and ecstatic. R. J. Kaufmann points out, with particular reference to this tragedy, that "Ford's [romantic] characters are all self-defining and nonpolitical. They do not so much defy society as deny its relevance to their lives."[52] It is in this context that Giovanni reacts to his sister's lapse into repentance and conventional morality as a betrayal of their mutual dedication to a higher truth; and, like Othello, he must kill the thing he loves to preserve forever the perverse mystical absolute of which he has made her the human embodiment. When his projection of self insists on a will and mind of its own, he must destroy it to prevent the implied violation of psychic oneness. Thus Giovanni's evisceration of Annabella's heart—an abhorrent literalization of Petrarchan imagery—becomes a religious sacrifice to his narcissistic conception of purity.

VI

The happy and unhappy resolutions of the two plays by Beaumont and Fletcher and by Ford may be taken to illustrate alternative paradigms of the incest problem in Renaissance drama. In *A King and No King* the collaborating dramatists validate the impulse toward incest mechanically, by expediently removing the impediment of consanguinity at the eleventh hour (as Brome does for Philocles and Placilla in *The Lovesick Court*). But this somewhat facile maneuver, which becomes a cliché of incest plots, may be interpreted to imply that the taboo itself stimulates the imagination to creative displacements and substitutions—strategies, so to say, that make it possible to heal the breach between the erotic and spiritual drives indigenous to our nature. Robert Stein, a disciple of Jung, not only regards the propension to incest as a fundamental of human love but also sees in it a symbolic expression of man's need to reconcile his passional with his intellectual and spiritual requirements, his body with his soul.[53] Looked at in this way, Arbasces, by legitimately marrying Panthea after he has incestuously lusted for her, frees the static and deadening opposition between the instinctual and rational components of his personality and unifies them fluidly in a fertile and generative interchange. He breaks free of the enchaining divisions that had kept his physical and idealizing natures asunder, and overcomes his narcissism by granting Panthea an independent identity complementary to, and co-equal with, his own—an identity endowed with its own creative potential.

'Tis Pity She's a Whore dramatizes a more tragic model of incest. As Giovanni becomes ever more obsessively narcissistic in his passion for Annabella, he moves increasingly toward a terrifying obliteration of identity—first hers and finally his own. The bloody heart impaled on his dagger is a "heart," as he tells us so grotesquely, "in which is mine entombed" (V.vi.27). This play suggests that if love isolates itself too completely from objective reality, it feeds on, and ultimately consumes, itself. Its perverse and rarefied specialness Platonizes or abstracts itself out of existence. What may look from inside the temple of narcissism like religious mystery and sacrificial rite is seen by the sane who live outside as madness, depravity, monstrous egotism, unnatural lust, and sanguinary dismemberment. The savage mutilation of Annabella's body becomes an emblem of psychic violation and the disintegration of integrity.

These contrasting images of incest portray the paradoxical interrelatedness of separation and union, not only within the psyche but also in erotic alliances between people. They point respectively toward order and toward chaos, toward life and toward death. The abiding mystery of incest has always lain somehow in our instinctive perception of its simultaneous strangeness and familiarity, in its power to repel and to attract, in its intimations of a numinous oneness and in its threat of annihilation. It is therefore small wonder that the great playwrights of the Renaissance saw in it the stuff of drama. At its most probing and exploratory, it became a way of vitalizing in the theatre that perennial paradox to which Shakespeare gave such lyrical expression in "The Phoenix and the Turtle":

> Property was thus appalled,
> That the self was not the same;
> Single nature's double name
> Neither two nor one was called.
>
> Reason, in itself confounded,
> Saw division grow together,
> To themselves yet either neither,
> Simple were so well compounded,
>
> That it cried, "How true a twain
> Seemeth this concordant one!"
> (Ll. 37–46)

Incest, as the image of the phoenix suggests, could contain the double, even mutual, possibilities of self-immolation and self-renewal. Sixteenth- and seventeenth-century drama, a drama of which erotic passion is so significant a component, could scarcely fail to take account of concerns as close to the human heart as these.

Notes
Index

Notes

1. Shakespeare's Theatrical Symbolism and Its Function in *Hamlet*

1. Stage-consciousness and theatrical self-reference as prominent aspects of Elizabethan dramatic convention have been variously explored by many scholars. See, for instance, Reuben Brower, "The Mirror of Analogy: *The Tempest*," in *The Fields of Light* (New York: Oxford University Press, 1951), pp. 95–122; Anne Righter, *Shakespeare and the Idea of the Play* (London: Chatto and Windus, 1962); Clifford Lyons, "Stage Imagery in Shakespeare's Plays," in *Essays on Shakespeare and Elizabethan Drama in Honor of Hardin Craig*, ed. Richard Hosley (Columbia: University of Missouri Press, 1962), pp. 261–274; Herbert Weisinger, "Theatrum Mundi: Illusion as Reality," in *The Agony and the Triumph* (East Lansing: Michigan State University Press, 1964), pp. 58–70; Thomas B. Stroup, *Microcosmos: The Shape of the Elizabethan Play* (Lexington: University of Kentucky Press, 1965); Norman Rabkin, "The Great Globe Itself," in *Shakespeare and the Common Understanding* (New York: Free Press, 1967), pp. 192–233; Jackson I. Cope, "The Rediscovery of Anti-Form in the Renaissance," *Comparative Drama*, 2 (1968), 155–171; Thelma N. Greenfield, *The Induction in Elizabethan Drama* (Eugene: University of Oregon Books, 1969); James L. Calderwood, *Shakespearean Metadrama* (Minneapolis: University of Minnesota Press, 1971) and *Metadrama in Shakespeare's Henriad* (Berkeley: University of California Press, 1979); Robert Egan, *Drama within Drama: Shakespeare's Sense of His Art in "King Lear," "The Winter's Tale," and "The Tempest"* (New York: Columbia University Press, 1975); and Coburn Freer, *The Poetics of Jacobean Drama* (Baltimore: Johns Hopkins University Press, 1981). See also chap. 3, n. 3.

For Shakespeare's awareness of his own craft with particular reference to *Hamlet*, see especially Maynard Mack, "The World of *Hamlet*," *Yale Review*, 41 (1952), 502–523; G. C. Thayer, "*Hamlet*: Drama as Discovery and as Metaphor," *Studia Neophilologica*, 28 (1956), 118–129; Richard Foster, "*Hamlet* and the Word," *University of Toronto Quarterly*, 30 (1961), 229–245; and Alvin B. Kernan, "Politics and Theatre in *Hamlet*," *Hamlet Studies*, 1 (1979), 1–12.

2. The theatrical trope is ancient. Ernst Robert Curtius in *European Literature and the Latin Middle Ages*, trans. W. R. Trask (New York: Pantheon Books, 1953), pp. 138–144, traces its permutations from Plato to Hofmannsthal.

3. S. L. Bethell, *Shakespeare and the Popular Dramatic Tradition* (London: Staples Press, 1944), pp. 31–41.

4. Properly speaking, the device of play-within-play adds another plane of reality, making the response a triple or (if the anagogical level is included) a quadruple one. Looked at in this way, the gradations of actuality resemble a Platonic ladder, for the play-within-play is an image of an

image of an image. Real actors pretend to be actors entertaining an actor-audience, who, in turn, entertain a real audience, who are metaphorically actors on the world's stage and hence "walking shadows" of an ultimate cosmic reality of which they are but dimly aware. In reverse, the movement can be graphed as follows: ULTIMATE REALITY → ACTUAL WORLD → PLAY WORLD → PLAY-WITHIN-PLAY WORLD.

5. I am indebted for some of the ideas in this essay to my undergraduate tutor, Mr. H. V. D. Dyson of Merton College, Oxford. See especially "The Emergence of Shakespeare's Tragedy," *Proceedings of the British Academy*, 36 (1950), 69–93.

6. For a full explication of the player's speech and its symbolic relation to major themes in *Hamlet*, see Harry Levin, *Kenyon Review*, 12 (1950), 273–296. Levin reprinted his "An Explication of the Player's Speech" in *The Question of Hamlet* (New York: Oxford University Press, 1959), pp. 138–164, 168.

7. Ulysses describing Patroclus as an actor (*Troilus and Cressida*, I.iii.151–161), Buckingham satirizing the "ham" (*Richard III*, III.v.5–11), and Hamlet giving advice to the players (*Hamlet*, III.ii.2–14) are typical examples.

8. Hamlet, of course, has the distinct advantage in this contest of acting. He knows or, rather, strongly suspects Claudius's secret; but the king is kept guessing about Hamlet until the "mouse-trap," and even then, he is not sure *how much* his nephew knows.

9. Even Polonius can see a ray of truth through Hamlet's disguise, although the disguise itself deceives him: "How pregnant sometimes his replies are! A happiness that often madness hits on, which reason and sanity could not so prosperously be deliver'd of" (II.ii.208–211).

10. It is very possible that Shakespeare reinforced the connection at this point by another actual allusion to the Globe Theatre, the emblem of which is traditionally thought to have been a figure of Hercules carrying the world on his shoulders: "*Hamlet.* Do the boys carry it away? *Rosencrantz.* Ay, that they do, my lord—Hercules and his load too" (II.ii.360–362). If so, the effect would be to enhance audience participation in the symbolism.

11. See n. 6 above.

12. George Lyman Kittredge in his famous edition of *Hamlet* (Boston: Ginn and Co., 1939) notes that the exaggerated style of the speech itself is quite necessary to preserve the distinction between the two fictional levels of art and art-within-art (pp. 197–198).

13. To achieve this symbolic effect in modern production, the actor who plays the Ghost should actually appear upon the stage. The audience know by this time that he is neither a figment of Hamlet's imagination nor a "goblin damn'd" (I.iv.40) but a truthful reality—and so does Hamlet himself. To represent the prince as having some kind of special x-ray vision violates the whole intention of the scene, for if the audience do not share the spectacle, they are put most awkwardly in the position of sharing the queen's moral blindness. The multi-consciousness must be able to operate freely.

14. J. V. Cunningham in *Woe or Wonder: The Emotional Effect of Shakespearian Tragedy* (Denver: University of Denver Press, 1951) points out that the word *act* often has the special significance of "chance" or "fortune" in contexts of tragic catastrophe (p. 17). The theatrical connotation, however, is present also.

15. Ibid., p. 33.

2. *Titus Andronicus, Hamlet,* and the Limits of Expressibility

1. Christopher Marlowe, *Tamburlaine the Great*, ed. J. S. Cunningham (Manchester: Manchester University Press, 1981), pp. 200–201.

2. "Hamlet" in *Selected Essays* (London: Faber and Faber, 1951), p. 145. In an important rejoinder, "An Objective Correlative for T. S. Eliot's Hamlet," *Journal of Aesthetics and Art Criticism*, 13 (1954), 69–79, David L. Stevenson argues that we can accept the idea of disequilibrium between plot and character, between fact and emotion, in Shakespeare's tragedy without

pronouncing the play "an artistic failure." Stevenson sees the lack of "objective correlative" in *Hamlet* as a deliberate strategy, a way of focusing upon the prince's emotional turmoil for its own sake and not merely as a means of forwarding the plot.

3. The dates cited here are essentially those assigned by Alfred Harbage and Samuel Schoenbaum in *Annals of English Drama, 975–1700* (Philadelphia: University of Pennsylvania Press, 1964).

4. Thomas Kyd, *The Spanish Tragedy*, ed. Philip Edwards (London: Methuen, 1959), pp. 42–43. All other quotations of the play are taken from this edition.

5. In the extant 1592 edition Hieronimo gives an elaborate explanation of his revenge, then, mentioning a previous (and unexplained) vow to be silent, declines under threat of torture to reveal to the court what he has just told them. Edwards believes that Kyd, in order to shorten the tragedy, revised the original ending (printed in an earlier, lost edition of 1592), and that the printer of the second 1592 edition conflated the longer ending with Kyd's manuscript revision, thus producing the present contradiction. This ingenious hypothesis may be correct, but it is possible to make *dramatic*, as opposed to strictly logical, sense of the scene as it stands. The court have been profoundly shocked by the holocaust of the play-within-the-play and the grotesque "show" of Horatio's unburied corpse. Even if they have fully taken in Hieronimo's earlier words, they might wish, if only for emotional reasons, to hear them amplified. Their grieved need for volubility now corresponds precisely to Hieronimo's earlier need for it, as Hieronimo himself senses when he addresses the dumbfounded Viceroy: "Speak, Portuguese, whose loss resembles mine: / If thou canst weep upon thy Balthazar, / 'Tis like I wail'd for my Horatio" (IV.iv.114–116). Hieronimo's shift from the eloquence of a "tongue . . . tun'd to tell his latest tale" (IV.iv.85) to "harmless silence" (IV.iv.181) may be regarded as a psychological aspect of his revenge, a calculated means of imposing his own linguistic frustrations upon his victims. For a suggestive analysis of the style of Kyd's play, see Jonas A. Barish, "*The Spanish Tragedy*, or the Pleasures and Perils of Rhetoric," in John Russell Brown and Bernard Harris, eds., *Elizabethan Theatre*, Stratford-upon-Avon Studies 9 (London: Edward Arnold, 1966), pp. 58–85.

6. Quotations from *Alphonsus, Emperor of Germany* are taken from Thomas Marc Parrott, ed., *The Plays and Poems of George Chapman: The Tragedies*, 2 vols. (London: Routledge and Sons, 1910; rpt. New York: Russell and Russell, 1961), II, 401–471, 683–711.

7. *Alphonus* shows additional signs of the influence of *Titus Andronicus*. In this same scene Saxony echoes Aaron's words, "Blood and revenge are hammering in my head" (*Titus Andronicus*, II.iii.39), when he says to Edward, "Unprincely thoughts do hammer in thy head" (IV.iii.142). Then he dashes out the brains of Hedewick's bastard child, insisting that Edward be fed nothing but the "newly born" (IV.iii.160) remains, and stabs his daughter. The Thyestean cannibalism and the death of the violated daughter at the hands of her father both find parallels in Shakespeare's play.

8. Parrott, ed., *Plays and Poems of George Chapman*, p. 691.

9. John Marston, *Antonio's Revenge*, ed. W. Reavley Gair (Manchester: Manchester University Press, 1978), p. 55. All other quotations of the play are taken from this edition.

10. The text of Henry Chettle's *Tragedy of Hoffman* cited is that of the Malone Society, ed. Harold Jenkins (Oxford: Oxford University Press, 1951). Jenkins numbers the lines consecutively throughout. For the sake of clarity, I add designations of act and scene, modernize the long *s*, and, in a few cases, alter punctuation.

11. In at least one detail Chettle's tragedy corresponds to the degenerate German play, *Der Bestrafte Brudermord* (*Fratricide Punished*), perhaps, in part, a derivant of the *Ur-Hamlet*, and probably acted by English players on the Continent between 1660 and 1690. Fearing that Lucibella has committed suicide by throwing herself off a cliff, Mathias describes how he "did percaiue her . . . Clambering vpon the steepenes of the rocke" (ll. 1926–1927; V.i). This is curiously like the Queen's account in *Fratricide Punished* of how "Ophelia has climbed a high hill, and cast herself down and taken her own life." See Geoffrey Bullough, ed., *Narrative and Dramatic Sources of Shakespeare*, 8 vols. (London: Routledge and Kegan Paul, 1957–75), VII, 156.

12. Bullough, *Narrative and Dramatic Sources of Shakespeare*, VI, 42.

13. Ibid., p. 53.

14. Ibid., p. 55.

15. Ibid., p. 71.

16. *Hippolytus*, ll. 606–607, 671–672; see F. J. Miller, ed. and trans., *Seneca's Tragedies*, 2 vols., Loeb Classical Library (London: William Heinemann, 1917), I, 364–367, 372–373.

17. Eliot, *Selected Essays*, p. 145.

18. It is worth recording that in the 1987–88 Royal Shakespeare Company production of *Titus Andronicus*, directed by Deborah Warner and performed at the Swan Theatre in Stratford-upon-Avon and at the Pit Theatre in London, the actors who spoke these elaborate speeches (Donald Sumpter as Marcus and Brian Cox as Titus) managed to rivet the audience in a kind of horrified amazement without eliciting anything like embarrassed tittering or laughter.

19. Eugene M. Waith, "The Metamorphosis of Violence in *Titus Andronicus*," *Shakespeare Survey*, 10 (1957), 39–49.

20. See *The Memoirs of Giacomo Casanova di Seingalt*, trans. Arthur Machen, 12 vols. (London: The Casanova Society, 1922), V, 22–23.

21. Albert H. Tricomi argues that Shakespeare sometimes exposes "the euphemisms of metaphor by measuring their falseness against the irrefutable realities of dramatized events"; see "The Aesthetics of Mutilation in *Titus Andronicus*," *Shakespeare Survey*, 27 (1974), 13.

22. My count includes the variants and derivatives of these words; see Marvin Spevack, *A Complete and Systematic Concordance to the Works of Shakespeare*, 6 vols. (Hildesheim: Georg Olms, 1968–75), III, 272, 295. That the word *hand* outnumbers *tongue* in the vocabulary of the tragedy by roughly three to one would seem to suggest the limited potential of mere language as opposed to action. But the symbolism of hands in *Titus* is complex: as agents of the written word and of gesture, they also represent extensions of the power of speech. Titus himself plays on the dual significance when he addresses his daughter: "Speak, Lavinia, what accursed hand / Hath made thee handless in thy father's sight?" (III.i.66–67).

23. A. C. Hamilton in *The Early Shakespeare* (San Marino, Calif.: Huntington Library, 1967) points out how the "posture of kneeling . . . is repeated throughout the play" to express the futility of pleading (p. 83). Lawrence N. Danson in a stimulating essay remarks "the prevailing deafness to the human voice in its cries for mercy or justice" that "is made to seem endemic to the play's world"; see "The Device of Wonder: *Titus Andronicus* and Revenge Tragedies," *Texas Studies in Literature and Language*, 16 (1974), 30.

24. See chap. 7.

25. James L. Calderwood in *Shakespearean Metadrama* (Minneapolis: University of Minnesota Press, 1971) goes so far as to claim that *Titus Andronicus* "presents us with a rape of language" (p. 29).

26. See Ann Haaker, *"Non Sine Causa*: The Use of Emblematic Method and Iconology in the Thematic Structure of *Titus Andronicus*," *Research Opportunities in Renaissance Drama*, 13–14 (1970–71), 143–168.

27. Titus's attempt to displace emotion through art recalls Hieronimo's encounter with the painter in *The Spanish Tragedy*. The lines also anticipate Richard II's famous release of emotion when he sits upon the ground to "tell sad stories of the death of kings" (*Richard II*, III.ii.156).

28. H. E. Butler, ed. and trans., *Institutio Oratoria*, 4 vols., Loeb Classical Library (London: William Heinemann, 1921), III, 507.

29. Tom Stoppard, *Rosencrantz and Guildenstern Are Dead* (New York: Grove Press, 1968), p. 62.

30. Spevack's count is as follows: 11,563 words; 2,631 different words; 1,507 lines; 357 speeches; 39.12 percent of the words of the play; 37.28 percent of the lines of the play; 31.42 percent of the speeches of the play. The closest competitor to Hamlet is Richard III, whose figures,

のNotes to Pages 35–53

in respective order, are 8,826; 2,072; 1,145; 298; 31.17; 31.22; 27.44 (see *A Complete and Systematic Concordance*, II, 1027, and III, 834).

31. It is worth noticing that all the surviving dramatized versions of the Hamlet story insist on the idea of silence at the prince's death. In the so-called bad quarto of 1603, Hamlet says, "O, my heart sinks, Horatio; / Mine eyes have lost their sight, my tongue his use" (V.ii.101–102); see Albert B. Weiner, ed., *Hamlet: The First Quarto, 1603* (Great Neck, N.Y.: Barron's Educational Series, 1962), p. 166. In *Der Bestrafte Brudermord* Hamlet's final speech includes the words "My voice fails" (see Bullough, *Narrative and Dramatic Sources of Shakespeare*, VII, 158).

32. Lamb, "On the Tragedies of Shakespeare, Considered with Reference to Their Fitness for Stage Presentation" (1811), in *Shakespeare Criticism: A Selection*, ed. D. Nichol Smith (London: Oxford University Press, 1916), p. 195.

33. Polonius's cynical warning to his daughter that Hamlet's "tenders / Of . . . affection" (I.iii.100–101) are insincere and that his rank places the prince "out of [her] star" (II.ii.141) seems to be contradicted by Gertrude's words at Ophelia's burial: "I hop'd thou shouldst have been my Hamlet's wife" (V.i.244).

34. This detail appears also in *Der Bestrafte Brudermord*: King Erico (Claudius) explains to Leonhardus (Laertes) that Hamlet's "mother backs [the prince], and my subjects love him dearly" (Bullough, *Narrative and Dramatic Sources of Shakespeare*, VII, 152).

35. Tricomi, "The Mutilated Garden in *Titus Andronicus*," *Shakespeare Studies*, 9 (1976), 94.

36. For additional discussion of the nature theme in *Titus Andronicus* and *Hamlet*, see chap. 7.

37. Susan Snyder, *The Comic Matrix of Shakespeare's Tragedies* (Princeton: Princeton University Press, 1979), p. 94.

38. See Maurice Charney, *Style in "Hamlet"* (Princeton: Princeton University Press, 1969).

39. See chap. 1 for a detailed discussion of the theme of acting in *Hamlet*.

40. Samuel Johnson, *Lives of the English Poets*, ed. George Birkbeck Hill, 3 vols. (Oxford: Clarendon Press, 1905), I, 163. Johnson in fact believed with Theobald and other eighteenth-century scholars that *Titus* had been spuriously attributed to Shakespeare: "the colour of the stile is wholly different from that of the other plays"; see *Johnson on Shakespeare*, ed. Arthur Sherbo, in *The Yale Edition of the Works of Samuel Johnson*, 15 vols. incomplete (New Haven: Yale University Press, 1958-), VIII, 750.

3. Immediacy and Remoteness in *The Taming of the Shrew* and *The Tempest*

1. See especially G. Wilson Knight, " 'Great Creating Nature': An Essay on *The Winter's Tale*," in *The Crown of Life*, 2d ed. (London: Methuen, 1948), pp. 76–128.

2. E. M. W. Tillyard, *Shakespeare's Last Plays* (London: Chatto and Windus, 1938), p. 80.

3. Compare a similar play on words in *Hamlet* (I.v.98); see chap. 1, sec. II.

4. This issue has frequently been the subject of Shakespearean commentary. See especially Maynard Mack, "Engagement and Detachment in Shakespeare's Plays," in *Essays on Shakespeare and Elizabethan Drama in Honor of Hardin Craig*, ed. Richard Hosley (Columbia: University of Missouri Press, 1962), pp. 275–296; also Anne Righter, *Shakespeare and the Idea of the Play* (London: Chatto and Windus, 1962). Of more specialized relevance are Ejner J. Jensen, "Spying Scenes and the Problem Plays: A Shakespearean Strategy," *Tulane Studies in English*, 20 (1972), 23–40, and chap. 1. For a valuable study of the subject in relation to Jonson, see Henry E. Jacobs, "Theaters within Theaters: Levels of Dramatic Illusion in Ben Jonson's Comedy," Diss. Indiana University, 1973. See also chap. 1, n. 1.

5. For further discussion, see chap. 8.

4. Wit, Wisdom, and Theatricality in *The Book of Sir Thomas More*

1. Richard Simpson, "Are There Any Extant MSS. in Shakespeare's Handwriting?", *Notes and Queries*, 4th ser., 8 (1871), 1–3. Listed below are the most important and influential writings on the question: James Spedding, "Shakespeare's Handwriting," *Notes and Queries*, 4th ser., 10 (1872), 227–228; Alfred W. Pollard and J. Dover Wilson, eds., *Shakespeare's Hand in "The Play of Sir Thomas More"* (Cambridge: Cambridge University Press, 1923); R. C. Bald, "Addition III of *Sir Thomas More*," *Review of English Studies*, 7 (1931), 67–69; and *"The Booke of Sir Thomas More* and Its Problems," *Shakespeare Survey*, 2 (1949), 44–65; Peter W. M. Blayney, *"The Booke of Sir Thomas Moore* Reexamined," *Studies in Philology*, 69 (1972), 167–191; R. W. Chambers, "Some Sequences of Thought in Shakespeare and in the 147 Lines of *Sir Thomas More*," *Modern Language Review*, 26 (1931), 251–280, rev. in *Man's Unconquerable Mind* (London: Jonathan Cape, 1939), pp. 204–249; D. C. Collins, "On the Date of *Sir Thomas More*," *Review of English Studies*, 10 (1934), 401–411; Caroline F. E. Spurgeon, "Imagery in the *Sir Thomas More* Fragment," *Review of English Studies*, 6 (1930), 257–270; Samuel A. Tannenbaum, *The Booke of Sir Thomas Moore* (New York: Tenny Press, 1927); "More about *The Booke of Sir Thomas Moore*," *PMLA*, 43 (1928), 767–778; "Dr. Greg and the 'Goodal' Notation in *Sir Thomas Moore*," *PMLA*, 44 (1929), 934–938; and *Shakespere and "Sir Thomas Moore"* (New York: Tenny Press, 1929); Robert A. Law, "Is Heywood's Hand in *Sir Thomas More*?", *Studies in English* (University of Texas), 11 (1931), 24–31; W. W. Greg, "The Manuscript of *Sir Thomas More*," Malone Society Collections, vol. II, pt. 3 (Oxford: Oxford University Press, 1931), 233–234; "T. Goodal in *Sir Thomas More*," *PMLA*, 44 (1929), 633–634, and 46 (1931), 268–271; William H. Matchett, "Shylock, Iago, and *Sir Thomas More*: With Some Further Discussion of Shakespeare's Imagination," *PMLA*, 92 (1977), 217–230; Michael L. Hays, "Shakespeare's Hand in *Sir Thomas More*: Some Aspects of the Paleographic Argument," *Shakespeare Studies*, 8 (1975), 241–253; Carol A. Chillington, "Playwrights at Work: Henslowe's, Not Shakespeare's, *Book of Sir Thomas More*," *English Literary Renaissance*, 10 (1980), 439–479; D. J. Lake, "The Date of the *Sir Thomas More* Additions by Dekker and Shakespeare," *Notes and Queries*, NS, 24 (April, 1977), 114–116; MacD. P. Jackson, "Linguistic Evidence for the Date of Shakespeare's Addition to *Sir Thomas More*," *Notes and Queries*, NS, 25 (April, 1978), 154–156. See also Scott McMillin, *The Elizabethan Theatre and "The Book of Sir Thomas More"* (Ithaca: Cornell University Press, 1987), which absorbs, reviews, and discusses most of the recent scholarship; also Charles R. Forker, "Webster or Shakespeare? Style, Idiom, Vocabulary, and Spelling in the Additions to *Sir Thomas More*," in T. H. Howard-Hill, ed., *Shakespeare and "Sir Thomas More": Essays on the Play and Its Shakespearian Interest* (Cambridge: Cambridge University Press, 1989), pp. 151–170.

2. The seven hands have been identified as (1) Anthony Munday, (2) a playhouse scribe, who was probably not an author, (3) Henry Chettle, (4) perhaps but not certainly Thomas Heywood, (5) Thomas Dekker, (6) probably Shakespeare, and (7) Sir Edmund Tilney, Master of the Revels and censor of the play. See Bald, *"The Booke of Sir Thomas More* and Its Problems," pp. 44–65; also McMillin, *The Elizabethan Theatre and "The Book of Sir Thomas More,"* pp. 135–159.

3. The most authoritative definition of the biographical play (and the most thorough critical overview of its themes and techniques) is still that of Irving Ribner; see "The Biographical Play," in *The English History Play in the Age of Shakespeare*, rev. ed. (New York: Barnes and Noble, 1965), pp. 194–223.

4. McMillin argues that the condition of "wild disarray" that many scholars have discerned in the *More* manuscript is illusory and that its apparent confusions can be explained in great part on the hypothesis that the play was originally written for a large cast (Lord Strange's Men) for performance at the Rose in the early 1590s, then revised for a different troupe with fewer actors (the Admiral's Men) for performance in 1603 or later at the Fortune; see *The Elizabethan Theatre and "The Book of Sir Thomas More,"* pp. 53–112.

5. McMillin, *"The Book of Sir Thomas More*: A Theatrical View," *Modern Philology*, 68 (1970), 10–24; McMillin absorbs the substance of this essay into his book (see nn. 1 and 4 above). See also Judith Doolin Spikes, *"The Book of Sir Thomas More*: Structure and Meaning," *Moreana*, 43–44 (1974), 25–39; Spikes argues that the play is organized around the theme of responsibility.

6. Citations of *Sir Thomas More* are to the modernized text of the play prepared by Harold Jenkins in C. J. Sisson, ed., *William Shakespeare: The Complete Works* (New York: Harper and Row, 1953). In order to avoid misleading readers about insertions of my own, I have silently removed Jenkins's editorial brackets.

7. In passing, the Lord Mayor alludes to More as "he that drove rebellion from our door" (III.iii.84), a reference to the quelling of the May Day insurrection; but the scene resolutely eschews an emphasis on politics.

8. Compare *A Midsummer Night's Dream*, V.i.209–215; and see chap. 3, sec. IV.

9. See *The Complete Works of Saint Thomas More*, ed. Richard S. Sylvester et al., 15 vols. incomplete (New Haven: Yale University Press, 1963-), II, 81.

10. William Roper, *The Lyfe of Sir Thomas Moore, Knighte*, ed. Elsie Vaughan Hitchcock, Early English Text Society (London: Oxford University Press, 1935), p. 5.

11. See my discussion of *The Tempest* in chap. 3, especially sec. III.

12. In this connection, see Stephen Greenblatt's chap., "At the Table of the Great: More's Self-Fashioning and Self-Cancellation," in *Renaissance Self-Fashioning: From More to Shakespeare* (Chicago: University of Chicago Press, 1980), pp. 11–73.

13. W. B. Yeats, *Memoirs*, ed. Denis Donoghue (London: Macmillan, 1972), p. 151.

14. Tillyard, *Shakespeare's History Plays* (London: Chatto and Windus, 1944), p. 121.

15. Scott McMillin disagrees with those who have assumed the unstageability of *Sir Thomas More* and thinks, in any case, that Tilney's strictures would no longer be relevant to a production after 1603; see *The Elizabethan Theatre and "The Book of Sir Thomas More"* (p. 94) and n. 4 above.

16. If the play was revived after Elizabeth's death, as McMillin suggests, the political sensitivity of the subject matter might be somewhat lessened, but even then, the topic could hardly be considered safe.

5. "All the World's a Stage": Multiple Perspectives in Arden

1. Harold Jenkins in *"As You Like It,"* *Shakespeare Survey*, 8 (1955), calls the foundation of the story "flimsy" and its disguisings "inconsequential" (p. 14); Anne Barton in *"As You Like It* and *Twelfth Night*: Shakespeare's Sense of an Ending," *Shakespearian Comedy*, ed. David Palmer and Malcolm Bradbury, Stratford-upon-Avon Studies, 14 (London: Edward Arnold, 1972), refers to the "plotlessness" of the play (p. 163); Agnes Latham in her introduction to the new Arden edition (London: Methuen, 1975) echoes these judgments: "at a superficial level, very little seems to happen" (p. lxxx).

2. Norman Rabkin, *Shakespeare and the Common Understanding* (New York: Free Press, 1967); see especially pp. 1–19.

3. A. S. P. Woodhouse, "Nature and Grace in *The Faerie Queene*," *ELH*, 16 (1949), 196, 218.

4. Marvell, "The Mower against Gardens" (ll. 33–34), in H. M. Margoliouth, ed., *The Poems and Letters of Andrew Marvell*, 3d ed. (Oxford: Clarendon Press, 1971), I, 44.

5. Jay L. Halio devotes an entire essay to the topic: "'No Clock in the Forest': Time in *As You Like It*," *Studies in English Literature*, 2 (1962), 197–207; rpt. in *Twentieth-Century Interpretations of "As You Like It,"* ed. Jay L. Halio (Englewood Cliffs, N.J.: Prentice-Hall, 1968), pp. 88–97. For a discussion of the theme of time in Shakespeare's chronicle plays, see chap. 9.

6. Henry David Thoreau, *Walden*, ed. J. Lyndon Shanley (Princeton: Princeton University Press, 1971), p. 98.

7. Edwin Greenlaw, Charles Grosvenor Osgood, Frederick Morgan Padelford, et al., eds., *The Works of Edmund Spenser: A Variorum Edition*, 10 vols. (Baltimore: Johns Hopkins Press, 1932–57), VI, 180.

8. John Russell Brown in a chapter to which I am heavily indebted develops this point; see "Love's Order and the Judgement of *As You Like It*," in *Shakespeare and His Comedies* (London: Methuen, 1957), pp. 141–159.

9. Walter R. Davis perceptively analyzes the relation of disguise to self-discovery in Shakespeare's major source, Lodge's *Rosalynde*; see "Masking in Arden," *Studies in English Literature*, 5 (1965), 151–163. Since in the prose romance Arden represents the adjustment of the actual to the ideal, masking or deliberate role-playing serves "the interests of ethical clarification" (p. 155).

10. Edwin Wilson, ed., *Shaw on Shakespeare* (New York: E. P. Dutton, 1961), p. 32.

6. Shakespeare's Chronicle Plays as Historical-Pastoral

1. The phrase is T. S. Eliot's; see Eliot, "Four Elizabethan Dramatists," in *Selected Essays* (London: Faber and Faber, 1951), p. 114.

2. Readers familiar with the voluminous scholarship on Shakespeare's histories will recognize my considerable indebtedness to such important standard works as J. Dover Wilson's introductions to his new Cambridge editions of the individual plays; E. M. W. Tillyard's *Shakespeare's History Plays* (London: Chatto and Windus, 1944); Irving Ribner's *The English History Play in the Age of Shakespeare*, rev. ed. (New York: Barnes and Noble, 1965); Alfred Harbage's *As They Liked It: A Study of Shakespeare's Moral Artistry* (New York: Macmillan, 1947); M. M. Reese's *The Cease of Majesty* (London: Edward Arnold, 1961); and Lily B. Campbell's *Shakespeare's "Histories": Mirrors of Elizabethan Policy* (San Marino, Calif.: Huntington Library, 1947). I have also found useful W. W. Greg's *Pastoral Poetry and Pastoral Drama* (London: A. H. Bullen, 1906), Edwin Greenlaw's "Shakespeare's Pastorals," *Studies in Philology*, 13 (1916), 122–154, and Madeleine Doran's *Endeavors of Art* (Madison: University of Wisconsin Press, 1954).

3. At the time this essay was originally written in 1963 there had been (to my knowledge) only one occasion in the English-speaking world when all ten plays had been performed consecutively; this was in 1935 when the Pasadena Playhouse of California staged the series. Since 1963, stage and television performances of at least parts of the cycle have become much more common in both Great Britain and North America. The Royal Shakespeare Theatre at Stratford-upon-Avon devoted its four hundredth anniversary season (1964) to a series of seven plays that embraced both tetralogies, the three parts of *Henry VI* being abridged into two plays the second of which was renamed *Edward IV*. Productions of the three parts of *Henry VI*, of the two parts of *Henry IV*, and indeed of one or both tetralogies at the same time are now fairly standard. The tradition of producing Shakespeare's histories in series received an indirect stimulus from John Barton's popular *The Hollow Crown: An Entertainment by and about the Kings and Queens of England*, first presented by the Royal Shakespeare Company at the Aldwych Theatre, London, on 19 March 1961. This is a group of musical selections and readings—poetry, speeches from plays, letters, excerpts from the English chronicles, and the like—designed to highlight the historical panoply of English royalty from William the Conqueror to Queen Victoria. It opens, as might be predicted from the title, with the famous speech of Richard II: "For God's sake let us sit upon the ground / And tell sad stories of the death of kings!" (*Richard II*, III.ii.155–170); see Barton, *The Hollow Crown* (London: Samuel French, 1962).

4. One of the best modern discussions of this aspect of the histories, to which I am indebted in what follows, is Una Ellis-Fermor's "Shakespeare's Political Plays," in *The Frontiers of Drama*, 3d ed. (London: Methuen, 1948), pp. 34–55.

5. I quote Graham Hough's translation of Tasso's words from his illuminating analysis of the Italian poet's *Discorsi dell' Arte Poetica e in particolare sopra il poema eroico*; see Hough, *A*

Preface to "The Faerie Queene" (London: Gerald Duckworth, 1962), p. 55. Tasso's remarks appear to have served him as a prolegomenon to *Jerusalem Delivered*.

6. Some critics, of course, have tended to ignore *Henry VIII* as a history play, influenced in most cases by the much disputed claim for Fletcher's partial authorship and by the play's remove in time and style from the earlier histories. An influential exception is G. Wilson Knight's important essay in *The Crown of Life*, 2d ed. (London: Methuen, 1948), pp. 256–336, which argues with force, incidentally, that the play is Shakespeare's unaided work. But Tillyard omits *Henry VIII* from consideration in *Shakespeare's History Plays*, as does Lily B. Campbell in *Shakespeare's "Histories,"* while R. A. Foakes in his new Arden edition (London: Methuen, 1957) asserts "that it cannot be fitted into the scheme of the earlier histories" (p. xlii). Reese in *The Cease of Majesty* says that "In the main" it "is conceived in the spirit of the later romances, with a good deal of pageantry and spectacle," and that here Shakespeare "does not trouble to revive the political themes" of the earlier plays (p. 333). No one, I think, would now deny the important thematic and stylistic relationship to Shakespeare's other "last plays," but from the standpoint of genre in the Renaissance sense, such considerations are secondary. Heminge and Condell classed *Henry VIII* with the other English histories because, obviously, it contained native historical characters, dealt with historical events, and in the birth of Elizabeth and Cranmer's prophecy dramatized the fulfillment of those national hopes for "smiling plenty, and fair prosperous days" (*Richard III*, V.v.34) that had concluded the preceding play in the Folio collection. And if this was not sufficient reason to group *Henry VIII* with the other histories, there were additional grounds; for the most prominent theme of the drama, the rise and fall of persons of state, was one that had preoccupied Shakespeare continuously throughout all nine of the earlier dramas.

7. In *Macbeth* Malcolm lists these "as justice, verity, temp'rance, stableness, / Bounty, perseverance, mercy, lowliness, / Devotion, patience, courage, fortitude" (IV.iii.92–94).

8. It is worth noticing that Marlowe employs similar imagery in *Edward II* in which the young prince (the future Edward III) is referred to as "a lamb, encompassèd by wolves [i.e., Mortimer and his adherents], / Which in a moment will abridge his life" (V.i.41–42); see Irving Ribner, ed., *Christopher Marlowe's "Edward II": Text and Major Criticism* (New York: Odyssey Press, 1970), p. 56. Although Shakespeare's indebtedness to Marlowe is well established (*Edward II* clearly influenced the conception of *Richard II*), the trilogy on Henry VI (c. 1590–91) probably antedates Marlowe's chronicle play (c. 1592). The precise relationship of Shakespeare's earliest histories to Marlowe's drama is a complex problem (see the edition of *Edward II* by H. B. Charlton and R. D. Waller, revised by F. N. Lees [London: Methuen, 1955], pp. 6–27), but in any case, sheep-wolf imagery in political contexts is commonplace.

9. Frye, *Anatomy of Criticism: Four Essays* (Princeton: Princeton University Press, 1957), p. 143.

10. Edward Hall, *Hall's Chronicle; Containing the History of England during the Reign of Henry the Fourth, and the Succeeding Monarchs, to the End of the Reign of Henry the Eighth,* [ed. Sir Henry Ellis] (London: J. Johnson, 1809), p. 112.

11. Robert Greene, *The Scottish History of James IV*, ed. Norman Sanders (London: Methuen, 1970), p. 49.

12. *The Reign of King Edward III*, ed. James Winny, in *Three Elizabethan Plays* (London: Chatto and Windus, 1959), p. 27.

13. *The Dramatic Works and Poems of James Shirley*, ed. W. Gifford and A. Dyce, 6 vols. (London: John Murray, 1833), I, 65.

14. I cite this phrase from the stage directions in J. Dover Wilson's new Cambridge edition of *King John* (Cambridge: Cambridge University Press, 1954), pp. 32, 34.

15. Izaak Walton, *The Compleat Angler, 1653–1676*, ed. Jonquil Bevan (Oxford: Clarendon Press, 1983), p. 234. It is interesting that Venator's reminiscence is provoked by a singing of Marlowe's popular pastoral lyric, "Come live with me, and be my Love," and Raleigh's answer. Like Shakespeare and Walton, John Webster also imported the contrast between pastoral and royal

status into his work. In *The Duchess of Malfi*, just before she is strangled, Bosola taunts the heroine, reminding her in her agony: "Thou art some great woman, sure, for riot begins to sit on thy forehead, clad in gray hairs, twenty years sooner than on a merry milkmaid's" (IV.ii.135–137); see John Russell Brown, ed., *The Duchess of Malfi* (London: Methuen, 1964), p. 124.

16. Caroline F. E. Spurgeon in *Shakespeare's Imagery and What It Tells Us* (New York: Macmillan, 1936), pp. 216–224, calls attention to the vegetative imagery that pervades the histories. She fails, however, to explore its significance very deeply. Richard D. Altick's "Symphonic Imagery in *Richard II*," *PMLA*, 62 (1947), 339–365, contains a splendid treatment of the earth-husbandry imagery and its relation to other themes in the single play he discusses. See also Robert K. Presson, "Some Traditional Instances of Setting in Shakespeare's Plays," *Modern Language Review*, 61 (1966), 12–22.

17. The quartos and Folio, of course, rarely specify locations of scene in the form of stage directions. Garden settings, like most other settings in Shakespeare, are more reliably and more effectively established by references to place in the dialogue itself. In the following analysis I have tried to provide the necessary evidence of setting in each case by means of appropriate quotation, or, at least, of specific reference to Shakespeare's own words.

18. Although I would argue that this technique has a special appropriateness to the history plays, where the theme of social and political order is so heavily stressed, it is by no means unique there, for Shakespeare also uses natural settings symbolically in both the comedies and tragedies. In *The Merchant of Venice* (V.i), for instance, a landscape near Portia's house stirs the romantic Lorenzo to lyrical reflections on the relationship of love, music, and cosmic harmony. Clearly the idyllic atmosphere in which "the sweet wind . . . gently kiss[es] the trees" (V.i.2) and "the moonlight sleeps upon this bank" (V.i.54) reinforces an ideal of natural and moral order against which the unnatural values of Shylock are ultimately measured. And it is not difficult to find similar examples in the tragedies. The romantic orchard in *Romeo and Juliet* where the moon "tips with silver all these fruit-tree tops" (II.ii.108) serves to emphasize the central contrast between young love and old hatred; and Shakespeare heightens the unnaturalness of King Hamlet's murder by having the crime committed with symbolic irony in an orchard. Kyd in *The Spanish Tragedy* had already used the latter device: Horatio is suddenly hanged in the leafy arbor where he has been making love to Bel-Imperia, and his grief-crazed mother later chops it down and curses the entire garden in an act of symbolic retribution. See chap. 7 for more extended discussion of green-world settings in the early comedies and tragedies.

19. See Ernst Robert Curtius, *European Literature and the Latin Middle Ages*, trans. W. R. Trask (New York: Pantheon Books, 1953), pp. 183–202; also D. W. Robertson, Jr., "The Doctrine of Charity in Mediaeval Literary Gardens: A Topical Approach through Symbolism and Allegory," *Speculum*, 26 (1951), 24–49.

20. Frye goes so far as to recognize "a secular Eucharist symbol in the red and white rose" (*Anatomy of Criticism*, p. 284); he points to their historical union in "the reigning head of the church" (p. 195) and quotes *Richard III* (p. 363): "And then, as we have ta'en the sacrament, / We will unite the white rose and the red" (V.v.18–19).

21. The quarto of 1594 (entitled *The First Part of the Contention betwixt the Two Famous Houses of York and Lancaster*) specifies that the conjurors are brought to "the backside of [Eleanor's] Orchard" (I.ii) and mentions a tower to which she ascends. The Folio text omits this detail, but it is clear from the action that the same setting applies. In the sixteenth century, "garden" and "orchard" were often interchangeable terms (see *OED*).

22. See Arthur Colby Sprague, *Shakespeare's Histories: Plays for the Stage* (London: Society for Theatre Research, 1964), pp. 88–89.

23. Ross, "The Meaning of Strawberries in Shakespeare," *Studies in the Renaissance*, 7 (1960), 229.

24. Ibid., p. 233.

25. See R. A. Foakes's new Arden edition of *Henry VIII* (London: Methuen, 1957), pp. xxxi, 176.

26. Dryden, "An Essay of Dramatic Poesy," in *Essays of John Dryden*, ed. W. P. Ker, 2 vols. (Oxford: Clarendon Press, 1900), I, 79.

27. See Barber, *Shakespeare's Festive Comedy* (Princeton: Princeton University Press, 1959), pp. 192–221.

28. Empson, *Some Versions of Pastoral* (London: Chatto and Windus, 1950), pp. 27–86. Readers will recognize my particular debt here to the chap. "Double Plots: Heroic and Pastoral in the Main Plot and Sub-Plot."

29. Theobald's famous emendation has of course been challenged, but no one has yet suggested words so appropriately *in character*—both for the fat knight himself and for the ignorant woman who, with such a rich combination of pathos and unconscious comedy, narrates the circumstances of his death. Falstaff knew his Bible, as he reveals when he refers to "Pharaoh's lean kine" (*1 Henry IV*, II.iv.468) and to "Dives that liv'd in purple" (III.iii.32); and that he could imagine himself as a weaver singing psalms (see II.iv.130–131) accords well with Theobald's inference that what Mistress Quickly fails to recognize in his feverish "babbling" is a deathbed recitation of Psalm 23. Sir Walter Greg has defended the reading persuasively on paleographical grounds in "Principles of Emendation in Shakespeare," *Proceedings of the British Academy*, 14 (1928), 147–216.

7. The Green Underworld of Early Shakespearean Tragedy

1. Northrop Frye, of course, coined the phrase "drama of the green world," applying it specifically to the romantic comedies of Shakespeare; see "The Argument of Comedy," in *English Institute Essays, 1948* (New York: Columbia University Press, 1949), pp. 58–73, and *Anatomy of Criticism* (Princeton: Princeton University Press, 1957), pp. 182–184. Frye includes all the comedies alluded to here (*The Two Gentlemen of Verona, Love's Labor's Lost, A Midsummer Night's Dream, The Merchant of Venice, As You Like It*, and *The Winter's Tale*).

2. See chap. 6 for the theme of the green world in relation to the English histories; also John Wilders, *The Lost Garden: A View of Shakespeare's English and Roman History Plays* (Totowa, N.J.: Rowman and Littlefield, 1978).

3. Frye notes that "tragedy is really implicit or uncompleted comedy," and that "comedy contains a potential tragedy within itself" ("The Argument of Comedy," p. 65); see also Susan Snyder, *The Comic Matrix of Shakespeare's Tragedies* (Princeton: Princeton University Press, 1979). C. L. Barber discusses the fruitful relation between comic and tragic material in *1* and *2 Henry IV*; see "Rule and Misrule in *Henry IV*," in *Shakespeare's Festive Comedy* (Princeton: Princeton University Press, 1959), pp. 192–221.

4. See Frye, *Anatomy of Criticism*, and *A Natural Perspective* (New York: Columbia University Press, 1965); Barber, *Shakespeare's Festive Comedy*; and McFarland, *Shakespeare's Pastoral Comedy* (Chapel Hill: University of North Carolina Press, 1972).

5. It may be objected that *A Midsummer Night's Dream* does in fact include this darker perspective. Lysander could almost be describing the action of *Romeo and Juliet* when he speaks of romance, "short as any dream, / Brief as the lightning in the collied sky," and of "bright things" coming quickly "to confusion" (*A Midsummer Night's Dream*, I.i.144–149). Moreover, Titania, in accusing Oberon of infidelity, attributes floods, bad weather, seasonal change, and other "evils" (II.i.115) in nature to the couple's habitual quarreling. Lysander's speech does indeed remind us of the tragic pressures to which love is heir, but these belong to the world of Hermia's father, the world from which the Maying excursion into the woods is an obvious escape. The jealous spat between the fairy king and queen, though also negative in theme, is part of what Barber calls the

"playful mythopoesis" (*Shakespeare's Festive Comedy*, p. 122) that informs the forest episodes as a group and clearly belongs to the world of dreams, fancy, comic irrationality, and magical metamorphosis. We are therefore encouraged to suppress feelings of pessimism and regard the dispute with bemused detachment, invoking the same "pert and nimble spirit of mirth" (I.i.13) that the play as a whole celebrates.

6. For a discussion of antipastoral attitudes in Shakespearean comedy, see Peter Lindenbaum, *Changing Landscapes: Anti-Pastoral Sentiment in the English Renaissance* (Athens: University of Georgia Press, 1986), pp. 91–135. See also my analysis of *As You Like It* in chap. 5.

7. See Albert H. Tricomi, "The Mutilated Garden in *Titus Andronicus*," *Shakespeare Studies*, 9 (1976), 89–105.

8. These same antitheses also tend to inform the imagery and settings of Shakespeare's chronicle plays; see chap. 6, sec. II.

9. Nothing in Shakespeare's main source for this scene, Plutarch's *Life of Marcus Brutus*, suggests a garden setting; and indeed the only sense of location that can be deduced from Shakespeare's dialogue is that Brutus, who cannot sleep and has been trying to study the stars on a cloudy night for signs of dawn, is speaking somewhere on the grounds of his own house. The designation of an "orchard" (here a synonym for "garden") appears only in the Folio stage direction for Brutus's entrance. Brutus sends his boy Lucius for a taper (an obvious means of indicating darkness and obscurity on a daylight stage), which action then leaves him alone to deliver his important soliloquy during which he makes the tragic decision to assassinate Caesar. The main reason for the orchard setting is privacy—first, for Brutus by himself while he struggles with his conflict between idealism and policy, and later, for the conspirators as they gather to work out their plans. The total absence of vegetative detail may be a deliberate way of suggesting the unnaturalness of the politics being dramatized, and in any case, the darkness precludes much specificity; but usually Shakespeare gives his audience more help in orienting them to a particular sense of place—if the place is to have thematic or symbolic significance.

10. Many critics have assumed that all Shakespearean plays, including the tragedies, imply a cosmology of universal order at some level and, within this, a belief in natural law. George C. Herndl, for instance, in *The High Design: English Renaissance Tragedy and the Natural Law* (Lexington: University Press of Kentucky, 1970), takes Shakespeare as his point of departure in analyzing how post-Shakespearean tragedians increasingly undermined or departed from an essentially medieval concept of nature. Readers more skeptical than Herndl, however, have detected evidences of this shift not only *after* but also *during* Shakespeare's career. See especially Arthur Sewell, *Character and Society in Shakespeare* (Oxford: Clarendon Press, 1951); and William R. Elton, *"King Lear" and the Gods* (San Marino, Calif.: Huntington Library, 1966).

8. Perdita's Distribution of Flowers and the Function of Lyricism in *The Winter's Tale*

1. See *The Complete Works of William Hazlitt*, ed. P. P. Howe, 21 vols. (London: J. M. Dent and Sons, 1930–34), IV, 35; Hazlitt also discussed the same passage appreciatively in *The Atlas* (8 March 1829), *Works*, XX, 209–211.

2. *The Defence of Poesie* in *Miscellaneous Prose of Sir Philip Sidney*, ed. Katherine Duncan-Jones and Jan Van Dorsten (Oxford: Clarendon Press, 1973), p. 80. The union of the pictorial and the verbal is also evident in such locutions as Marlowe's "The shepherd nipped with biting winter's rage / Frolicks . . . to see the painted spring" (*Edward II*, II.ii.61–62); see Irving Ribner, ed., *Christopher Marlowe's "Edward II": Text and Major Criticism* (New York: Odyssey Press, 1970), p. 26. *"Pictus"* (literally, "painted") was a common classical metaphor for "flowery," as in *prata picta* (flowery meadows).

3. W. W. Greg, *Pastoral Poetry and Pastoral Drama* (London: A. H. Bullen, 1906), p. 411.

E. M. W. Tillyard also observes that "the country life is given the fullest force of actuality"; see *Shakespeare's Last Plays* (London: Chatto and Windus, 1938), p. 43. It has often been noted that Shakespeare increases the sense of realism in the pastoral section of the play by reversing Greene's contrast between the two kingdoms: Sicily, the traditional location of Arcadia, becomes the place of the jealous king's court, while the homeland of his boyhood friend, where the abandoned princess grows up, is transferred to rustic Bohemia.

4. Henry VI's "molehill" speech (*3 Henry VI*, II.v.1–54) and Richard II's prison soliloquy (*Richard II*, V.v.1–66) are cases in point.

5. J. H. P. Pafford in his new Arden edition of *The Winter's Tale* (London: Methuen, 1963) believes that "in the pastoral scene the season approaches winter" (pp. liv, lxix); Ernest Schanzer in his new Penguin edition (Harmondsworth: Penguin Books, 1969) avers that June "is, no doubt, the time-setting" (p. 206).

6. See William O. Scott, "Seasons and Flowers in *The Winter's Tale*," *Shakespeare Quarterly*, 14 (1963), 411–417.

7. See Schanzer, ed., *The Winter's Tale*, p. 197.

8. M. M. Mahood, *Shakespeare's Wordplay* (London: Methuen, 1957), pp. 161–163.

9. D. A. Traversi, *An Approach to Shakespeare*, 2d ed. (New York: Doubleday Anchor, 1956), p. 274.

10. C. H. Herford and Percy and Evelyn Simpson, eds., *Ben Jonson*, 11 vols. (Oxford: Clarendon Press, 1925–52), VII, 188.

11. Rosalie Colie, *The Resources of Kind: Genre-Theory in the Renaissance*, ed. Barbara K. Lewalski (Berkeley: University of California Press, 1973), p. 8.

12. See J. M. Nosworthy, "Music and Its Function in the Romances of Shakespeare," *Shakespeare Survey*, 11 (1958), 60–69.

13. Lytton Strachey, "Shakespeare's Final Period," rpt. from the *Independent Review*, 3 (1904), 405–418, in *Books and Characters, French and English* (New York: Harcourt, Brace, 1922), p. 64.

14. George Puttenham, *The Arte of English Poesie* (London, 1589), p. 5; Henry Peacham, *The Garden of Eloquence* (London, 1593), sig. ABiii. Peacham's metaphorical title is worth noting in the context of Perdita's flower speech. In his "Epistle Dedicatorie" the idea is developed further: "euen as by the power of the Sun beames, the nature of the roote is shewed in the blossome, & the goodnesse of the sap tasted in the sweetnesse of the frute, euen so the precious nature, and wonderfull power of wisedome, is by the commendable Art and vse of eloquence, produced and brought into open light" (sig. ABiii).

15. Margreta de Grazia, "Shakespeare's View of Language: An Historical Perspective," *Shakespeare Quarterly*, 29 (1978), 374–388.

16. Richard A. Lanham, *The Motives of Eloquence: Literary Rhetoric in the Renaissance* (New Haven: Yale University Press, 1976), p. 161.

9. The Idea of Time in Shakespeare's Second Historical Tetralogy

1. This point has been developed *in extenso* by David Scott Kastan in *Shakespeare and the Shapes of Time* (London: Macmillan, 1982), pp. 23–27, 37–55. Kastan, in turn, builds upon the work of Tom Driver and Ricardo Quinones; see Driver, *The Sense of History in Greek and Shakespearean Drama* (New York: Columbia University Press, 1960), and Quinones, *The Renaissance Discovery of Time* (Cambridge, Mass.: Harvard University Press, 1972).

2. See Lily B. Campbell, *Shakespeare's "Histories": Mirrors of Elizabethan Policy* (San Marino, Calif.: Huntington Library, 1958); also David Bevington, *Tudor Drama and Politics: A Critical Approach to Topical Meaning* (Cambridge, Mass.: Harvard University Press, 1968).

3. As Henry Ansgar Kelly has usefully demonstrated, this formulation of the so-called Tudor

myth, heavily indebted to E. M. W. Tillyard's influential *Shakespeare's History Plays* (London: Chatto and Windus, 1944), represents a historiographical oversimplification. Kelly refers to it as "an ex post facto Platonic Form, made up of many fragments that were never fitted together into a mental pattern until they felt the force of [Tillyard's] synthesizing energy"; see Kelly, *Divine Providence in the England of Shakespeare's Histories* (Cambridge, Mass.: Harvard University Press, 1970), p. 298.

4. Although Falstaff and Hotspur seem almost to personify the opposed spirits of comedy and tragedy at a specific moment in the battle scene, we must not on this account oversimplify two profoundly realized and psychologically complex characters, each of whom elsewhere in the play reminds us of his potential for embodying some of the qualities that define his polar opposite in the symbolic contrast. Hotspur, as every actor knows, can be richly comic in his own right, and our awareness of the irreverent lightheartedness that is part of his nature contributes powerfully to our sense of loss at his death. By the same token, Falstaff increasingly reveals a strain of pathos, borne of failure and disappointment, that becomes an essential aspect of the comic vision he projects. The cowardly knight and the honor-driven nobleman are complementary as well as opposed; despite their obvious differences of age, physique, and outlook, each contains (or at least reflects) a suggestion of the other.

5. Although the apparent simultaneity of Richard's violation of Bolingbroke's rights and the latter's armed invasion of England might be explained, to quote Bevington, as "owing to Shakespeare's characteristic compression of historic time," we nevertheless "gain the impression of an already-existing plot" against the king; see David Bevington, ed., *The Complete Works of Shakespeare* (Glenview, Ill.: Scott, Foresman, 1980), p. 756.

10. "A Little More than Kin, and Less than Kind": Incest, Intimacy, Narcissism, and Identity in Elizabethan and Stuart Drama

1. William Aldis Wright, ed., *Roger Ascham: English Works* (Cambridge: Cambridge University Press, 1904), p. 231.

2. (*a*) Giovanni Battista Basile's *Pentameron*, 2 vols. (III, 2; trans. Benedetto Croce, ed. N. M. Penzer [New York: Dutton, 1932], I, 232–240) includes the tale of "The Girl with the Maimed Hands" in which a brother's proposal of marriage to his own sister causes her to cut off her hands, which she sends him as a gift.

(*b*) Bandello's large collection of novelle contains two incest stories (I, 44; II, 35); see the translation by John Payne in *The Novels of Matteo Bandello . . . Now First Done into English Prose and Verse*, 6 vols. (London: Villon Society, 1890), II, 242–252; V, 4. The first narrative (which may be a source for the relationship of the Duchess and the Duke's bastard son in *The Revenger's Tragedy*; see L. G. Salingar, "*The Revenger's Tragedy*: Some Possible Sources," *Modern Language Review*, 60 [1965], 5–9) recounts how a teenage count and his young stepmother, a marchioness, were discovered in bed together by the father-husband and beheaded; the second is a retelling from Marguerite's *Heptameron* of a young man who unwittingly sleeps with his mother and marries his daughter (I discuss Marguerite's version of the tale later in this essay).

(*c*) Cinthio's *Hecatommithi*, famous for the stories on which *Othello* and *Measure for Measure* are partly based, relates the unhappy love affair of Oronte, a commoner, and Princess Orbecche, whose mother and brother were executed for the crime of incest by her father King Sulmone. Cinthio used the same story (II, 2) for his widely influential Senecan tragedy, *Orbecche* (1541)— a story, in either its dramatic or narrative version, that could have influenced Webster's *Duchess of Malfi* (see *Hecatommithi ouero Cento Novelle di Gio. Battista Giraldi Cinthio* [Venice: Deuchino & Pulciani, 1608], pp. 187–199; also Gunnar Boklund, "*The Duchess of Malfi*": *Sources, Themes, Characters* [Cambridge, Mass.: Harvard University Press, 1962], pp. 28–31). P. R. Horne discusses the incest motif in both the play and the novella (see *The Tragedies of Giambattista Cinthio Giraldi* [London: Oxford University Press, 1962], pp. 51–52, 58–59).

(*d*) Book IV of Jorge de Montemayor's popular romance *Diana* (translated by Bartholomew Yong) contains the interpolated tale of the noble Moor Abdynaraez and his beloved Xarifa, who are reared together as brother and sister, fall in love, and only later discover that they are not blood relatives (see Judith M. Kennedy, ed., *A Critical Edition of Yong's Translation of George of Montemayor's "Diana" and Gil Polo's "Enamoured Diana"* [Oxford: Clarendon Press, 1968], pp. 166–184).

3. Richard III attempts to marry his own niece, Elizabeth of York (*Richard III*, IV.iv.297–298); Hamlet's uncle marries Gertrude, his own sister-in-law; Lear in his madness rails against an imaginary hypocrite, "thou simular of virtue / That art incestuous!" (*King Lear*, III.ii.54–55), apparently with the unnaturalness of his own daughters in mind; Adriana mistakes her brother-in-law (Antipholus of Syracuse) for her own husband and tries to treat him as her mate (*The Comedy of Errors*, II.ii); Isabella speaks of Angelo's attempt to barter her brother's life for her virginity as "a kind of incest" (*Measure for Measure*, III.i.138); and Antiochus sleeps with his daughter (*Pericles*, I.i.126–132). Mark Taylor discusses father-daughter relationships in *Shakespeare's Darker Purpose: A Question of Incest* (New York: AMS Press, 1982), discovering repressed incestuous desire almost everywhere; the preponderance of his "inferences" (p. xi) regarding the unconscious motivation of men toward their female children seems to me unduly strained and fanciful; see Joseph Candido's judicious review, *Shakespeare Studies*, 20 (1988), 323–332.

4. Lois E. Bueler lists forty-two Renaissance plays that involve the incest motif, categorizing them according to whether the incest is actual or imagined only, and whether it is witting or unwitting (see "The Structural Uses of Incest in English Renaissance Drama," *Renaissance Drama*, ed. Leonard Barkan, NS, 15 [1984], 115–145). Including cases of symbolic and metaphorical incest as well as elements of plot, we may expand Bueler's roster of plays to embrace the following dramas: Gascoigne's *Jocasta* (1566), Hughes's *The Misfortunes of Arthur* (1588), Peele's *Edward I* (1591), Jonson's *The Case Is Altered* (1597), Marston's *The Malcontent* (1604), Chapman's *The Tragedy of Charles, Duke of Byron* (1608), Beaumont and Fletcher's *Cupid's Revenge* (1608), Jonson's *Catiline* (1611), Fletcher's *Monsieur Thomas* (1615), Massinger's *The Bondman* (1623), Shirley's *The Opportunity* (1634), Ford's *The Fancies Chaste and Noble* (1635), Shirley's *The Coronation* (1635), *The Gentleman of Venice* (1639), and *The Court Secret* (1642). The dates given here and throughout are those of Alfred Harbage in *Annals of English Drama, 975–1700*, revised by S. Schoenbaum (London: Methuen, 1964).

5. Denis Gauer, "*Heart and Blood*: Nature and Culture in *'Tis Pity She's a Whore*," *Cahiers Elisabethains*, 31 (April 1987), 45.

6. Sigmund Freud, *Civilization and Its Discontents*, trans. James Strachey (New York: Norton, 1961), p. 51.

7. David F. Aberle and his colleagues conveniently summarize the leading anthropological theories on the origins and importance of the incest taboo; see "The Incest Taboo and the Mating Patterns of Animals" in Paul Bohannan and John Middleton, eds., *Marriage, Family and Residence* (Garden City, N.Y.: Natural History Press, 1968), pp. 5–11. The most widely promulgated of these theories tend to account for the nearly universal prohibition of incest in terms either of order *within* the family or of stability and social advantage *between* families in the larger social order. The incest taboo, for instance, is said to regulate the erotic impulses of the developing child, forcing him to direct these impulses outside the nuclear family and so learn social maturity and responsibility; or, it is held, the taboo outlaws sexual competition within the home with a view to preventing familial disruption, internal chaos, and self-destruction. A third hypothesis asserts that the collective good of a broader social organism (the securing of internal peace, economic benefits, and reciprocal assistance; the making of common cause, defensively or offensively, against an enemy group) necessitates the barrier against incest. Even the widely discredited view that inbreed-

ing necessarily threatens the genetic health of the family has lately been garnering fresh support, although such a view, whatever its scientific validity, would be largely irrelevant to the analysis of pre-Darwinian cultures.

Probably the most influential theory of incest for students of literature has been that of Claude Lévi-Strauss, who argued in his famous *Elementary Structures of Kinship* (trans. James Harle Bell, John Richard von Sturmer, and Rodney Needham [Boston: Beacon Press, 1969]) that the taboo arises from the need to control the exchange of women in society with something like equality, and to prevent their monopolization by a selfish few. Lévi-Strauss's principle of sexual reciprocity thus explains the need for exogamy, although often within a limited collectivity: "neither fraternity nor paternity can be put forward as claims to a wife, but . . . the sole validity of these claims lies in the fact that all men are in equal competition for all women, their respective relationships being defined in terms of the group, and not the family" (p. 42). To quote Lévi-Strauss's summation of the "rule of reciprocity," "The woman whom one does not take, and whom one may not take, is, for that very reason, offered up" (p. 51). Lévi-Strauss's formulation has been faulted on the ground that it does not properly distinguish between sexual relations and marriage (see, for instance, Francis Korn, *Elementary Structures Reconsidered: Lévi-Strauss on Kinship* [London: Tavistock Publications, 1973], pp. 13–16); but Renaissance plays, particularly those with comic endings, usually make as little practical distinction between the two as the French anthropologist.

René Girard brings us full circle by attempting to fuse the insights of Freud with those of cultural anthropology. Girard, beginning with an analysis of Freud's *Totem and Taboo*, relates both murder and incest to the traditions of ritual violence and the scapegoat, or surrogate victim, in primitive religion. As societies cure their tendency to internal violence by choosing for ritual sacrifice a victim from outside the group, who nevertheless represents the group symbolically, so they cure their desire for sexual conquest within the family by substituting an outside partner for the insider forbidden them: "The problem is always the same: violence is both the disease (inside) and the cure (outside). Violence, like sexual desire, must be forbidden wherever its presence is incompatible with communal existence" ("*Totem and Taboo* and the Incest Prohibition," in René Girard, *Violence and the Sacred*, trans. Patrick Gregory [Baltimore: Johns Hopkins University Press, 1977], p. 220).

8. (*a*) For Plato's views on incest, see *Plato: The Republic* (V), trans. Paul Shorey, 2 vols., Loeb Classical Library (London: William Heinemann, 1935), I, 459–469; the quotation appears on pp. 467–469.

(*b*) For Nero, see Tacitus, *Annals* (XIII, 13; XIV, 2), trans. John Jackson, 4 vols., Loeb Classical Library (London: William Heinemann, 1937), IV, 21, 109; also Suetonius, *The Lives of the Caesars* (VI, 28), trans. J. C. Rolfe, 2 vols., Loeb Classical Library (London: William Heinemann, 1914), II, 133.

(*c*) For Caligula, Claudius, and Domitian, see Suetonius, *The Lives of the Caesars*, 2 vols. (IV, 24; V, 26; VIII, 22), trans. Rolfe, I, 441; II, 55, 383.

(*d*) For Clodia and her brother, see Cicero, *Pro Caelio* (XIII, 32; XIV, 35; XV, 36) in *Cicero: The Speeches*, trans. R. Gardner, 2 vols., Loeb Classical Library (London: William Heinemann, 1958), II, 445, 449, 451.

(*e*) For Catiline, see Quintus Cicero, *Commentariolum Petitionis* (9), trans. Mary Isobel Henderson, in *Cicero: Letters to His Friends*, 4 vols., Loeb Classical Library (London: William Heinemann, 1972), IV, 756–757; Asconius's commentary on Cicero's oration *In Toga Candida* (82), in A. C. Clark, ed., *Q. Asconii Pediani Orationum Ciceronis Quinque Ennarratio* (Oxford: Clarendon Press, 1907), pp. 91–92; and Plutarch's *Life of Cicero* (X), in *The Lives of the Noble Grecians and Romanes*, trans. Sir Thomas North, 5 vols. (London: Nonesuch Press, 1929–30), IV, 203.

(*f*) For Seneca, see Thomas Newton, ed., *Seneca, His Tenne Tragedies*, with an introduction by T. S. Eliot (1927; rpt. Bloomington: Indiana University Press, [1966]). *Jocasta* by George Gascoigne and Francis Kinwelmersh has been edited by John W. Cunliffe in *Early English Classical Tragedies* (Oxford: Clarendon Press, 1912), pp. 65–159.

(*g*) For Juvenal's references to incest, see *Satire I* (ll. 75–78) and *Satire II* (ll. 29–33) in *Juvenal and Persius*, trans. G. G. Ramsay, Loeb Classical Library (London: William Heinemann, 1918), pp. 9, 18–21. For the imitation by Marston, see *The Scourge of Villanie* (*Satyre I*, ll. 13, 32–40) in Arnold Davenport, ed., *The Poems of John Marston* (Liverpool: Liverpool University Press, 1961), pp. 103–104, 268, 271; in *Satyre II* (ll. 21–25), Marston, following Chapman's *Hero and Leander* (V, 5–10), also alludes to the incest of Phoebus and Aurora, who were brother and sister (ed. Davenport, pp. 106, 180).

(*h*) Preston's immediate source for *Cambyses* was Richard Taverner's *Second Booke of the Garden of Wysedome* (London, 1539), which, in turn, derived from Herodotus (see Robert Carl Johnson, ed., *A Critical Edition of Thomas Preston's "Cambises"* [Salzburg: Institut für Englische Sprache und Literatur, 1975], pp. 6–11, 192); the Greek historian treats Cambyses' incestuous marriage in Book III, 31–32 (see *Herodotus*, trans. A. D. Godley, 4 vols., Loeb Classical Library [London: William Heinemann, 1938], II, 41–43.

(*i*) The quotation from Dio Cassius is from *Dio's Roman History* (XLIII, 27), trans. Earnest Cary, 9 vols., Loeb Classical Library (London: William Heinemann, 1914–27), IV, 261.

(*j*) For the Harpalyce-Clymenus incest, see G. A. Hirschig, ed., *Parthenii Erotica* (13), in *Erotici Scriptores* (Paris: Firmin Didot, 1856), p. 12; also H. J. Rose, ed., *Hygini Fabulae* (Lugduni Batavorum: A. W. Sijthoff, [1934]), p. 143.

(*k*) The quotation from Fulgentius appears in *On the Ages of the World and of Man* (3) in Leslie George Whitbread, trans., *Fulgentius the Mythographer* (Columbus: Ohio State University Press, 1971), p. 194; P. R. Horne discusses Manfredi's *Semiramis* briefly in *The Tragedies of Giambattista Cinthio Giraldi* (London: Oxford University Press, 1962), p. 154.

9. Versions of the story differ; see Robert Graves, *The Greek Myths*, 2 vols. (New York: George Braziller, 1955), I, 160–161. Ovid confines himself to the tragic incest of Macareus and Canace.

10. Citations of the *Metamorphoses* are taken throughout from Arthur Golding's translation, ed. W. H. D. Rouse (New York: W. W. Norton, 1966).

11. Henry Peacham in two different emblems associates the animal kingdom—specifically the cock—with incest. See fig. 3; also *Minerva Britanna, or a Garden of Heroical Deuises* (Leeds: Scolar Press, 1969), pp. 48, 118. Peacham may have chosen the male fowl to represent forbidden sexual intercourse because of the proximity of sisters, daughters, and other kindred that an enclosed pen or barnyard necessitates. Compare Chaucer who, in *The Nun's Priest's Tale*, suggests that Chauntecleer commits incest: "This gentil cok hadde in his governaunce / Sevene hennes for to doon al his pleasaunce, / Whiche were his sustres and his paramours . . ." (ll. 2865–2867); see Larry D. Benson, gen. ed., *The Riverside Chaucer*, 3d ed. (Boston: Houghton Mifflin, 1987), p. 254. In the second of the emblems from *Minerva Britanna* (p. 118; not reproduced in this book), a cat, symbolic of the forces of moral repression, catches the bird in his paws, intending to devour him. But the cock wittily defends his supposedly unnatural lust (apparently without success) on grounds of economic utility to his human owner. The implication of the cock's argument is that his chief function in the scheme of things, apart from serving as "the Plowmans clock, / Whom I awake betime, to daily paine," is to increase his "maisters gaine," that is, to fertilize eggs and thus produce more laying hens as well as more chickens for the farmer's table and for market. Thus Peacham cleverly captures a divided popular response to incest: on the one hand it is a mortal sin deserving the harshest punishment, but on the other, it is a reasonable practice that can be supported from a commonsense, utilitarian point of view. Of course the tradition of the beast fable, upon which both emblems obviously draw, deliberately blurs the moral and sexual distinction between animals and human beings that the quotation from Ovid articulates.

12. Robert K. Turner, Jr., ed., *A King and No King* (Lincoln: University of Nebraska Press,

1963), p. 102. I cite this text throughout. Similar Ovidian reasoning, as Bueler points out, occurs in Tourneur (*The Atheist's Tragedy*, IV.iii.124–130), in Brome (*The Lovesick Court*, III.iii), and in Suckling (*Aglaura*, II.iii.5–18).

13. Derek Roper, ed., *'Tis Pity She's a Whore* (London: Methuen, 1975), p. 8. I cite this text throughout.

14. Graves, *The Greek Myths*, I, 160; Kennedy, ed., *Montemayor's "Diana,"* p. 169. See nn. 2 (*d*) and 9 above.

15. Bueler notices the importance of the incest motif as a convenient device for complicating and resolving plots in Renaissance plays as well as for defining moral character. The plots that involve unwitting incest frequently allow courtly dramatists to demonstrate that aristocratic honor and idealistic love cannot finally conflict with each other, since the doctrine that "true love . . . results from the urge to seek honor" ("The Structural Uses of Incest," p. 125) is written, as it were, into the code of cavalier values. Bueler regards the efficient switching of partners (in denouements to which unwittingly incestuous courtships have been the prelude) as bearing out Lévi-Strauss's account of the incest taboo with its correlative principle of reciprocity, or exchange of women, as necessary to the sexual economy of a healthy society (see n. 7 above).

16. Lawrence Stone, *The Family, Sex and Marriage in England, 1500–1800* (London: Weidenfeld and Nicolson, 1977), p. 86. See also Natalie Zemon Davis, "Ghosts, Kin, and Progeny: Some Features of Family Life in Early Modern France," *Daedalus*, 106 (1977), 87–114; Davis discusses incest in relation to marriage customs and family identity (pp. 102–105). In addition to her essay, I am indebted to Professor Davis for a provocative private conversation in which some of the ideas contained in this paper germinated.

17. Stone, *The Family, Sex and Marriage*, p. 115. In corroboration of Stone, David Bergeron points to the close personal affection between Prince Henry and Princess Elizabeth at James I's court, whereas the king himself tended to be jealous of his oldest son's popularity. Charles (Henry's younger brother), being more studious and less athletic than the heir to the throne, was also more distant toward him; see Bergeron, *Shakespeare's Romances and the Royal Family* (Lawrence: University of Kansas Press, 1985), pp. 58, 62. It should be pointed out, however, that Stone's generalizations about the emotional environment of the Renaissance family have not gone unchallenged. For a feminist critique of Stone's popular book, a critique that argues that the author's "masculine perspective distorts his understanding of early modern family, sex, and marriage" (p. 391), see Lois G. Schwoerer, "Seventeenth-Century English Women Engraved in Stone?", *Albion*, 16 (1984), 389–403.

18. Whigham, "Sexual and Social Mobility in *The Duchess of Malfi*," *PMLA*, 100 (1985), 169.

19. J. R. Mulryne, ed., *Women Beware Women* (London: Methuen, 1975), p. 39; all further citations of the play are from this edition.

20. Daniel Dodson, "Middleton's Livia," *Philological Quarterly*, 27 (1948), 378–380.

21. T. J. B. Spencer, ed., *The Broken Heart* (Manchester: Manchester University Press, 1980), p. 76; all further citations are from this edition.

22. Robert Burton, *The Anatomy of Melancholy*, ed. Holbrook Jackson, 3 vols. (London: Dent, 1964), III, 281.

23. Oliver Lawson Dick, ed., *Aubrey's Brief Lives* (London: Secker & Warburg, 1968), p. 139. I owe this, as well as several additional references, to George Robin Schore, "'Incest? Tush!': Jacobean Incest Tragedy and Jacobean England," Diss. State University of New York at Stony Brook, 1982, p. 43.

24. See Richard Burn, *The Ecclesiastical Law*, 4 vols. (London: Sweet, Stevens, and Norton, 1842), II, 439–451; also W. K. Lowther Clarke and Charles Harris, eds., *Liturgy and Worship: A Companion to the Prayer Books of the Anglican Communion* (London: Society for Promoting Christian Knowledge, 1932), pp. 470–471.

25. Richard outrageously proposes the marriage to his sister-in-law, Queen Elizabeth: "If I have kill'd the issue of your womb, / To quicken your increase, I will beget / Mine issue of your blood

upon your daughter," to which the queen responds that God, not to mention "the law, my honor, and her love," expressly "forbids" such alliances between close kindred (*Richard III*, IV.iv.296–298, 341–346). Richard's earlier marriage to Lady Anne Nevill also involved a family relationship, for Richard's father, the Duke of York, and Anne's grandfather, the Earl of Salisbury, were brothers-in-law. Richard and Anne were thus cousins by marriage. See Charles Ross, *The Wars of the Roses: A Concise History* (London: Thames and Hudson, 1976), table II.

26. For the family relationship of Henry VII and Elizabeth of York, see Ross, *The Wars of the Roses*, tables I and II; also Charles Ross, *Edward IV* (Berkeley: University of California Press, 1974), tables I, II, and III. For the degrees of relationship and the papal dispensation, see J. A. Twemlow, *Calendar of Entries in the Papal Registers Relating to Great Britain and Ireland: Papal Letters 1484–1492*, XIV (London: Her Majesty's Stationery Office, 1960), 1–2, 14–27; also William Campbell, ed., *Materials for a History of the Reign of Henry VII*, 2 vols. (London: Her Majesty's Stationery Office, 1873–77; rpt. Kraus, 1965), I, 392–398; also S. B. Chrimes, *Henry VII* (Berkeley: University of California Press, 1972), pp. 330–331. It is a pleasure to acknowledge the assistance of Professor Kenneth G. Madison of Iowa State University with the historical background of Henry VII's marriage.

27. See Horace Howard Furness, ed., *A New Variorum Edition of Shakespeare: Hamlet*, 2 vols. (Philadelphia: J. B. Lippincott, 1877), I, 33. Hamner was uncertain about the proverb, but it is no longer in doubt; see Morris Palmer Tilley, *A Dictionary of the Proverbs in England in the Sixteenth and Seventeenth Centuries* (Ann Arbor: University of Michigan Press, 1950), K38.

28. One sign of how heavily the obsession with incest weighs upon Hamlet is his allusion to Nero as he approaches the interview with his mother in her closet: "Let not ever / The soul of Nero enter this firm bosom. / Let me be cruel, not unnatural; / I will speak daggers to her, but use none" (III.ii.392–395). The conscious reference, of course, is to Nero's murder of his mother Agrippina; but the Roman emperor's incest with her was almost equally notorious. It is just possible, too, that the choice of Claudius as the name for Hamlet's uncle, a strangely Roman name for a Danish usurper, was influenced by the memory of the emperor Claudius, who (as noted previously) had married Nero's mother incestuously; see n. 8 (*b*) above. The best treatment of the moral and theological implications of incest in the play is that of Jason P. Rosenblatt in "Aspects of the Incest Problem in *Hamlet*," *Shakespeare Quarterly*, 29 (1978), 349–364.

29. Toleration, of course, was by no means universal. Roland Mushat Frye cites several cases of incest between brothers and sisters-in-law for which public penance in church and "a sizable fine" were the penalty; see *The Renaissance Hamlet: Issues and Responses in 1600* (Princeton: Princeton University Press, 1984), pp. 80–81. By the reign of Charles I, some of the laxity that had characterized the morality of his father's court was disappearing. In 1631, for instance, the second Earl of Castlehaven was executed for a whole catalogue of sexual deviations that included, in addition to wife rape, sodomy, voyeurism, and sadism, the attempt, at least, to debauch his own daughter-in-law when she was but twelve years old as well as commanding a servant to copulate with her; see T. B. Howell, ed., *A Complete Collection of State Trials*, 33 vols. (London: Longman, Hurst, Rees, Orme, and Brown, 1816–26), III, 401–418. In addition, Stuart P. Sherman suggests that the plot of Ford's *'Tis Pity* may glance at the case of Sir Giles Allington, who was found guilty of having married his half sister, the procurer of the license being fined £2,000; see Sherman, ed., " *'Tis Pity She's a Whore" and "The Broken Heart"* (Boston: Heath, 1915), p. xxxvi.

30. Rosenblatt, in the essay cited above, discusses this contrast.

31. J. C. Flügel, "On the Character and Married Life of Henry VIII," *International Journal of Psycho-Analysis*, 1 (1920), 24–55; rpt. in Bruce Mazlish, ed., *Psychoanalysis and History* (Englewood Cliffs, N. J.: Prentice-Hall, 1963), pp. 124–149.

32. For the case of Alessandro de Medici, see Henry Edward Napier, *Florentine History*, 6 vols. (London: Edward Moxon, 1846–47), V, 1–64; also John Stewart Carter, ed., *The Traitor* (Lincoln: University of Nebraska Press, 1965), pp. ix-x.

33. See Norman Egbert McClure, ed., *The Letters of John Chamberlain*, 2 vols. (Philadelphia: American Philosophical Society, 1939), II, 144–145, 217–218.

34. Quoted by J. E. Neale, *Elizabeth I and Her Parliaments, 1584–1601* (London: Jonathan Cape, 1957), p. 171. I owe this reference to Professor Franklin M. Wright of Rhodes College, Memphis, Tenn.

35. The classic treatment of the debate appears in J. J. Scarisbrick, "The Canon Law of Divorce," in *Henry VIII* (Berkeley: University of California Press, 1968), pp. 163–197.

36. "If brethren dwell together, and one of them die, and have no child, the wife of the dead shall not marry without unto a stranger: her husband's brother shall go in unto her, and take her to him to wife, and perform the duty of an husband's brother unto her.

"And it shall be, that the firstborn which she beareth shall succeed in the name of his brother which is dead, that his name be not put out of Israel."

37. Charles Tyler Prouty, gen. ed., *The Dramatic Works of George Peele*, 3 vols. (New Haven: Yale University Press, 1952–70), III, 202, 204.

38. "If whoredome had not beene sinne, Surely Saint *Iohn* Baptist would neuer haue rebuked king *Herod* for taking his brothers wife, but he told him plainely, that it was not lawfull. . . . he would rather suffer death . . . then to suffer whoredome to be unrebuked, euen in a king. . . . truly *Iohn* had beene more then twise mad, if hee would haue had the displeasure of a king . . . and lost his head for a trifle"; see Mary Ellen Rickey and Thomas B. Stroup, eds., *Certaine Sermons or Homilies* (Gainesville, Fla.: Scholars Facsimiles Reprints, 1968), p. 80.

39. Continuation of the race or the founding of a new dynasty might perhaps, as in Lot's case, be thought to mitigate or even excuse incest; yet Tourneur in *The Atheist's Tragedy* made D'Amville, the atheist of the title, attempt to seduce his daughter-in-law with a similar motive. Clearly Tourneur used the incestuous impulse of his villain as simply another facet of the character's unambiguous depravity.

40. See Henry Snyder Gehman, ed., *The New Westminster Dictionary of the Bible* (Philadelphia: Westminster Press, 1970), pp. 321–322.

41. The first English text of this narrative appeared by an anonymous translator in *The Queene of Nauarres Tales, Containing, Verie pleasant Discourses of fortunate Louers . . .* (London: V[alentine] S[ims], 1597). I quote throughout from the modern translation by P. A. Chilton: *Marguerite de Navarre: The Heptameron* (Harmondsworth: Penguin Books, 1984).

42. N. W. Bawcutt, ed., *The Changeling* (London: Methuen, 1958), p. 108.

43. *Montaigne's Essayes*, trans. John Florio, I, 29; see the edition by L. C. Harmer, 3 vols. (London: Dent, 1965), I, 211.

44. *The Dramatic Works of Richard Brome Containing Fifteen Comedies Now First Collected*, 3 vols. (London: John Pearson, 1873; rpt. New York: AMS Press, 1966), II, 102. This edition prints each play with separate pagination but without line numbers; all further citations of *The Lovesick Court* are given parenthetically in the text by act and scene, followed by the page number for this play within volume II.

45. Bueler would have us read the entire play as a late parody of the fantastic plotting and unbelievable romanticism—of the clichés, in other words—that increasingly characterized so much cavalier drama in the Caroline period. Although there is much absurdity in *The Lovesick Court*, Brome seems to build a recognition of this factor into his subplot in which the servants Varillus and Tersulus (in their rivalry over Doris, a waiting-woman) act out a deliberately comic, below-stairs version of the contest between Philocles and Philargus. If the principals themselves were meant to be taken as a joke, the satire of the underplot would, in a sense, be deprived of its function. This is not to deny that, at specific moments, the highborn romantic lovers invite mockery in the extremity of their plight, but such irreverence is intermittent rather than sustained.

46. W. H. S. Jones, trans., *Pausanias: Description of Greece*, 5 vols., Loeb Classical Library (London: William Heinemann, 1935), IV, 311.

47. Kennedy, ed., *Diana* (IV), pp. 169–170.

48. See my *Skull Beneath the Skin: The Achievement of John Webster* (Carbondale: Southern Illinois University Press, 1986), pp. 310–311, 328. I have restated this idea in somewhat altered form in " 'Three Fair Medals Cast in One Figure': *Discordia Concors* as a Principle of Characterization in *The Duchess of Malfi*," *Iowa State Journal of Research*, 61 (1987), 373–381.

49. William Shullenberger, "Wrestling with the Angel: *Paradise Lost* and Feminist Criticism," *Milton Quarterly*, 20 (1986), 78.

50. Ibid., pp. 79–80.

51. Roper, ed., *'Tis Pity She's a Whore*, p. xlv.

52. R. J. Kaufmann, "Ford's Tragic Perspective," *Texas Studies in Literature and Language*, 1 (1960), 534.

53. Robert Stein, *Incest and Human Love: The Betrayal of the Soul in Psychotherapy*, 2d ed. (Dallas: Spring Publications, 1984).

Index

Works mentioned or discussed in this book (as distinguished from those merely cited in the notes for purposes of documentation) are listed by both author and title with cross-references; anonymous works and those of doubtful authorship appear under their titles only.

White Devil, The. See Webster, John

Wilders, John, 181 n. 2

Wilkins, George

—*Miseries of Enforced Marriage, The*, strained family relations in, 147; warm brother-sister relations in, 148

William I, the Conqueror (king of England), 178 n. 3

Wilson, Arthur, 142

Wilson, J. Dover, 176 n. 1, 178 n. 2, 179 n. 14

Winter's Tale, The. See Shakespeare, William

Wolsey, Thomas, Cardinal, 59. *See also* Cavendish, George

Women Beware Women. See Middleton, Thomas

Women Pleased. See Fletcher, John

Woodhouse, A. S. P., 72, 177 n. 3

Wordsworth, William, 88

Wright, Franklin M., 190 n. 34

Yeats, William Butler, 66, 177 n. 13

Yong, Bartholomew (trans. of Montemayor's *Diana*), 185 n. 2

Charles R. Forker, Professor of English at Indiana University, has taught at the universities of Wisconsin and Michigan, at Dartmouth College, and at Concordia University, Montréal, Québec. He has edited Shirley's *Cardinal*, Shakespeare's *Henry V*, and is currently at work on a critical edition of Marlowe's *Edward II*. His most recent books are *Henry V: An Annotated Bibliography* (with Joseph Candido), 1983, and *Skull Beneath the Skin: The Achievement of John Webster*, 1986, besides which he has contributed numerous essays and reviews to scholarly journals. He serves on the editorial boards of *Hamlet Studies* and *Medieval and Renaissance Drama in England*.